THREE ELIZABETHAN PAMPHLETS

THE
THIRDE

and laſt Part of Conny-
catching.

WITH THE NEW DEVISED
knauiſh Art of Foole-taking.

*The like Coſenages and Villenies neuer before
diſcouered.*

By R. G.

Imprinted at London by *Thomas Scarlet* for
Cutberd Burbie, and are to be ſolde at his ſhoppe in the
Poultrie, by S. Mildreds Church. 1592.

By courtesy of the Bodleian Library

Three Elizabethan Pamphlets

EDITED BY

GEORGE RICHARD HIBBARD

Select Bibliographies Reprint Series

BOOKS FOR LIBRARIES PRESS
FREEPORT, NEW YORK

First published 1951 as part of the Life,
Literature, & Thought Library by
George G. Harrap & Co. Ltd.

Reprinted 1969 by arrangement

STANDARD BOOK NUMBER:
8369-5034-8

LIBRARY OF CONGRESS CATALOG CARD NUMBER:
74-80622

PRINTED IN THE UNITED STATES OF AMERICA

FOREWORD

THIS series aims at presenting in an attractive form English texts which have not only intrinsic merit as literature but which are also valuable as manifestations of the spirit of the age in which they were written. The plan was inspired by the desire to break away from the usual annotated edition of English classics and to provide a series of books illustrating some of the chief developments in English civilization since the Middle Ages. Each volume will have a substantial introduction, which will relate the author to the main currents of contemporary life and thought, and which will be an important part of the book. Notes, where given, will be brief, stimulating, and designed to encourage the spirit of research in the student. It is believed that these books will be of especial value to students in universities and in the upper forms of schools, and that they will also appeal very much to the general reader.

Grateful acknowledgment is made of the valuable help given to the series in its early stages by Mr S. E. Buckley.

VIVIAN DE SOLA PINTO
General Editor,
Life, Literature
And Thought Library

ACKNOWLEDGMENTS

I WISH to express my thanks to Mr Colin B. McKerrow for permission to make use of the late R. B. McKerrow's edition of *The Works of Thomas Nashe*, to which I owe an enormous debt, particularly evident in the Notes, and to Messrs John Lane, The Bodley Head, Ltd, for permission to consult their reprints of *The Thirde and Last Part of Conny Catching* and of *The Wonderfull Yeare*, both edited by G. B. Harrison.

I must also thank the officials of the British Museum and the Bodleian Library for their unfailing help and courtesy.

G. R. H.

CONTENTS

INTRODUCTION

THE NATURE AND PURPOSE OF THE PAMPHLET

ROBERT GREENE begins one of his cony-catching stories with these words:

> Not far from Charing Cross dwelleth an honest young man, who being not long since married and having more rooms in his house than himself occupieth, either for term time or the Court lying so near, as divers do, to make a reasonable commodity, and to ease house-rent, which as the world goeth now is none of the cheapest, letteth forth a chamber or two, according as it may be spared.[1]

This passage, with its exact, circumstantial detail, sets the story that follows firmly and surely in the life of the times, and it takes one straight to what is the most fascinating feature of the three pamphlets that make up this volume—the vivid, realistic picture they give of the daily life of ordinary men and women in London during the last decade or so of Elizabeth's reign.

Greene, in particular, writing for what was primarily a London audience, and intent on giving the impression that his stories are fact not fiction, takes the utmost care to ensure that every detail of setting and manners is right. From what he says in the first of the stories in *The Third and Last Part of Cony-Catching* it is almost possible to draw a plan of the citizen's house, with the shop occupying the ground floor, the living-room, the maids' and children's bedroom, and the

[1] See below, p. 53.

master's own bedroom on the next floor, and, finally, the apprentices' sleeping-quarters in the garret, the whole being built end-on to the street. Even more interesting than the setting, however, is the behaviour of the people who live in it. The friendly relations between mistress and servant, the Sunday-afternoon stroll to Finsbury Fields, the desire of the mistress to be well spoken of among her maid's friends in the country—all these things and many more are combined to produce a remarkably complete and delightful picture of a typical London tradesman's home.

From this very appropriate starting-point, for the merchants were the strongest and most important element in the population of Elizabethan London, the picture grows and expands. Greene goes on to write of the life of the streets, with their ballad-singers, of the tavern and the playhouse, and, above all, of the London underworld. Nashe extends the scope of the picture still further with his satirical portraits of contemporary types—the upstart, the usurer, the merchant's wife, the affected traveller, and so on—and by the fact that his rambling, digressive manner enables him to touch on nearly everything that interested people at the time—the behaviour of foreigners, religion, politics, morals, demonology, poetry, and plays. His picture of life is not confined to London, not even to England, but London is nevertheless at the centre of it. And, finally, Dekker shows the way in which London life was disrupted and its citizens scattered by the outbreak of the plague in 1603.

In the middle of this picture stands Old St Paul's. It is here that Greene's cony-catchers meet to discuss their plans and to carry out some of their exploits; it is here, too, that Pierce Penilesse, after searching vainly for the devil among the lawyers at Westminster Hall and among the merchants at the Exchange, eventually encounters him in the shape of a professional perjurer, a knight of the post. Once again Greene and Nashe are being true to the life of the times.

St Paul's was in many ways the real centre of sixteenth-century London; its great central aisle was the most popular of meeting-places. To it came the lounger in search of news, the lawyer in search of clients, the merchant in search of business, the unemployed man in search of a job, the ruined gentleman or discharged soldier in search of an acquaintance to stand him a meal, the cony-catcher in search of a victim. John Earle, in his *Microcosmography* (1628), describes it as follows:

Paul's Walk is the land's epitome, or you may call it the lesser isle of Great Britain. It is more than this, the whole world's map, which you may here discern in its perfectest motion, justling and turning. It is a heap of stones and men, with a vast confusion of languages; and were the steeple not sanctified, nothing liker Babel. The noise in it is like that of bees, a strange humming or buzz mixed of walking tongues and feet: it is a kind of still roar or loud whisper. It is the great exchange of all discourse, and no business whatsoever but is here stirring and afoot. It is the synod of all pates politic, jointed and laid together in most serious posture, and they are not half so busy at the Parliament. . . . It is the general mint of all famous lies, which are here like the legends of Popery, first coined and stamped in the Church. All inventions are emptied here, and not few pockets. The best sign of a temple in it is, that it is the thieves' sanctuary, which rob more safely in the crowd than a wilderness, whilst every searcher is a bush to hide them. It is the other expense of the day, after plays, tavern, and a bawdy-house; and men have still some oaths left to swear here. It is the ears' brothel, and satisfies their lust and itch. The visitants are all men without exceptions, and the principal inhabitants and possessors are stale knights and captains out of service; men of long rapiers and breeches, which, after all, turn merchants here and traffic for news. Some make it a preface to their dinner and travel for a stomach; but thriftier men make it their ordinary and board here very cheap. Of all such places it is least haunted with hob-goblins, for if a ghost would walk more, he could not.[1]

[1] *A Book of Characters*, edited by Richard Aldington (Routledge, 1924), p. 228.

London itself was growing rapidly; according to G. M. Trevelyan in his *English Social History*, the population doubled itself during Elizabeth's reign (1558–1603) from about 100,000 people at the beginning to 200,000 at the end. At first this increasing population could still be housed within the bounds of the medieval city, where the Dissolution of the Monasteries had released a good deal of land for building purposes. By about 1570, however, all available building space within the City had been taken up, and London began to expand outward into suburbs. This expansion was not welcomed either by the City Authorities or the Government. The City Authorities resented the fact that the suburbs were largely outside their control; the Government feared that the growth of London would lead to a depopulation of the rest of the country; and both were very much aware that the crowded, ill-built shacks and houses beyond the City walls were centres of infection. Dekker, in *The Wonderful Year*, makes it plain that the plague of 1603 began in the suburbs, "the sinfully-polluted suburbs," as he calls them, and from there made its way into the City.

During the latter half of Elizabeth's reign numerous attempts were made to restrict this growth, but all were unavailing, because the increase in population was the result very largely of economic forces that were not understood at the time. England was just beginning to feel the effects of that profound change in her position with respect to the rest of the world that had come with the discovery of the Americas. From being a country on the very edge of a world based on the Mediterranean she was becoming the centre of a world based on the Atlantic. The change was accelerated by the wars in the Netherlands, which hindered the development of Antwerp as a centre of world commerce, so that the initiative passed to London. The building of the Royal Exchange, completed in 1568, marks the emergence of London as a world trading centre.

The growing wealth of the City would have attracted people in any case, but during the sixteenth century there were other reasons as well to draw, and even to drive, people from the country to the large and thriving town. There was, first, a gradual increase in population without a corresponding increase in the demand for rural labour. On the contrary, there had been a decline in that demand. Enclosure in the sixteenth century was not on a large scale, but it was sufficient, nevertheless, to turn considerable numbers of ploughmen into sturdy beggars. To these were added the servants and hangers-on of the monasteries, who found themselves homeless and unemployed when the monasteries were dissolved; and, finally, during the last years of Elizabeth's reign the wars in the Netherlands and in Ireland produced a crop of discharged soldiers, many of them maimed, who could not easily be reabsorbed into the life of the nation. These people, roaming the country and living as best they could by begging, and often by cheating and stealing, are remembered in the nursery-rhyme:

> Hark, hark,
> The dogs do bark,
> The beggars are coming to town.

They formed one of the most serious problems that the Tudors had to deal with. Not unnaturally many members of "these rowsey, ragged rabblement of rakehells," as they are called by the Elizabethan sociologist Thomas Harman, drifted to London, and became part of the underworld that Robert Greene describes so well.

In reading Greene's cony-catching stories one soon becomes aware of a certain discrepancy between profession and practice. Greene says that his purpose in writing is to warn his fellow-citizens against the devices and stratagems of the rogues. In fact, however, his sympathies are with the rogues rather than with their victims, who come almost entirely from the trading and professional middle class. He writes from the point of view of the citizen, but he does not like him. This bias against the bourgeoisie, implicit in Greene, is quite explicit in Nashe. *Pierce Penilesse* is a very comprehensive satire; on one score or another Nashe attacks nearly every social class, but his main target throughout is the merchant, the man whose mind is set on making money and rising in the social scale. Of the three, Greene, Nashe, and Dekker, only Dekker is genuinely sympathetic towards the citizen, and even he regards the usurer as a legitimate figure of fun.

In part, this anti-bourgeois bias can be explained on personal grounds. Greene and Nashe, both of them graduates of Cambridge and men of ability, could not help comparing their own precarious existence with the security and the comfort enjoyed by the prosperous merchant community. Nashe says as much at the beginning of *Pierce Penilesse*. After describing his own penniless state he goes on:

> Thereby I grew to consider how many base men, that wanted those parts which I had, enjoyed content at will and had wealth at command. I called to mind a cobbler, that was worth five hundred pound; an hostler, that had built a goodly inn, and might dispend forty pound yearly by his land; a car-man in a leather pilch, that had whipped out a thousand pound out of his horse tail: and have I more wit than all these? thought I to myself, am I better born? am I better brought up? yea, and better favoured? and yet am I a beggar? What is the cause? how am I crossed? or whence is this curse?[1]

But while the personal element counts for something, the pamphleteers, writing for the general public, reflect to a large extent that public's attitude, and the second interest of their work is this, that it shows the reaction of ordinary people to the profound social and economic changes which were altering the whole shape and structure of life and society at the time.

In theory both the social organization and the economic activity of this country during the sixteenth and early seven-

[1] See below, p. 75.

teenth centuries conformed to the medieval pattern. The medieval church, in an attempt to show the whole of life as part of the divine purpose, had accepted the organization of life as it was, and rationalized it. Professor Tawney, in *Religion and the Rise of Capitalism*,[1] puts it in this way:

> The gross facts of the social order are accepted, in all their harshness and brutality. They are accepted with astonishing docility, and, except on rare occasions, there is no question of reconstruction. What they include is no trifle. It is nothing less than the whole edifice of feudal society—class privilege, class oppression, exploitation, serfdom. But these things cannot, it is thought, be treated as simply alien to religion, for religion is all-comprehensive. They must be given some ethical meaning, must be shown to be the expression of some larger plan. The meaning given them is simple. The facts of class status and inequality were rationalised in the Middle Ages by a functional theory of society, as the facts of competition were rationalised in the eighteenth by the theory of economic harmonies; and the former took the same delight in contemplating the moral purpose revealed in social organisation, as the latter in proving that to the curious mechanism of human society a moral purpose was superfluous or disturbing. Society, like the human body, is an organism composed of different members. Each member has its function, prayer, or defence, or merchandise, or tilling the soil. Each must receive the means suited to its station, and must claim no more. Within classes, there must be equality; if one takes into his hand the living of two, his neighbour will go short. Between classes there must be inequality; for otherwise a class cannot perform its function, or—a strange thought to us—enjoy its rights. Peasants must not encroach on those above them. Lords must not despoil peasants. Craftsmen and merchants must receive what will maintain them in their calling, and no more.

Into this scheme of things the merchant, impelled by the desire for profit—that is to say, for more means than were suited to his station in life—never fitted very comfortably.

[1] John Murray (1926), p. 22.

B

The medieval church consistently condemned the pursuit of wealth for its own sake or as a means to social advancement; and, above all, it condemned the lending of money at a fixed rate of interest, since charging interest on a loan implies a desire to profit from the necessities of one's neighbour, the sin of avarice. A fourteenth-century schoolman, quoted by Tawney, writes:

> He who has enough to satisfy his wants and nevertheless ceaselessly labours to acquire riches, either in order to obtain a higher social position, or that subsequently he may have enough to live without labour, or that his sons may become men of wealth and importance—all such are incited by a damnable avarice, sensuality or pride.[1]

Even during the Middle Ages, of course, the facts of life did not square with the theory. Merchants did pursue profit as a means of security and social advancement; they did lend money at interest. Chaucer's Pardoner preaches a sermon on the text "Radix malorum est cupiditas," for the express purpose of getting people to buy his worthless relics, so making a personal gain. But, while the facts did not fit the theory, the theory nevertheless remained dominant in the minds of ordinary men until well on into the seventeenth century. It is not surprising that it did so, since it continued to enjoy the official approval both of the State and of the State Church. One of the clearest and fullest expressions of this conception of a static, hierarchical, interdependent society is to be found in *The Book of Homilies*, published in 1562, with orders that they should be read in all churches. The tenth of these homilies, *An Exhortation to Obedience*, begins like this:

> Almighty God hath created and appointed all things, in heaven, earth, and waters, in a most excellent and perfect order. In heaven he hath appointed distinct (or several) orders, and states of archangels and angels. In earth, he hath assigned and

[1] Tawney, *op. cit.*, p. 34.

appointed kings and princes, with other governors under them, all in good and necessary order. The water above is kept, and raineth down in due time and season. The sun, moon, stars, rainbow, thunder, lightning, clouds, and all birds of the air, do keep their order. The earth, trees, seeds, plants, herbs, corn, grass and all manner of beasts, keep themselves in their order. All the parts of the whole year, as winter, summer, months, nights and days, continue in their order. All kinds of fishes in the sea, rivers and waters, with all fountains and springs, yea, the seas themselves, keep their comely course and order. And man himself also hath all his parts both within and without, as soul, heart, mind, memory, understanding, reason, speech, with all and singular corporal members of his body, in a profitable, necessary, and pleasant order. Every degree of people, in their vocation, calling, and office, hath appointed to them their duty and order. Some are in high degree, some in low; some kings, and princes, some inferiors and subjects; priests and laymen, masters and servants, fathers and children, husbands and wives, rich and poor; and every one have need of other.[1]

Society as organized in the State is seen here as part of the divine plan. No class is independent of the rest, each has responsibilities towards the whole, and it is the duty of the individual to remain in that station in life to which it has pleased God to call him, doing the labour that station demands, and expecting no more in return than is due to him.

This, then, is what the Elizabethans heard in their churches; these were the notions with which they grew up. They only had to look about them, however, to see an ever-increasing gulf between theories and facts. In particular, they could not help being aware of the growing strength and importance of the middle class both in town and country, a growth that took place at the expense both of the peasantry at one end of the scale and of the landed aristocracy at the other. The reasons for it are various. In part it was due to Tudor policy: the early Tudors deliberately encouraged the development of

[1] *Certain Sermons or Homilies* (S.P.C.K., 1890), p. 109.

the middle class, while depressing the power and influence of the old aristocracy, in order to ensure that there should be no repetition of the Wars of the Roses. More important even than this, however, was the fact that world affairs were propitious for a middle-class advance. As has been pointed out already, England was becoming a world trading centre. Merchants got together to send out expeditions to trade with Russia, the Levant, the East Indies, and the Americas. Such expeditions were risky, but when they succeeded enormously profitable. The main article of export was cloth. The country gentry enclosed lands in order to breed sheep for their wool, instead of producing wheat. Some of the profits came back directly to the land, but, as well as this, the growing wealth of the merchants led the country gentlemen to borrow capital from them for the further improvement of their estates. Roughly speaking, the middle class of town and country worked together for their mutual advantage. Their rise was assisted by the fact that the reign of Elizabeth was accompanied by a steady rise in prices. The Spaniards brought large quantities of gold and silver from America to Europe. There was no corresponding increase in the production of the necessities of life; prices therefore rose. The gainers in this process were the merchants and the middle-class gentry who farmed their own estates. The losers were the labouring class of town and country, who received no corresponding increase in wages, the peasants who were dispossessed to make way for the sheep, and many of the aristocracy.

The rise in prices hit the great landed aristocracy because their main source of income was from rents. Many of these rents were fixed by long leases and could not be raised to keep pace with the rising cost of living. This in itself would not have affected their position seriously had they been willing to cut down on their expenditure. In fact, they did the opposite. The period 1580–1603 saw an enormous increase in ostentatious waste on the part of the nobility. They built themselves great houses, surrounded themselves with retinues of servants, spent money lavishly on entertainments, hospitality, and clothes. The Earl of Leicester died £85,000 in debt, yet his funeral alone cost £3000. Gambling was rife among them, and those who served the Crown as public servants, ambassadors, or leaders of military expeditions had to find their expenses out of their own pockets. In a brilliant article in the *Economic History Review*, vol. xviii, 1948, Lawrence Stone shows that of the nineteen earls and marquesses in the country in 1600 only five were not deeply in debt.

In these difficulties members of the landed aristocracy had recourse to the money-lenders—*i.e.*, to the merchants and business-men of the City of London. They mortgaged their lands recklessly, and in due course many of these lands passed into the hands of the money-lenders, who established themselves as country gentlemen, so climbing the social ladder. In fact, a social revolution was taking place; the old rigid divisions between classes were disappearing. The possession of land was still the basis of social distinction, but it was the possession of money in the shape not only of ready cash, but of bonds, mortgages, and investments, that was becoming increasingly the true source of power and influence; and money was concentrated in the hands of the middle class.

People change their ways of living more easily and more rapidly than they change their ways of thinking and feeling. So great was the demand for credit in Elizabethan England that the merchants all over the country were almost forced to become money-lenders. What was emerging was an acquisitive society, in which money-making became more and more divorced from moral considerations, in which one man took into his hand the living of two or more; but people in general naturally tended to see it all from the old moral point of view. What impressed them was not the growing wealth of the country as a whole, but the spectacle of the great man plunged into debt, and of his estates passing into the hands of a London alderman. The moral conscience of the age saw the money-lender or userer, as it preferred to call him, as a monster, an agent of the devil, engaged in turning the old order of things upside down.

And so when Thomas Nashe, in *Pierce Penilesse*, directs his satire at the London of his day it is the usurer, the upstart, the proud merchant's wife—the moneyed middle class, in fact—that he singles out for special attention, and the framework of his satire is provided by the medieval conception of the Seven Deadly Sins. In the name of the old order Nashe condemns the new. But, while he is so very much aware of the power of the new merchant class, he is not blind to the way in which the folly of the aristocracy and their love of luxury were contributing to their downfall. His portrait of the prodigal young master is a penetrating piece of social criticism, which incidentally throws a great deal of light on the motives which sent the Elizabethan gentleman on voyages to distant parts of the world:

> A young heir or cockney, that is his mother's darling, if he have played the waste-good at the Inns of the Court or about London, and that neither his student's pension nor his unthrift's credit will serve to maintain his college of whores any longer, falls in a quarrelling humour with his fortune, because she made him not King of the Indies, and swears and stares, after ten in the hundred, that ne'er a such peasant as his father or brother shall keep him under: he will to the sea, and tear the gold out of the Spaniards' throats, but he will have it, byrlady. And when he comes there, poor soul, he lies in brine, in ballast, and is lamentable sick of the scurvies; his dainty fare is turned to a hungry feast of dogs and cats, or haberdine and poor John at the most, and, which is lamentablest of all, that without mustard.

The survival of medieval ways of thinking, so evident in Nashe's use of the Seven Deadly Sins, is apparent again in his long disquisition on devils, which is a counterblast to the more daring speculations of men like Marlowe. It is there, too, in Dekker's attitude to the plague, which he sees as God's visitation on London for its pride and luxury.

From a more specifically literary point of view the interest of these pamphlets is twofold, lying in the form that they take and the English in which they are written. The great attraction of the pamphlet for the Elizabethans lay in the fact that it was a new literary form. There were no models to be followed, no rules to be adhered to; the creative artist could do as he liked with it. George Orwell, in his introduction to *British Pamphleteers*, vol. i (1948), says this of the pamphlet:

> Probably a true pamphlet will always be somewhere between five hundred and ten thousand words, and it will always be unbound and obtainable for a few pence. A pamphlet is never written primarily to give entertainment or to make money. It is written because there is something one wants to say *now*, and because one believes there is no other way of getting a hearing. Pamphlets may turn on points of ethics or theology, but they always have a clear political implication. A pamphlet may be written either *for* or *against* somebody or something, but in essence it is always a protest.

This definition is too narrow. All three pamphlets reprinted here were written by professional writers to give entertainment and to make money. Not one of them is directly political, though all three are moral, and while the element of protest is strong in Nashe, it is less so in the other two. What each found in the pamphlet form was a means of self-expression and a field for experiment. Greene says that his purpose in writing the cony-catching stories is to expose the ways of cheats and to warn his fellow-citizens; it soon becomes apparent that he is really out to entertain, that he is using his knowledge of low life and his reading to produce a series of short stories, which hang together because they all deal with the same kind of activity, and are set in the same milieu.

Dekker, again, devotes the second half of *The Wonderful Year* to short stories, this time of a grim, macabre kind, recalling the gravediggers' scene in *Hamlet*, all of which illustrate his main theme of the plague. But in his case these short stories, dealing with particular incidents and related in a vivid, colloquial prose, are preceded by a general picture of the state of London in 1603 and of the coming of the plague, for which he uses a very different prose style, highly coloured and rhetorical, to bring out the contrast between the general and the particular.

Nashe is the most experimental and the most exuberant of the three. In *Pierce Penilesse* the supplication itself, based on the conception of the Seven Deadly Sins, has its antecedents in the medieval sermon; Chaucer's poor parson would have been thoroughly at home with the general plan of it. But within the old framework Nashe innovates; his telling satirical portraits of contemporary types—the prodigal young master, the proud merchant's wife, the counterfeit politician, and so on—anticipate some of the main features of the Theophrastan character as it was to be written by Hall, Overbury, and Earle in the seventeenth century. The defence of plays takes him into the field of literary criticism, while his inset anecdotes, such as "A Tale of a Wise Justice," or "A Rare Witty Jest of Doctor Watson," belong to the jest-book, which was so popular at the time. Outside the supplication proper the most striking feature both of the beginning and the end of *Pierce Penilesse* is the way in which Nashe takes an intimate friendly tone with his reader, even addressing him on one occasion as "gentle reader." The unbuttoned ease of this looks forward to the manner of an essayist like Cowley, and even more to that of Sterne. Indeed, with its rambling, digressive construction, its self-conscious virtuosity, and its parade of odd and out-of-the-way learning, all held together by the personality of the man behind it, *Pierce Penilesse* has much in common with *Tristram Shandy*.

In all three pamphlets there are qualities which suggest that it is here that journalism has its beginnings. This is clearest

in the case of *The Wonderful Year*, which is primarily a piece
of reporting. Dekker produces an account of the most
important events of 1603 for the benefit of the people who had
lived through those events, and the changes that he made in
one of his stories for the second edition would seem to show
that some of them are based on fact. In the first edition of the
work the story of the sexton of Stepney, who was frightened
out of his wits at finding a living man in one of his graves,
ends with Dekker reporting the death of the sexton. In the
second edition of *The Wonderful Year*, however, Dekker
alters this, having presumably learnt in the meantime that the
sexton was still alive, and instead of writing "he died in a
short time after," he now writes "he had like to have died
presently after."

There is something of the journalist, too, in the efforts that
these writers make to keep themselves in the public eye and
to advertise their own works. Greene tells one and the same
story in both *The Second Part of Cony-Catching* and *The Third
Part of Cony-Catching*, with a good deal of added detail at the
second telling—the story of how a cutpurse got a cutler to
make a special knife for him and then cut his purse with it.
Greene's aim in doing this is twofold. He gives the impression
that his stories are pieces of reporting, transcripts from life,
and that he is a reliable witness; and at the same time, when
he retells the story in *The Third Part of Cony-Catching*, he
advertises the earlier work. At the end of the second and
longer version he writes very virtuously:

> This tale, because it was somewhat misreported before, upon
> talk had with the poor cutler himself, is set down now in true
> form and manner how it was done; therefore is there no offence
> offered, when by better consideration, a thing may be enlarged
> or amended, or at least the note be better confirmed.

Indeed, in a subsequent pamphlet, *A Disputation between a
he Cony-Catcher and a she Cony-Catcher*, Greene goes so far
as to suggest that his pamphlets have spread terror in the

underworld, and that his life is in danger. Nevertheless he promises to continue his work and to publish a *Black Book*, containing the names of the most notorious rogues of the day. Whether Greene ever intended to write the *Black Book* it is impossible to say, because he died in 1592, the year that the *Disputation* was published. What is important is that in his work the sensational and the topical are carefully and deliberately exploited, as they are again in the work of Nashe, who carried the process of self-advertisement as far as it could be carried in his literary quarrel with Gabriel Harvey.

Far from being limited in the way that George Orwell suggests, the pamphlet, in the hands of the men who were using it round about the year 1600, was the most elastic of forms. Within it there was room for things as varied as the essay, the character sketch, the short story, the political pamphlet, and reportage, not to mention burlesque and personal invective.

This same vigour and fertility of invention and this same refusal to be cramped into any kind of formal strait-jacket appear again in the style of these writers. Their prose shows a considerable variety within itself. That of Greene is smooth-flowing and lucid; it is clearly based on the colloquial idiom of the day. That of Nashe is highly individual—a virtuoso display of verbal pyrotechnics. In his case the style is very much the man. That of Dekker falls between the two: he strains after effect as Greene does not; he does not invariably produce the effect he aims at, as Nashe always does; the second of his little poems on the death of Queen Elizabeth in *The Wonderful Year* is a collection of most ridiculous conceits.

Different as their styles are, all of them have one thing in common, which marks their prose off from that of a man like Addison, and, indeed, from all prose written since the Restoration: none of them feels that there is a written language, as distinct from the spoken language. They write for the ear rather than the eye, and in everything they say one is aware of

the human voice. It does not matter to them whether a word
is learned or low: if it expresses what they want to say they
use it. This is particularly evident in the work of Nashe, whose
style is largely the result of the way in which he brings together
the far-sought word and the commonplace word, the learned
phrase drawn from Latin and the homely phrase caught from
the lips of the people. His vocabulary is full of neologisms;
he makes up verbs in *-ize* at will—'adulterize,' 'citizenize,'
'sirenize,' 'tragedize,' etc.; needing a more expressive word
than 'gossip,' he coins 'chatmate'; seeking something more
picturesque than 'belly' he produces 'pudding-house.' Many
words now in common use in the language seem to have been
introduced by him; for many others that he uses the *Oxford
English Dictionary* has only one entry; they were never used
before and have never been used since. Alongside these words
Nashe sets words and phrases taken from the living speech of
the time, which in their expressiveness are a kind of natural
poetry. This can be best illustrated, not from *Pierce Penilesse*,
evident though it is there, but from the most mature of his
works, *Nashe's Lenten Stuff*, where in a burlesque version of
the Hero and Leander story he writes as follows (I give the
original spelling):

> The nurse or mother Mampudding, that was a cowring on
> the backe side whiles these things were a tragedizing [*i.e.*, the
> deaths of Hero and Leander] led by the scritch or outcry to the
> prospect of this sorrowfull heigho, as soone as through the raveld
> button holes of her bleare eyes, she had suckt in and received
> such a revelation of Domesday, and that she saw her mistris
> mounted a cockhorse, and hoysted away to hell or to heaven,
> on the backs of those rough headed ruffians [the waves], down
> she sunk to the earth as dead as a doore nail, and never mumpt
> crust after.[1]

The tendency has been for the written language to cut itself
off more and more from the vivid, slangy phrase, represented

[1] *Works of Thomas Nashe*, edited by R. B. McKerrow (1904–10), vol. iii, p. 200.

here by such things as "this sorrowfull heigho," or "never mumpt crust after," yet "mumpt" expresses the motion of toothless jaws as no other word does. Only in the Elizabethan Age would anyone have thought of translating "Hinc illae lachrymæ" as Dekker does: "She wept her bellyful for all this." Point, balance, and elegance are not qualities to be found in the prose of the Elizabethan pamphlets; what one finds instead is a vocabulary and a style that convey the look, the sound, and the feel of things with a peculiar sharpness and immediacy. It is essentially a poetical as opposed to a scientific use of language; the words smell of the soil from which they spring, the life of the times. Compared with later prose, that of men like Greene and Nashe and Dekker lacks precision; in particular, they use pronouns laxly, as we still do in conversation; 'he' may refer to any one of two or three people, but this lack of precision is more than compensated by the gain in vigour and expressiveness.

THE RISE OF THE PAMPHLET

The pamphlet is the result of a union between the old and the new, between the sermon, the chief vehicle for popular instruction during the Middle Ages, and the printing-press, which provided the preacher with what he had always wanted —the means of reaching a larger and a wider audience. The earliest works which can be described as pamphlets are, in fact, printed sermons published about the time of the Reformation. A typical example is a sermon by Bishop Fisher, *The Sermon of John, the Bishop of Rochester, made against the Pernicious Doctrine of Martin Luther*, which was printed by Wynkyn de Worde in 1521. This has the controversial quality that we associate with the pamphlet to-day, but the sober and dignified way in which Fisher argues his case is hardly that of the pamphleteer. Furthermore, this sermon was clearly written to be preached, and only published subsequently.

The earliest true pamphlet that I know, written for publi-
cation with the intention of influencing public opinion for a
practical end, is *A Supplication for the Beggars*, by Simon Fish,
which was published in 1529 and addressed to Henry VIII.
Into fewer than eleven pages (in a modern reprint) Fish packs
a brilliant piece of violent and outspoken anti-clerical propaganda, calling for the dissolution of the monasteries. The
Roman Catholic clergy are attacked on economic grounds, as
the engrossers of half the national income, which they do
nothing to earn; on political grounds, because they owe
allegiance to a foreign Power, the Papacy; on moral grounds,
because they spend their excessive leisure in debauching women;
and on religious grounds, because much of their teaching is
based on the idea of purgatory, which is not even mentioned
in the Bible. The argument is good, but it was the force and
violence with which it was expressed that made the work so
influential at the time, and which marked it out as the first true
pamphlet. Fish asks:

Who is she that will set her hands to work to get threepence
a day and may have at least twenty pence a day to sleep an hour
with a friar, a monk, or a priest? What is he that would labour
for a groat a day and may have at least twelve pence a day to be
bawd to a priest, a monk, or a friar? What a sort are there of
them that marry priests' sovereign ladies but to cloak the priest's
incontinency and that they may have a living of the priest themselves for their labour? How many thousands doth such lubricity
bring to beggary, theft and idleness, which should have kept their
good name and have set themselves to work had not been this
excess treasure of the spirituality? What honest man dare take
any man or woman in his service that hath been at such a school
with a spiritual man? Oh, the grievous shipwreck of the commonwealth, which in ancient time before the coming in of these
ravenous wolves was so prosperous: that then there were but few
thieves: yea, theft was at that time so rare that Cæsar was not
compelled to make penalty of death upon felony, as your grace
may well perceive in his institutes. There was also at that time

but few poor people and yet they did not beg, but there was given them enough unasked, for there was at that time none of these ravenous wolves to ask it from them as it appeareth in the Acts of the Apostles. Is it any marvel though there be now so many beggars, thieves and idle people? Nay truly.[1]

From this time onward the pamphlet became the main instrument of controversy and propaganda in an age which was rapidly discovering the power of the printed word. The chief source of controversy throughout the sixteenth century and well on into the seventeenth was religion. During the reign of Elizabeth the State Church was assailed from the one side by the Catholics living in exile on the Continent, and from the other by the Puritans at home, and the power the pamphleteers exercised is evidenced by the steps that the Government took against them. Everything possible was done to prevent the import and circulation of Catholic pamphlets; and when in the years 1588–89 an illegal Puritan press issued a series of witty and influential anti-episcopalian pamphlets, written under the pseudonym of Martin Marprelate, the Government not only pursued the printing-press itself with unrelenting rigour from one part of the country to another, eventually running it to earth in Manchester, but also took the unusual step of hiring professional writers, of whom Nashe was probably one, to answer the Martinists in their own style.

While religion was the main topic of pamphleteering during the sixteenth century, however, it was by no means the only one. *A Supplication for the Beggars* shows how intimately religious, political, social, economic, and moral problems were involved with one another, and all these topics were dealt with in subsequent pamphlets. Throughout the century there was a steady widening of the uses to which the pamphlet was put, and by the end of Elizabeth's reign stage-plays, witchcraft, the lot of the soldier, and even tobacco-smoking had all been the subjects of paper battles, while the

[1] *A Supplicacyon for the Beggers*, edited by E. Arber (1878), p. 8.

most famous literary quarrel of the age, that between Nashe and Gabriel Harvey, was carried on by the same means.

Nor was the pamphlet restricted to controversy. About the year 1552, or possibly somewhat earlier, one Gilbert Walker, about whom nothing is known, produced a pamphlet entitled: *A Manifest Detection of the most vile and detestable use of Diceplay.* Written in the form of a conversation in the "Church of Pauls," this gives a most interesting and detailed account of the way in which professional dice-players and card-sharpers, using weighted dice and marked cards, fleeced foolish young gentleman who had more money than sense. The author's purpose is to give information, and in this he succeeds. *A Manifest Detection* makes it plain that by the middle of the sixteenth century there already existed a large and well-organized London underworld, living by its wits and extending its activities to other parts of the country. There is nothing controversial about it at all, but the lively way in which it is written and the use of anecdote suggest that it was intended to entertain as well as to inform.

The same two purposes lie behind John Awdeley's *The Fraternity of Vagabonds*, which appeared in 1561. This is the first attempt in English to describe the methods used by the landless men, the sturdy rogues and vagabonds, to obtain by force and by cheating the living that society denied them. Awdeley's work is brief, and seems to be a mixture of fact and fiction. Its importance lies in two things: first, it had the effect of directing the attention of others to the study of vagabonds and their ways, and, secondly, the details that Awdeley gives about the canting language used by the rogues of the time caught the fancy of an age which was interested in words and the possibilities of language as no age has been since.

Out of this grew something much bigger and more important, *A Caveat or Warning for Common Cursitors, vulgarly called Vagabonds, set forth by Thomas Harman, Esquire, for the Utility and Profit of his Natural Country*, published in 1566. Harman was a country magistrate, living at Crayford, in Kent. A born sociologist, he made it his business to elicit all the information he could from the rogues and vagabonds who came to his house for charity and advice. This information he analysed and classified and finally set out in his book. His method is to give a description of a particular type of rogue, followed by an anecdote illustrating that rogue's methods. Harman denies that he has any literary ability; he says of himself, "Eloquence have I none; I never was acquainted with the Muses: I never tasted of Helicon. But according to my plain order, I have set forth this work, simply and truly, with such usual terms as is among us well known and frequented." In fact, however, Harman's "plain order" produces a most convincing narrative style, and it is not surprising that four editions of the work came out in seven years. A good example of his method is provided by his description of "A Hooker, or Angler":

> These hookers, or anglers, be perilous and most wicked knaves, and be derived or proceed forth from the upright-men. They commonly go in frieze jerkins and gallyslops, pointed beneath the knee. These, when they practise their pilfering, it is all by night; for, as they walk a day-times from house to house to demand charity, they vigilantly mark where or in what place they may attain to their prey, casting their eyes up to every window, well noting what they see there, whether apparel or linen, hanging near unto the said windows, and that they will be sure to have the next night following. For they customably carry with them a staff of five or six foot long, in which, within one inch of the top thereof, is a little hole bored through in which hole they put an iron hook, and with the same they will pluck unto them quickly anything that they may reach therewith, which hook in the day-time they covertly carry about with them, and is never seen or taken out till they come to the place where they work their feat.
> Such have I seen at my house, and have oft talked with them and have handled their staves, not then understanding to what

use or intent they served, although I had and perceived by their talk and behaviour great likelihood of evil suspicion in them. They will either lean upon their staff, to hide the hole thereof, when they talk with you or hold their hand upon the hole. And what stuff, either woollen or linen, they thus hook out, they never carry the same forthwith to their stalling kens, but hides the same a three days in some secret corner, and after conveys the same to their houses above said, where their host or hostess giveth them money for the same, but half the value that it is worth, or else their doxies shall afar off sell the same at the like houses. I was credibly informed that a hooker came to a farmer's house in the dead of the night, and putting back a draw window of a low chamber, the bed standing hard by the said window, in which lay three persons (a man and two big boys), this hooker with his staff plucked off their garments, which lay upon them to keep them warm, with the coverlet and sheet, and left them lying asleep naked saving their shirts, and had away all clean, and never could understand where it became. I verily suppose that when they were well waked with cold, they surely thought that Robin Goodfellow, according to the old saying, had been with them that night.[1]

To make his work thoroughly serviceable Harman adds an alphabetical list of the names of such rogues as he had met, or heard of, and a canting dictionary.

Intending to produce a social document, Harman had, in fact, produced a 'best-seller.' What he wrote as a warning to the plain citizen to be on his guard, and as a plea to the Government to take more stringent action, was read for much the same reasons that certain Sunday newspapers are read to-day.

The final development with which we are concerned in this kind of literature came about 1590, when Robert Greene, who had an unerring instinct for what the public of the day required, turned his back on the Euphuistic romances, which he had been writing for the previous six or seven years, and began to exploit the appeal of the underworld. Greene knew this

---

[1] *The Elizabethan Underworld*, edited by A. V. Judges (Routledge, 1930), p. 73.

C

underworld well—he had been living in it since 1585—and in the cony-catching pamphlets which he now produced he says again and again that his aim is didactic. The motto on the title-page of the first of them, *Nascimur pro patria*, is in effect a Latinized version of Harman's phrase "for the utility and profit of his natural country." Nevertheless one has only to read them to see that Greene's purpose is not to warn or to teach, but to entertain. What he does is to use his own knowledge of London and its more disreputable characters, and to combine this with the material provided by Walker and Harman to produce a series of fascinating stories. The brief anecdote, which Harman had used by way of illustration, is expanded by Greene and becomes the staple of his work. In the first two cony-catching pamphlets, *A Notable Discovery of Cozenage* and *The Second Part of Cony-Catching*, published in 1591, there is still a certain amount of factual information in the manner of Harman, though it is cut down to a minimum. In the pamphlets that followed it disappears altogether. In *The Third and Last Part of Cony-Catching* the process is complete. From being the vehicle for controversy only the pamphlet has now become the vehicle for creative, imaginative writing also.

SOURCE OF THE TEXT

The text, which has been modernized, is based on that of the earliest extant editions. The copies used are the following:

> *The Thirde and Last Part of Conny Catching.* The copy of the edition of 1592 in the Bodleian Library (Malone 575).
>
> *Pierce Penilesse his Supplication to the Divell.* The copy of the third edition of 1592 in the British Museum (C. 40. d. 19).
>
> *The Wonderfull Yeare.* The copy of the first edition of 1603 in the Bodleian Library (Wood 616 (i)).

THE THIRD AND LAST PART OF CONY-CATCHING

WITH THE NEW-DEVISED KNAVISH ART OF FOOL-TAKING

*The like cozenages and villainies
never before discovered*

BY

ROBERT GREENE, M.A.

*To all such as have received either pleasure or profit by
the two former published books of this argument, and
to all beside that desire to know the wonderful sly
devices of this hellish crew of cony-catchers*

In the time of King Henry the Fourth, as our English
chroniclers have kept in remembrance, lived divers sturdy and
loose companions in sundry places about the City of London,
who gave themselves to no good course of life, but, because
the time was somewhat troublesome, watched diligently when,
by the least occasion of mutiny offered, they might prey upon
the goods of honest citizens and so by their spoil enrich themselves. At that time likewise lived a worthy gentleman, whose
many very famous deeds (whereof I am sorry I may here make
no rehearsal, because neither time nor occasion will permit
me) renown his name to all ensuing posterities, he being

called Sir Richard Whittington, the founder of Whittington College in London, and one that bore the office of Lord Mayor of this city three several times. This worthy man, well noting the dangerous disposition of that idle kind of people, took such good and discreet order (after he had sent divers of them to serve in the king's wars, and they, loath to do so well, returned to their former vomit) that in no place of or about London they might have lodging or entertainment, except they applied themselves to such honest trades and exercises as might witness their maintaining was by true and honest means. If any to the contrary were found they were in justice so sharply proceeded against as the most hurtful and dangerous enemies to the commonwealth.

In this quiet and most blissful time of peace, when all men, in course of life, should shew themselves most thankful for so great a benefit, this famous city is pestered with the like, or rather worse kind of people, that bear outward shew of civil, honest, and gentlemanlike disposition, but in very deed their behaviour is most infamous to be spoken of. And as now by their close villainies they cheat, cozen, prig, lift, nip, and such like tricks now used in their cony-catching trade to the hurt and undoing of many an honest citizen and other: so if God should in justice be angry with us, as our wickedness hath well deserved, and, as the Lord forfend, our peace should be molested as in former time—even as they did, so will these be the first in seeking domestical spoil and ruin; yea, so they may have it, it skills not how they come by it. God raise such another as was worthy Whittington, that in time may bridle the headstrong course of this hellish crew and force them live as becometh honest subjects, or else to abide the reward due to their looseness.

By reading this little treatise ensuing you shall see to what marvellous subtle policies these deceivers have attained, and how daily they practise strange drifts for their purpose. I say no more, but if all these forewarnings may be regarded, to the

benefit of the well minded, and just control of these careless
wretches, it is all I desire and no more than I hope to see.

Yours in all he may,

R. G.

THE THIRD AND LAST PART OF
CONY-CATCHING

BEING by chance invited to supper, where were present divers,
both of worship and good account, as occasion served for
intercourse of talk, the present treacheries and wicked devices
of the world was called in question. Amongst other most
hateful and well worthy reprehension, the wondrous villainies
of loose and lewd persons, that bear the shape of men yet are
monsters in condition, was specially remembered; and not only
they, but their complices, their confederates, their base-
natured women, and close compacters were noted; namely,
such as term themselves cony-catchers, cross-biters, with their
appertaining names to their several cozening qualities, as
already is made known to the world by two several imprinted
books, by means whereof the present kind of conference was
occasioned.

Quoth a gentleman sitting at the table, whose deep step
into age deciphered his experience, and whose gravity of
speech reported his discretion; quoth he: "By the two published books of cony-catching I have seen divers things
whereof I was before ignorant; notwithstanding, had I been
acquainted with the author, I could have given him such notes
of notorious matters that way intenting, as in neither of the
pamphlets are the like set down. Beside, they are so necessary
to be known, as they will both forearm any man against such
treacherous vipers, and forewarn the simpler sort from conversing with them."

The gentleman being known to be within Commission of
the Peace, and that what he spake of either came to him by

examinations, or by riding in the circuits as other like officers do, was entreated by one man above the rest, as his leisure served him, to acquaint him with those notes, and he would so bring it to pass, as the writer of the other two books should have sight of them, and if their quantity would serve, that he should publish them as a third and more necessary part than the former were.

The gentleman replied: "All such notes as I speak, are not of mine own knowledge, yet from such men have I received them, as I dare assure their truth; and but that by naming men wronged by such mates, more displeasure would ensue than were expedient, I could set down both time, place and parties. But the certainty shall suffice without any such offence. As for such as shall see their injuries discovered and, biting the lip, say to themselves, 'Thus was I made a cony,' their names being shadowed, they have no cause of anger, in that the example of their honest simplicity beguiled may shield a number more endangered from tasting the like. And seeing you have promised to make them known to the author of the former two books, you shall the sooner obtain your request; assuring him thus much upon my credit and honesty, that no one untruth is in the notes, but every one credible, and to be justified if need serve."

Within a fortnight or thereabout afterward the gentleman performed his promise, in several papers sent the notes, which here are in our book compiled together. When thou hast read say if ever thou heardest more notable villainies discovered. And if thou or thy friends receive any good by them, as it cannot be but they will make a number more careful of themselves, thank the honest gentleman for his notes, and the writer that published both the other and these for general example.

*A pleasant tale how an honest substantial citizen was
made a cony, and simply entertained a knave that
carried away his goods very politicly.*

What laws are used among this hellish crew, what words
and terms they give themselves and their copesmates are at
large set down in the former two books; let it suffice ye then
in this, to read the simple true discourses of such as have by
extraordinary cunning and treachery been deceived, and,
remembering their subtle means there, and sly practices here,
be prepared against the reaches of any such companions.

Not long since, a crew of cony-catchers meeting together
and in conference laying down such courses as they severally
should take to shun suspect and return a common benefit
among them; the carders received their charge, the dicers
theirs, the hangers about the court theirs, the followers of
sermons theirs, and so the rest to their offices. But one of
them especially, who at their wonted meetings, when report
was made how every purchase was gotten, and by what policy
each one prevailed, this fellow in a kind of priding scorn,
would usually say:

"In faith, masters, these things are prettily done, common
sleights, expressing no deep reach of wit, and I wonder men
are so simple to be so beguiled. I would fain see some rare
artificial feat indeed, that some admiration and fame might
ensue the doing thereof. I promise ye, I disdain these base
and petty paltries, and—may my fortune jump with my
resolution—ye shall hear, my boys, within a day or two, that
I will accomplish a rare stratagem indeed, of more value than
forty of yours, and when it is done shall carry some credit
with it."

They, wondering at his words, desired to see the success of
them, and so, dispersing themselves as they were accustomed,
left this frolic fellow pondering on his affairs.

A citizen's house in London, which he had diligently eyed and aimed at for a fortnight's space, was the place wherein he must perform this exploit; and having learned one of the servant maids' name of the house, as also where she was born and her kindred, upon a Sunday in the afternoon, when it was her turn to attend on her master and mistress to the garden in Finsbury Fields to regard the children while they sported about, this crafty mate, having duly watched their coming forth and seeing that they intended to go down St Laurence Lane, stepped before them, ever casting an eye back lest they should turn some contrary way. But, their following still fitting his own desire, near unto the conduit in Aldermanbury he crossed the way and came unto the maid and, kissing her, said: "Cousin Margaret, I am very glad to see you well; my uncle your father, and all your friends in the country are in good health, God be praised."

The maid, hearing herself named and not knowing the man, modestly blushed, which he perceiving, held way on with her amongst her fellow apprentices, and thus began again: "I see, cousin, you know me not, and I do not greatly blame you, it is so long since you came forth of the country; but I am such a one's son," naming her uncle right, and his son's name, which she very well remembered but had not seen him in eleven years. Then, taking forth a bowed groat and an old penny bowed, he gave it to her as being sent from her uncle and aunt, whom he termed to be his father and mother. "Withal," quoth he, "I have a gammon of bacon and a cheese from my uncle your father, which are sent to your master and mistress, which I received of the carrier, because my uncle enjoined me to deliver them, when I must entreat your mistress that at Whitsuntide next she will give you leave to come down into the country."

The maid, thinking simply all he said was true, and as they so far from their parents are not only glad to hear of their welfare but also rejoice to see any of their kindred—so this poor maid, well knowing her uncle had a son so named as he called himself and thinking from a boy, as he was at her leaving the country, he was now grown such a proper handsome young man, was not a little joyful to see him. Beside, she seemed proud that her kinsman was so neat a youth, and so she held on questioning with him about her friends; he soothing each matter so cunningly, as the maid was confidently persuaded of him.

In this time, one of the children stepped to her mother and said, "Our Marget, mother, hath a fine cousin come out of the country, and he hath a cheese for my father and you." Whereon she, looking back, said: "Maid, is that your kinsman?" "Yea, forsooth, mistress," quoth she, "my uncle's son, whom I left a little one when I came forth of the country."

The wily treacher, being master of his trade, would not let slip this opportunity, but courteously stepping to the mistress (who, loving her maid well, because indeed she had been a very good servant and from her first coming to London had dwelt with her, told her husband thereof) coined such a smooth tale unto them both, fronting it with the gammon of bacon and the cheese sent from their maid's father, and hoping they would give her leave at Whitsuntide to visit the country, as they with very kind words entertained him, inviting him the next night to supper, when he promised to bring with him the gammon of bacon and the cheese. Then framing an excuse of certain business in the town, for that time he took his leave of the master and mistress and his new cousin Margaret, who gave many a look after him, poor wench, as he went, joying in her thoughts to have such a kinsman.

On the morrow he prepared a good gammon of bacon, which he closed up in a soiled linen cloth, and sewed an old card upon it, whereon he wrote a superscription unto the master of the maid, and at what sign it was to be delivered, and afterwards scraped some of the letters half out that it might seem they had been rubbed out in the carriage. A good cheese he prepared likewise, with inscription accordingly on it, that it could not be discerned but that some unskilful writer in the country had done it, both by the gross proportion of the letters, as also the bad orthography, which amongst plain husbandmen is very common in that they have no better instruction. So, hiring a porter to carry them, between five and six in the evening he comes to the citizen's house and entering the shop receives them of the porter, whom the honest-meaning citizen would have paid for his pains; but this his maid's new-found cousin said he was satisfied already, and so, straining courtesy, would not permit him. Well, up are carried the bacon and the cheese, where—God knows— Margaret was not a little busy to have all things fine and neat against her cousin's coming up. Her mistress likewise, as one well affecting her servant, had provided very good cheer, set all her plate on the cupboard for shew, and beautified the house with cushions, carpets, stools, and other devices of needlework, as at such times divers will do to have the better report made of their credit amongst their servants' friends in the country; albeit at this time, God wot, it turned to their own after-sorrowing.

The master of the house, to delay the time while supper was ready, he likewise shews this dissembler his shop; who, seeing things fadge so pat to his purpose, could question of this sort and that well enough, I warrant you, to discern the best from the worst and their appointed places, purposing a further reach than the honest citizen dreamed of. And to be plain with ye, such was this occupier's trade, as though I may not name it, yet thus much I dare utter, that the worst thing he could carry away was worth above twenty nobles, because he dealt altogether in whole and great sale, which made this companion forge this kindred and acquaintance, for an hundred pound or twain was the very least he aimed at.

At length the mistress sends word supper is on the table, whereupon up he conducts his guest. And after divers wel-

comes, as also thanks for the cheese and bacon, to the table
they sit; where, let it suffice, he wanted no ordinary good fare,
wine, and other knacks, beside much talk of the country—
how much his friends were beholding for his cousin Margaret,
to whom by her mistress' leave he drank twice or thrice, and
she, poor soul, doing the like again to him with remembrance
of her father and other kindred, which he still smoothed very
cunningly. Countenance of talk made them careless of the
time, which slipped from them faster than they were aware
of; nor did the deceiver hasten his departing, because he
expected what indeed followed, which was that being past
ten of the clock, and he feigning his lodging to be at Saint
Giles in the Field, was entreated both by the good man and
his wife, to take a bed there for that night. For fashion sake,
though very glad of this offer, he said he would not trouble
them, but, giving them many thanks, would to his lodging
though it were further. But wonderful it was to see how
earnest the honest citizen and his wife laboured to persuade
him, that was more willing to stay than they could be to bid
him, and what dissembled willingness of departure he used
on the other side, to cover the secret villainy intended! Well,
at the length, with much ado, he is contented to stay, when
Margaret and her mistress presently stirred to make ready his
bed, which—the more to the honest man's hard hap, but all
the better for this artificial cony-catcher—was in the same
room where they supped, being commonly called their hall;
and there, indeed, stood a very fair bed, as in such sightly
rooms it may easily be thought citizens use not to have anything mean or simple.

The mistress, lest her guest should imagine she disturbed
him, suffered all the plate to stand still on the cupboard; and
when she perceived his bed was warmed, and everything else
according to her mind, she and her husband, bidding him
goodnight, took themselves to their chamber, which was on
the same floor, but inward, having another chamber between

them and the hall, where the maids and children had their lodging. So desiring him to call for anything he wanted, and charging Margaret to look it should be so, to bed are they gone; when the apprentices having brought up the keys of the street door, and left them in their master's chamber as they were wont to do, after they had said prayers, their evening exercise, to bed go they likewise, which was in a garret backward over their master's chamber.

None are now up but poor Margaret and her counterfeit cousin, whom she, loath to offend with long talk, because it waxed late, after some few more speeches about their parents and friends in the country, she, seeing him laid in bed, and all such things by him as she deemed needful, with a low curtsy, I warrant ye, commits him to his quiet, and so went to bed to her fellows the maidservants.

Well did this hypocrite perceive the keys of the doors carried into the good man's chamber, whereof he being not a little glad, thought now they would imagine all things sure and therefore doubtless sleep the sounder. As for the keys, he needed no help of them, because such as he go never unprovided of instruments fitting their trade, and so at this time was this notable treacher.

In the dead time of the night, when sound sleep makes the ear unapt to hear the very least noise, he forsaketh his bed, and having gotten all the plate bound up together in his cloak, goeth down into the shop; where, well remembering both the place and parcels, maketh up his pack with some twenty pounds' worth of goods more. Then, settling to his engine, he getteth the door off the hinges, and, being forth, lifteth close to again, and so departs, meeting within a dozen paces three or four of his companions that lurked thereabouts for the purpose. Their word for knowing each other, as is said, was *quest*, and this villain's comfortable news to them was *twag*, signifying he had sped. Each takes a fleece for easier carriage, and so away to *Bell brow*, which, as I have heard, is, as they interpret it, the house of a thief receiver, without which they can do nothing; and this house with an apt porter to it stands ready for them all hours of the night. Too many such are there in London, the masters whereof bear countenance of honest substantial men, but all their living is gotten in this order; the end of such, though they scape awhile, will be sailing westward in a cart to Tyburn.

Imagine these villains there in their jollity, the one reporting point by point his cunning deceit, and the other, fitting his humour, extolling the deed with no mean commendations.

But returning to the honest citizen, who, finding in the morning how dearly he paid for a gammon of bacon and a cheese and how his kind courtesy was thus treacherously requited, blames the poor maid, as innocent herein as himself, and imprisoning her, thinking so to regain his own, grief with ill cherishing there shortens her life. And thus ensueth one hard hap upon another, to the great grief both of master and mistress, when the truth was known, that they so wronged their honest servant. How it may forewarn others I leave to your own opinions, that see what extraordinary devices are nowadays to beguile the simple and honest liberal-minded.

Of a notable knave, who, for his cunning deceiving a gentleman of his purse, scorned the name of a cony-catcher and would needs be termed a fool-taker, as master and beginner of that new-found art.

A crew of these wicked companions being one day met together in Paul's Church (as that is a usual place of their assembly both to determine on their drifts as also to speed of many a booty) seeing no likelihood of a good afternoon (so they term it either forenoon or after when aught is to be done) some dispersed themselves to the plays, others to the bowling-alleys, and not past two or three stayed in the church.

Quoth one of them, "I have vowed not to depart, but something or other I'll have before I go; my mind gives me that this place yet will yield us all our suppers this night." The other, holding like opinion with him, there likewise walked up and down, looking when occasion would serve for some cash.

At length they espied a gentleman toward the law entering in at the little north door, and a country client going with him in very hard talk. The gentleman holding his gown open with his arms on either side, as very many do, gave sight of a fair purple velvet purse, which was half put under his girdle, which, I warrant you, the resolute fellow that would not depart without something had quickly espied. "A game," quoth he to his fellows, "mark the stand"; and so separating themselves walked aloof; the gentleman going to the nether step of the stairs that ascend up into the choir, and there he walked still with his client.

Oft this crew of mates met together, and said there was no hope of nipping the bung because he held open his gown so wide and walked in such an open place. "Base knaves," quoth the frolic fellow, "if I say I will have it, I must have it, though he that owes it had sworn the contrary." Then, looking aside, he spied his trug or quean coming up the church. "Away," quoth he to the other, "go look you for some other purchase, this wench and I are sufficient for this."

They go. He lessons the drab in this sort, that she should to the gentleman, whose name she very well knew, in that she had holp to cozen him once before, and pretending to be sent to him from one he was well acquainted with for his counsel, should give him his fee for avoiding suspicion, and so frame some wrong done her, as well enough she could; when her mate, taking occasion as it served, would work the mean, she should strike, and so they both prevail.

The quean, well inured with such courses, because she was one of the most skilful in that profession, walked up and down alone in the gentleman's sight, that he might discern she stayed to speak with him, and as he turned toward her, he saw her take money out of her purse, whereby he gathered some benefit was toward him; which made him the sooner dispatch his other client; when she, stepping to him, told such a tale of commendations from his very friend, that had sent her to him, as she said, that he entertained her very kindly. And giving him his fee, which before her face he put up into his purse and thrust it under his girdle again, she proceeded to a very sound discourse, whereto he listened with no little attention.

The time serving fit for the fellow's purpose, he came behind the gentleman, and as many times one friend will familiarly with another clap his hands over his eyes to make him guess who he is, so did this companion, holding his hands fast over the gentleman's eyes, said, "Who am I?" twice or thrice, in which time the drab had gotten the purse and put it up. The gentleman, thinking it had been some merry friend of his, reckoned the names of three or four, when, letting him go, the crafty knave, dissembling a bashful shame of what he had done, said: "By my troth, sir, I cry ye mercy; as I came in at the church door, I took ye for such a one (naming a man), a very friend of mine, whom you very much resemble: I beseech ye be not angry, it was very boldly done of me, but in penance of my fault, so please ye to accept it, I will bestow a gallon or two of wine on ye," and so laboured him earnestly to go with him to the tavern, still alleging his sorrow for mistaking him.

The gentleman, little suspecting how "Who am I?" had handled him, seeing how sorry he was, and seeming to be a man of no such base condition, took all in good part, saying, "No harm, sir, to take one for another, a fault wherein any man may easily err," and so excusing the acceptation of his wine because he was busy there with a gentlewoman, his friend.

The treacher with courtesy departed; and the drab (having what she would) shortening her tale (he desiring her to come to his chamber the next morning) went to the place where her copes-mate and she met, and not long after, divers other of the crew, who hearing in what manner this act was performed, smiled agood thereat, that she had both got the gentleman's purse, her own money again, and his advice for just nothing.

He that had done this tall exploit, in a place so open in view, so hardly to be come by, and on a man that made no mean esteem of his wit, bids his fellows keep the worthless name of a cony-catcher to themselves; for he henceforth would be termed a fool-taker, and such as could imitate this quaint example of his, which he set down as an entrance into that art, should not think scorn to become his scholars.

Night drawing on apace, the gentleman returned home, not all this while missing his purse; but being set at supper, his wife entreated a pint of sack, which he minding to send for, drew to his purse, and seeing it gone, what strange looks, beside sighs, were between him and his wife, I leave to your supposing. And blame them not; for, as I have heard, there was seven pound in gold, beside thirty shillings and odd white money in the purse. But in the midst of his grief he remembered him that said, "Who am I?"; wherewith he brake forth into a great laughter, the cause whereof his wife being desirous to know, he declared all that passed between him and the deceiver, as also how soon afterward the quean abbreviated her discourse and followed. "So by troth, wife," quoth he, "between 'Who am I?' and the drab, my purse is gone." Let his loss teach others to look better to theirs.

———————

Another tale of a cozening companion, who would needs
try his cunning in this new-invented art, and how by his
knavery at one instant he beguiled half a dozen and more.

Of late time there hath a certain base kind of trade been
used, who, though divers poor men, and doubtless honest,
apply themselves to only to relieve their need, yet are there
some notorious varlets do the same, being compacted with
such kind of people as this present treatise manifesteth to the
world; and what with outward simplicity on the one side,
and cunning close treachery on the other, divers honest citizens
and day-labouring men that resort to such places as I am to
speak of, only for recreation as opportunity serveth, have been
of late sundry times deceived of their purses. This trade, or
rather unsufferable loitering quality, in singing of ballads and
songs at the doors of such houses where plays are used, as
also in open markets and other places of this city, where is
most resort; which is nothing else but a sly fetch to draw many
together, who listening unto an harmless ditty, afterward
walk home to their houses with heavy hearts. From such as
are hereof true witnesses to their cost, do I deliver this example.

A subtle fellow, belike emboldened by acquaintance with the
former deceit, or else being but a beginner to practise the
same, calling certain of his companions together, would try
whether he could attain to be master of his art or no, by taking
a great many of fools with one train. But let his intent, and
what else beside, remain to abide the censure after the matter
is heard, and come to Gracious Street, where this villainous
prank was performed.

A roguing mate and such another with him were there got
upon a stall singing of ballads; which belike was some pretty
toy, for very many gathered about to hear it, and divers buying,
as their affections served, drew to their purses and paid the
singers for them. The sly mate and his fellows, who were

D

dispersed among them that stood to hear the songs, well noted where every man that bought put up his purse again. And to such as would not buy, counterfeit warning was sundry times given by the rogue and his associate, to beware of the cut-purse and look to their purses, which made them often feel where their purses were, either in sleeve, hose, or at girdle, to know whether they were safe or no. Thus the crafty copes-mates were acquainted with what they most desired; and as they were scattered, by shouldering, thrusting, feigning to let fall something, and other wily tricks fit for their purpose, here one lost his purse, there another had his pocket picked, and, to say all in brief, at one instant, upon the complaint of one or two that saw their purses were gone, eight more in the same company found themselves in like predicament. Some angry, others sorrowful, and all greatly discontented, looking about them knew not who to suspect or challenge, in that the villains themselves that had thus beguiled them, made shew that they had sustained like loss. But one angry fellow, more impatient than all the rest, he falls upon the ballad singer, and, beating him with his fists well favouredly, says, if he had not listened his singing, he had not lost his purse; and therefore would not be otherwise persuaded, but that they two and the cutpurses were compacted together. The rest that had lost their purses likewise, and saw that so many complain together, they jump in opinion with the other fellow, and begin to tug and hale the ballad singers; when one after one the false knaves began to shrink away with the purses. By means of some officer then being there present the two rogues were had before a Justice; and, upon his discreet examination made, it was found that they and the cutpurses were compacted together, and that by this unsuspected villainy they had deceived many. The fine fool-taker himself, with one or two more of that company, was not long after apprehended, when I doubt not but they had their reward answerable to their deserving; for I hear of their journey westward, but not of their return. Let this forewarn those that listen singing in the streets.

———————

Of a crafty mate, that brought two young men unto a tavern, where, departing, with a cup, he left them to pay both for the wine and the cup.

A friend of mine sent me this note, and assuring me the truth thereof, I thought necessary to set it down amongst the rest, both for the honest simplicity on the one side and most cunning knavery used on the other; and thus it was:

Two young men of familiar acquaintance, who delighted much in music, because themselves therein were somewhat expert, as on the virginals, bandora, lute, and such like, were one evening at a common inn of this town, as I have heard, where the one of them shewed his skill on the virginals to the no little contentment of the hearers. Now as divers guests of the house came into the room to listen, so among the rest entered an artificial cony-catcher, who, as occasion served, in the time of ceasing between the several toys and fancies he played, very much commended his cunning, quick hand, and such qualities praiseworthy in such a professor.

The time being come, when these young men craved leave to depart, this politic varlet, stepping to them, desired that they would accept a quart of wine at his hand, which he would, most gladly he would, bestow upon them: besides, if it liked him that played on the virginals to instruct, he would help him to so good a place, as happily might advantage him for ever.

These kind words, delivered with such honest outward shew, caused the young men, whose thoughts were free from any other opinion than to be as truly and plainly dealt withal as themselves meant, accepted his offer, because he that played on the virginals was desirous to have some good place of service. And hereupon to the tavern they go, and, being set, the wily companion calleth for two pints of wine, a pint of white and a pint of claret, casting his cloak upon the table and falling to his former communication of preferring the young man. The wine is brought, and two cups withal, as is the usual manner; when drinking to them of the one pint, they pledge him, not unthankful for his gentleness. After some time spent in talk, and as he perceived, fit for his purpose, he takes the other cup, and tastes the other pint of wine; wherewith he finding fault, that it drank somewhat hard, said that rose-water and sugar would do no harm; whereupon he leaves his seat, saying he was well acquainted with one of the servants of the house, of whom he could have two pennyworth of rose-water for a penny, and so of sugar likewise, wherefore he would step to the bar unto him. So, taking the cup in his hand, he did, the young men never thinking on any such treachery as ensued, in that he seemed an honest man, and beside left his cloak lying on the table by them.

No more returns the younker with rose-water and sugar, but stepping out of doors, unseen of any, goes away roundly with the cup. The young men, not a little wondering at his long tarrying, by the coming of the servants to see what they wanted, who took no regard of his sudden departure, find themselves there left, not only to pay for the wine, but for the cup also, being rashly supposed by the master and his servants to be copartners with the treacherous villain. But their honest behaviour well known, as also their simplicity too much abused, well witnessed their innocency; notwithstanding they were fain to pay for the cup, as afterward they did, having nothing towards their charge but a threadbare cloak not worth two shillings.

Take heed how you drink wine with any such companions.

----

*Of an honest householder, which was cunningly
deceived by a subtle companion, that came to hire a
chamber for his master.*

Not far from Charing Cross dwelleth an honest young man,
who being not long since married and having more rooms in
his house than himself occupieth, either for term time or the
Court lying so near, as divers do, to make a reasonable commodity, and to ease house-rent, which as the world goeth
now is none of the cheapest, letteth forth a chamber or two,
according as it may be spared.

In an evening but a while since, came one in the manner of
a serving man to this man and his wife, and he must needs
have a chamber for his master, offering so largely, as the
bargain was soon concluded between them. His intent was to
have fingered some booty in the house, as by the sequel it
may be likeliest gathered; but belike no fit thing lying abroad,
or he better regarded than happily he would be, his expectation
that way was frustrate. Yet as a resolute cony-catcher indeed,
that scorneth to attempt without some success, and rather will
prey upon small commodity, than return to his fellows dis-
graced with a lost labour, he summons his wits together and
by a smooth tale overreached both the man and his wife.

He tells them that his master was a captain late come from
the sea, and had costly apparel to bring thither, which, for
more easy carriage, he entreats them lend him a sheet to bind
it up in. They suspecting no ill, because he required their boy
should go with him to help him carry the stuff, the good wife
steps unto her chest, where her linen lay finely sweetened with
roseleaves and lavender, and lends him a very good sheet
indeed.

This success made him bold to venture a little further, and
then he tells them his master had a great deal of broken sugar
and fine spices that lay negligently abroad in his lodging as it

was brought from the ship, all which he was assured his master would bestow on them, so he could devise how to get it brought thither.

These liberal promises prevailing with them that lightly believed, and withal were somewhat covetous of the sugar and spices, the woman demanded if a couple of pillow-beres would not serve to bring the sugar and spices in. "Yes, marry," quoth he, "so the sugar may best be kept by itself and the spices by themselves. And," quoth he, "because there are many crafty knaves abroad," (grieving that any should be craftier than himself) and in the evening the linen might quickly be snatched from the boy, for the more safety he would carry the sheet and pillow-beres himself, and within an hour or little more, return with the boy again, because he would have all things ready before his master came, who, as he said, was attending on the Council at the Court.

The man and his wife, crediting his smooth speeches, sends their boy with him, and so along toward Ivy Bridge go they. The cony-catcher seeing himself at free liberty, that he had gotten a very good sheet and two fine pillow-beres, steps to the wall, as though he would make water, bidding the boy go fair and softly on before. The boy, doubting nothing, did as he willed him, when presently he stepped into some house hard by fit to entertain him; and never since was he, his master, the sugar, spices, or the linen heard of.

Many have been in this manner deceived, as I hear; let this give them warning to beware of any such unprofitable guests.

Of one that came to buy a knife and made first proof of his trade on him that sold it.

One of the cunning nips about the town came unto a poor cutler to have a cuttle made according unto his own mind,

and not above three inches would he have both the knife and
the haft in length; yet of such pure metal as possible may be.
Albeit the poor man never made the like before yet being
promised four times the value of his stuff and pains, he was
contented to do this. And the day being come that he should
deliver it, the party came, who, liking it exceedingly, gave him
the money promised, which the poor man gladly put up into
his purse, that hung at a button-hole of his waistcoat before
his breast, smiling that he was so well paid for so small a
trifle. The party perceiving his merry countenance, and
imagining he guessed for what purpose the knife was, said,
"Honest man, whereat smile you?" "By my troth, sir,"
quoth the cutler, "I smile at your knife, because I never made
one so little before; and were it not offensive unto you, I
would request to know what use you will put it to." "Wilt
thou keep my counsel?" quoth the nip. "Yea on mine
honesty," quoth the cutler. "Then hearken in thy ear," said
the nip, and so rounding with him cut the poor man's purse
that hung at his bosom, he never feeling when he did it.
"With this knife," quoth the nip, "mean I to cut a purse."
"Marry, God forbid!" quoth the cutler, "I cannot think you
to be such a kind of man. I see you love to jest"; and so they
parted.

The poor man, not so wise as to remember his own purse,
when by such a warning he might have taken the offender
doing the deed, but rather proud, as it were, that his money
was so easily earned, walks to the alehouse, which was within
a house or two of his own, and finding there three or four of
his neighbours, with whom he began to jest very pleasantly,
swears by cock and pie he would spend a whole groat upon
them, for he had gotten it and more clearly by a good bargain
that morning.

Though it was no marvel to see him so liberal because
indeed he was a good companion, yet they were loath to put
him unto such cost; notwithstanding, he would needs do it,

and, so far as promise stretched, was presently filled in and set upon the board. In the drinking time often he wished to meet with more such customers as he had done that morning and commended him for a very honest gentleman, I warrant you. At length, when the reckoning was to be paid, he draws to his purse, where finding nothing left but a piece of the string in the button-hole, I leave to your judgment whether he was now as sorry as he was merry before.

Blank and all amort sits the poor cutler, and with such a pitiful countenance as his neighbours did not a little admire his solemn alteration, and desirous to know the cause thereof, from point to point he discourseth the whole manner of the tragedy, never naming his new customer but with such a far-fetched sigh, as soul and body would have parted in sunder. And in midst of all his grief, he brake forth in these terms:

"I'll believe a man the better by his word while I know him. The knife was bought to cut a purse indeed, and I thank him for it he made the first proof of the edge with me."

The neighbours grieving for his loss, yet smiling at his folly to be so overreached, were fain to pay the groat the cutler called in, because he had no other money about him; and spent as much more beside to drive away his heaviness.

This tale, because it was somewhat misreported before, upon talk had with the poor cutler himself, is set down now in true form and manner how it was done; therefore is there no offence offered, when by better consideration, a thing may be enlarged or amended, or at least the note be better confirmed.

Let the poor cutler's mishap example others, that they brag not over-hastily of gain easily gotten, lest they chance to pay now as dearly for it as he did.

Of a young nip that cuningly beguiled an ancient professor of that trade, and his quean with him, at a play.

A good fellow that was newly entered into the nipping craft and had not as yet attained to any acquaintance with the chief and cunning masters of that trade, in the Christmas holidays last came to see a play at the *Bull within Bishopsgate*, there to take his benefit as time and place would permit him. Not long had he stayed in the press, but he had gotten a young man's purse out of his pocket, which when he had he stepped into the stable to take out the money, and to convey away the purse, but looking on his commodity, he found nothing therein but white counters, a thimble and a broken threepence, which belike the fellow that ought it, had done of purpose to deceive the cutpurse withal, or else had played at the cards for counters, and so carried his winnings about him till his next sitting to play.

Somewhat displeased to be so overtaken, he looked aside and spied a lusty youth entering at the door, and his drab with him—this fellow he had heard to be one of the finest nippers about the town, and ever carried his quean with him, for conveyance when the stratagem was performed—he puts up the counters into the purse again, and follows close to see some piece of their service.

Among a company of seemly men was this lusty companion and his minion gotten, where both they might best behold the play and work for advantage; and ever this young nip was next to him, to mark when he should attempt any exploit, standing as it were more than half between the cunning nip and his drab, only to learn some part of their skill. In short time the deed was performed, but how the young nip could not easily discern; only he felt him shift his hand toward his trug to convey the purse to her. But she, being somewhat mindful of the play, because a merriment was then on the stage, gave no regard, whereby, thinking he had pulled her by the coat, he twitched the young nip by the cloak, who, taking advantage of this offer, put down his hand and received the purse of him. Then, counting it discourtesy to let him lose all his labour, he softly plucked the quean by the coat, which she feeling and imagining it had been her companion's hand, received of him the first purse with the white counters in it.

Then, fearing lest his stay should hinder him, and seeing the other intended to have more purses ere he departed, away goes the young nip with the purse he got so easily, wherein, as I have heard, was thirty-seven shillings and odd money, which did so much content him, as that he had beguiled so ancient a stander in that profession.

What the other thought when he found the purse, and could not guess how he was cozened, I leave to your censures; only this makes me smile, that one false knave can beguile another, which bids honest men look the better to their purses.

How a gentleman was craftily deceived of a chain of gold and his purse, in Paul's Church in London.

A gentleman of the country, who, as I have heard since the time of his mishap whereof I am now to speak, had about half a year before buried his wife, and, belike, thinking well of some other gentlewoman, whom he meant to make account of as his second choice, upon good hope, or otherwise persuaded, he came up to London to provide himself of such necessaries as the country is not usually stored withal. Besides silks, velvets, cambrics, and such like, he bought a chain of gold that cost him fifty-seven pounds and odd money; whereof, because he would have the maidenhead or first wearing himself, he presently put it on in the goldsmith's shop, and so walked therewith about London as his occasions served.

But let not the gentleman be offended, who, if this book come to his hands, can best avouch the truth of this discourse, if here by the way I blame his rash pride, or simple credulity; for between the one and the other, the chain he paid so dear for about ten of the clock in the morning, the cony-catchers the same day ere night shared amongst them, a matter whereat he may well grieve and I be sorry, in respect he is my very good friend.

But to the purpose. This gentleman walking in Paul's, with his chain fair glittering about his neck, talking with his man about some business, was well viewed and regarded by a crew of cony-catchers, whose teeth watered at his goodly chain, yet knew not how to come by it, hanging as it did; and therefore entered into secret conspiration among themselves, if they could not come by all the chain, yet how they might make it lighter by half a score pounds at the least. Still had they their eyes on the honest gentleman, who little doubted any such treason intended against his so late bought bargain; and they, having laid their plot, each one to be assistant in this enterprise, saw when the gentleman dismissed his servant, to go about such affairs as he had appointed him, himself still walking there up and down the middle aisle.

One of these mates, that stood most on his cunning in these exploits, followed the serving-man forth of the church calling him by divers names, as John, Thomas, William, etc., as though he had known his right name but could not hit on it; which whether he did or no I know not, but well I wot the serving-man turned back again, and seeing him that called him seemed a gentleman, booted and cloaked after the newest fashion, came with his hat in his hand to him, saying, "Sir, do ye call me?" "Marry do I, my friend," quoth the other, "dost not thou serve such a gentleman?" and named one as himself pleased. "No truly, sir," answered the serving-man, "I know not any such gentleman as you speak of." "By my troth," replied the cony-catcher, "I am assured I knew thee and thy master, though now I cannot suddenly remember myself." The serving-man fearing no harm, yet fitting the humour of this treacherous companion, told right his master's name whom he served, and that his master was even then walking in Paul's. "O' God's will," quoth the cony-catcher, repeating his master's name, "a very honest gentleman; of such a place is he not?" naming a shire of the country; for he must know both name, country and sometimes what gentlemen dwell near the party that is to be overreached, ere he can proceed. "No indeed, sir," answered the serving-man, with such reverence as it had been to an honest gentleman indeed, "My master is of such a place, a mile from such a town, and hard by such a knight's house." By which report the deceiver was half instructed because though he was ignorant of the fellow's master, yet well he knew the country and the knight named. So craving pardon that he had mistaken him, he returns again into the church, and the serving-man trudgeth about his assigned business.

Being come to the rest of the crew, he appoints one of them, whom he knew to be expert in deed, to take this matter in hand, for himself might not do it lest the serving-man should return and know him. He schooled the rest likewise what every man should do when the pinch came, and changing his cloak with one of his fellows walked by himself attending the feat. And everyone being as ready, the appointed fellow makes his sally forth, and coming to the gentleman, calling him by his name, gives him the courtesy and embrace, likewise thanking him for good cheer he had had at his house; which he did with such seemly behaviour and protestation as the gentleman, thinking the other to be no less, used like action of kindness to him.

Now as country gentlemen have many visitors, both with

near-dwelling neighbours, and friends that journey from far, whom they can hardly remember, but some principal one that serves as countenance to the other; so he, not discrediting the cunning mate's words, who still at every point alleged his kindred to the knight, neighbour to the gentleman, which the poor serving-man had, doubting no ill, revealed before, and that both there and at his own house in hawking time with that knight and other gentlemen of the country he had liberally tasted his kindness; desiring pardon that he had forgotten him, and offered him the courtesy of the city. The cony-catcher excused himself for that time, saying at their next meeting he would bestow it on him. Then seeming to have espied his chain and commending the fairness and workman-ship thereof, says, "I pray ye, sir, take a little counsel of a friend, it may be you will return thanks for it. I wonder," quoth he, "you dare wear such a costly jewel so open in sight, which is even but a bait to entice bad men to adventure time and place for it, and nowhere sooner than in this city, where, I may say to you, are such a number of cony-catchers, cozeners, and such like that a man can scarcely keep anything from them, they have so many reaches and sleights to beguile withal; which a very especial friend of mine found too true not many days since."

Hereupon he told a very solemn tale of villainies and knaveries in his own profession, whereby he reported his friend had lost a watch of gold; shewing how closely his friend wore it in his bosom, and how strangely it was gotten from him that the gentleman by that discourse waxed half afraid of his chain, and giving him many thanks for this good warning, presently takes the chain from about his neck, and tying it up fast in a handkerchief, put it up into his sleeve, saying: "If the cony-catcher get it here, let him not spare it."

Not a little did the treacher smile in his sleeve, hearing the rash security but indeed simplicity of the gentleman, and no sooner saw he it put up but presently he counted it sure his own, by the assistance of his complices, that lay in an ambuscado for the purpose. With embraces and courtesies on either side, the cony-catcher departs, leaving the gentleman walking there still; whereat the crew were not a little offended that he still kept in the church and would not go abroad.

Well, at length, belike remembering some business, the gentleman, taking leave of another that talked with him, hasted to go forth at the furthest west door of Paul's, which he that had talked with him and gave him such counsel perceiving, hied out of the other door, and got to the entrance ere he came forth, the rest following the gentleman at an inch. As he was stepping out the other stepped in and let fall a key, having his hat so low over his eyes, that he could not well discern his face, and, stooping to take up the key, kept the gentleman from going backward or forward, by reason his leg was over the threshold. The foremost cony-catcher behind, pretending a quarrel unto him that stooped, rapping out an oath, and drawing his dagger, said: "Do I meet the villain? Nay, he shall not scape me now," and so made offer to strike him.

The gentleman at his standing up, seeing it was he that gave him so good counsel, and pretended himself his very friend, but never imagining this train was made for him, stepped in his defence, when the other following tripped up his heels; so that he and his counsellor were down together, and two more upon them, striking with their daggers very eagerly. Marry, indeed the gentleman had most of the blows, and both his handkerchief with the chain, as also his purse with three and fifty shillings in it, were taken out of his pocket in this struggling, even by the man that himself defended.

It was marvellous to behold, how not regarding the villain's words uttered before in the church, nor thinking upon the charge about him, which after he had thus treacherously lost unwittingly, he stands pacifying them that were not discontented but only to beguile him. But they, vowing that they

would presently go for their weapons and so to the field, told
the gentleman he laboured but in vain, for fight they must and
would, and so, going down by Paul's Chain, left the gentleman made a cony going up towards Fleet Street, sorry for his
new counsellor and friend and wishing him good luck in the
fight; which indeed was with nothing but wine pots, for joy
of their late gotten booty.

Near to St Dunstan's Church the gentleman remembered
himself and feeling his pocket so light had suddenly more
grief at his heart than ever happen to him or any man again.
Back he comes to see if he could espy any of them, but they
were far enough from him. God send him better hap when he
goes next a wooing, and that this his loss may be a warning
to others.

---

*How a cunning knave got a trunk well-stuffed with
linen and certain parcels of plate out of a citizen's
house, and how the master of the house holp the deceiver
to carry away his own goods.*

Within the City of London dwelleth a worldly man who
hath very great dealing in his trade, and his shop very well
frequented with customers, had such a shrewd mischance of
late by a cony-catcher, as may well serve for an example to
others lest they have the like.

A cunning villain, that had long time haunted this citizen's
house, and gotten many a cheat which he carried away safely,
made it his custom when he wanted money, to help himself
ever where he had sped so often. Divers things he had which
were never missed, especially such as appertained to the
citizen's trade, but when any were found wanting they could
not devise which way they were gone, so politicly this fellow

always behaved himself. Well knew he what times of greatest business this citizen had in his trade; and when the shop is most stored with chapmen, then would he step up the stairs (for there was and is another door to the house besides that which entereth into the shop) and what was next hand came ever away with.

One time above the rest, in an evening about Candlemas, when daylight shuts in about six of the clock, he watched to do some feat in the house; and seeing the mistress go forth with her maid, the goodman and his folks very busy in the shop, up the stairs he goes as he was wont to do; and lifting up the latch of the hall portal door saw nobody near to trouble him, when stepping into the next chamber, where the citizen and his wife usually lay, at the bed's feet there stood a handsome trunk, wherein was very good linen, a fair gilt salt, two silver French bowls for wine, two silver drinking pots, a stone jug covered with silver, and a dozen of silver spoons. This trunk he brings to the stairs' head, and making fast the door again, draws it down the steps so softly as he could, for it was so big and heavy as he could not easily carry it. Having it out at the door, unseen of any neighbour or anybody else, he stood struggling with it to lift it up on the stall, which by reason of the weight troubled him very much.

The goodman coming forth of his shop, to bid a customer or two farewell, made the fellow afraid he should now be taken for all together. But calling his wits together to escape if he could, he stood gazing up at the sign belonging to the house, as though he were desirous to know what sign it was; which the citizen perceiving, came to him and asked him what he sought for.

"I look for the sign of the *Blue Bell*, sir," quoth the fellow, "where a gentleman having taken a chamber for this term-time, hath sent me hither with this his trunk of apparel." Quoth the citizen, "I know no such sign in this street, but in the next (naming it) there is such a one indeed, and there

dwelleth one that letteth forth chambers to gentlemen."
"Truly, sir," quoth the fellow, "that's the house I should
go to. I pray you, sir, lend me your hand but to help the
trunk on my back, for I, thinking to ease me a while upon
your stall, set it short, and now I can hardly get it up again."

The citizen, not knowing his own trunk, but indeed never
thinking on any such notable deceit, helps him up with the
trunk, and so sends him away roundly with his own goods.

When the trunk was missed, I leave to your conceits what
household grief there was on all sides, especially the goodman
himself, who, remembering how he helped the fellow up with
a trunk, perceived that hereby he had beguiled himself, and
lost more than in haste he should recover again. How this
may admonish others, I leave to the judgement of the indifferent opinion, that see when honest meaning is so craftily
beleaguered, as good foresight must be used to prevent such
dangers.

---

*How a broker was cunningly overreached by as crafty
a knave as himself, and brought in danger of the gallows.*

It hath been used as a common byword: "A crafty knave
needeth no broker"—whereby it should appear that there can
hardly be a craftier knave than a broker. Suspend your
judgements till you have heard this discourse ensuing, and
then, as you please, censure both the one and the other.

A lady of the country sent up a servant whom she might
well put in trust, to provide her of a gown answerable to such
directions as she had given him, which was of good price, as
may appear by the outside and lace, whereto doubtless was
every other thing agreeable. For the tailor had seventeen
yards of the best black satin could be got for money, and so
much gold lace, besides spangles, as valued thirteen pounds.

E

What else was beside, I know not, but let it suffice thus much was lost, and therefore let us to the manner how.

The satin and the lace being brought to the tailor that should make the gown, and spread abroad on the shop-board to be measured, certain good fellows of the cony-catching profession chanced to go by, who, seeing so rich lace and so excellent good satin, began to commune with themselves how they might make some purchase of what they had seen. And quickly it was to be done or not at all. As ever in a crew of this quality, there is some one more ingenious and politic than the rest, or at leastwise that covets to make himself more famous than the rest, so this instant was there one in this company that did swear his cunning should deeply deceive him, but he would have both the lace and satin. When having laid the plot with his companions, how and which way their help might stand him in stead, this way they proceeded.

Well noted they the serving-man that stood in the shop with the tailor, and gathered by his diligent attendance that he had some charge of the gown there to be made; wherefore by him must they work their treachery intended, and use him as an instrument to beguile himself. One of them sitting on a seat near the tailor's stall could easily hear the talk that passed between the serving-man and the tailor, where among other communication it was concluded that the gown should be made of the self-same fashion in every point as another lady's was, who then lay in the City; and that measure being taken by her, the same would fitly serve the lady for whom the gown was to be made. Now the serving-man intended to go speak with the lady, and upon a token agreed between them (which he carelessly spake so loud that the cony-catcher heard it) he would as her leisure served, certify the tailor, and he should bring the stuff with him, to have the lady's opinion both of the one and the other.

The serving-man being gone about his affairs, the subtle mate that had listened to all their talk acquaints his fellows

both with the determination and token appointed for the
tailor's coming to the lady. The guide and leader to all the
rest for villainy—though there was no[t] one but was better
skilled in such matters than [in] honesty—he appoints that
one of them should go to the tavern, which was not far off,
and laying two faggots on the fire in a room by himself and a
quart of wine filled for countenance of the treachery, another
of that crew should give attendance on him as if he were his
master, being bare-headed, and "Sir" humbly answering at
every word.

To the tavern goes this counterfeit gentleman and his
servant waiting on him, where everything was performed as
is before rehearsed, when the master-knave, calling the drawer,
demanded if there dwelt near at hand a skilful tailor that could
make a suit of velvet for himself; marry, it was to be done
with very great speed.

The drawer named the tailor that we now speak of, and
upon the drawer's commending his cunning the man in all
haste was sent for to a gentleman for whom he must make a
suit of velvet forthwith. Upon talk had of the stuff, how
much was to be bought of everything appertaining thereto, he
must immediately take measure of this counterfeit gentleman
because he knew not when to return that way again; afterwards
they would go to the mercer's.

As the tailor was taking measure on him bareheaded, as if
he had been a substantial gentleman indeed, the crafty mate
had cunningly gotten his purse out of his pocket, at the one
string whereof was fastened a little key and at the other his
signet ring. This booty he was sure of already, whether he
should get anything else or no of the mischief intended.
Stepping to the window he cuts the ring from the purse and
by his supposed man (rounding him in the ear) sends it to the
plot-layer of this knavery, minding to train the tailor along
with him, as it were to the mercer's, while he the meantime
took order for the other matter.

Afterward, speaking aloud to his man, "Sirrah," quoth he, "despatch what I bade you, and about four of the clock meet me in Paul's; by that time I hope the tailor and I shall have despatched." To Cheapside goeth the honest tailor with this notorious dissembler, not missing his purse for the space of two hours after, in less than half which time the satin and gold lace was gotten likewise by the other villian from the tailor's house in this order.

Being sure the tailor should be kept absent, he sends another mate home to his house, who abused his servants with this device: that the lady's man had met their master abroad, and had him to the other lady to take measure of her. And lest they should delay the time too long, he was sent for the satin and lace, declaring the token appointed, and withal giving their master's signet ring for better confirmation of his message. The servants could do no less than deliver it, being commanded (as they supposed) by so credible testimony. Neither did the leisure of anyone serve to go with the messenger, who seemed an honest young gentleman, and carried no cause of distrust in his countenance. Wherefore they delivered him the lace and satin folded up together as it was, and desired him to will their master to make some speed home, both for cutting out of work and other occasions.

To a broker fit for their purpose goes this deceiver with the satin lace, who, knowing well they could not come honestly by it, nor anything else he bought of that crew, as often before he had dealt much with them, either gave them not so much as they would have or at least as they judged they could have in another place; for which the ringleader of this cozenage vowed in his mind to be revenged on the broker.

The master-knave, who had spent two hours and more in vain with the tailor and would not like of any velvet he saw, when he perceived that he missed his purse and could not devise how or where he had lost it, shewed himself very sorry for his mishap and said in the morning he would send the

velvet home to his house, for he knew where to speed of better
than any he had seen in the shops.

Home goes the tailor very sadly, where he was entertained
with a greater mischance, for there was the lady's serving-man
swearing and stamping that he had not seen their master since
the morning they parted, neither had he sent for the satin and
lace. But when the servants justified their innocency, beguiled
both with the true token rehearsed and their master's signet
ring, it exceedeth my cunning to set down answerable words
to this exceeding grief and amazement on either part, but most
of all the honest tailor, who sped the better by the broker's
wilfulness, as afterward it happened, which made him the
better brook the loss of his purse.

That night all means were used that could be, both to the
mercers, brokers, goldsmiths, goldfiners, and such like, where
happily such things do come to be sold. But all was in vain.
The only help came by the inventor of this villainy, who, scant
sleeping all night, in regard of the broker's extreme gaining,
both by him and those of his profession, the next morning he
came by the tailor's house at what time he espied him with
the lady's serving-man coming forth of the doors; and into
the tavern he went to report what a mishap he had upon the
sending for him thither the day before.

As he was but newly entered his sad discourse, in comes the
party offended with the broker; and having heard all (whereof
none could make better report than himself) he takes the
tailor and serving-man aside, and pretending great grief for
both their causes, demands what they would think him worthy
of that could help them to their good again. On condition to
meet with such a friend, offer was made of five pound; and
after sundry speeches passing between them alone, he seeming
that he would work the recovery thereof by art, and they
promising not to disclose the man that did them good, he
drew forth a little book out of his bosom (whether it were
Latin or English it skilled not, for he could not read a word

on it) then desiring them to spare him alone a while, they should perceive what he would do for them.

Their hearts encouraged with some good hope, kept all his words secret to themselves; and not long had they sitten absent out of the room, but he called them in again, and seeming as though he had been a scholar indeed, said he found by his figure that a broker in such a place had their goods lost, and in such a place of the house they should find it, bidding them go thither with all speed; and as they found his words, so (with reserving to themselves how they came to knowledge thereof) to meet him again in the evening, and reward him as he had deserved.

Away in haste goes the tailor and the serving-man, and entering the house with the constable found them in the place where he that revealed it, knew the broker always laid such gotten goods. Of their joy again I leave you to conjecture, and think you see the broker with a good pair of bolts on his heels, ready to take his farewell of the world in a halter, when time shall serve. The counterfeit cunning man and artificial cony-catcher, as I heard, was paid his five pound that night. Thus one crafty knave beguiled another. Let each take heed of dealing with any such kind of people.

FINIS

PIERCE PENILESSE
HIS SUPPLICATION TO THE DEVIL

Barbaria grandis habere nihil

BY

THOMAS NASHE

———————

A private Epistle of the Author to the Printer,
wherein his full meaning and purpose in publishing
this book is set forth.

FAITH, I am very sorry, sir, I am thus unawares betrayed to
infamy. You write to me my book is hasting to the second
impression: he that hath once broke the ice of impudence
need not care how deep he wade in discredit. I confess it to
be a mere toy, not deserving any judicial man's view; if it
have found any friends, so it is; you know very well that it
was abroad a fortnight ere I knew of it, and uncorrected and
unfinished it hath offered itself to the open scorn of the world.
Had you not been so forward in the republishing of it you
should have had certain epistles to orators and poets to insert
to the latter end; as, namely, to the ghost of Machiavelli, of
Tully, of Ovid, of Roscius, of Pace, the Duke of Norfolk's
jester; and lastly to the ghost of Robert Greene, telling him
what a coil there is with pamphleting on him after his death.

These were prepared for *Pierce Penilesse* first setting forth, had not the fear of infection detained me with my lord in the country.

Now this is that I would have you to do in this second edition; first, cut off that long-tailed title, and let me not in the forefront of my book make a tedious mountebank's oration to the reader, when in the whole there is nothing praiseworthy.

I hear say there be obscure imitators that go about to frame a second part to it and offer it to sell in Paul's Churchyard and elsewhere, as from me. Let me request you, as ever you will expect any favour at my hands, to get somebody to write an epistle before it, ere you set it to sale again, importing thus much; that if any such lewd device intrude itself to their hands, it is a cozenage and plain knavery of him that sells it to get money, and that I have no manner of interest or acquaintance with it. Indeed if my leisure were such as I could wish I might haps, half a year hence, write the return of the knight of the post from hell, with the devil's answer to the supplication; but as for a second part of *Pierce Penilesse*, it is a most ridiculous roguery.

Other news I am advertised of, that a scald trivial lying pamphlet, called *Greene's Groatsworth of Witte*, is given out to be of my doing. God never have care of my soul, but utterly renounce me, if the least word or syllable in it proceeded from my pen or if I were any way privy to the writing or printing of it. I am grown at length to see into the vanity of the world more than ever I did, and now I condemn myself for nothing so much as playing the dolt in print. Out upon it, it is odious, specially in this moralising age, wherein everyone seeks to shew himself a politician by misinterpreting.

In one place of my book, Pierce Penilesse saith but to the knight of the post, "I pray how might I call you," and they say I meant one Howe, a knave of that trade, that I never heard of before.

The antiquaries are offended without cause, thinking I go

about to detract from that excellent profession, when, God is my witness, I reverence it as much as any of them all, and had no manner of allusion to them that stumble at it. I hope they will give me leave to think there be fools of that art as well as of all other. But to say I utterly condemn it as an unfruitful study, or seem to despise the excellent qualified parts of it, is a most false and injurious surmise. There is nothing that if a man list he may not wrest or pervert. I cannot forbid any to think villainously, *Sed caveat emptor*, let the interpreter beware; for none ever heard me make allegories of an idle text. Write who will against me, but let him look his life be without scandal; for if he touch me never so little, I'll be as good as *The Black Book* to him and his kindred.

Beggarly lies no beggarly wit but can invent. Who spurneth not at a dead dog? But I am of another metal; they shall know that I live as their evil angel, to haunt them world without end, if they disquiet me without cause.

Farewell, and let me hear from you as soon as it is come forth. I am the plague's prisoner in the country as yet: if the sickness cease before the third impression, I will come and alter whatsoever may be offensive to any man, and bring you the latter end.

Your friend,
THO. NASH

PIERCE PENILESSE HIS SUPPLICATION TO THE DEVIL

HAVING spent many years in studying how to live, and lived a long time without money, having tired my youth with folly and surfeited my mind with vanity, I began at length to look back to repentance and address my endeavours to prosperity. But all in vain I sat up late and rose early, contended with the cold, and conversed with scarcity; for all my labours turned

to loss, my vulgar Muse was despised and neglected, my pains
not regarded or slightly rewarded, and I myself, in prime of
my best wit, laid open to poverty.[1] Whereupon, in a malcontent humour, I accused my fortune, railed on my patrons,
bit my pen, rent my papers, and raged in all points like a
madman. In which agony tormenting myself a long time, I
grew by degrees to a milder discontent, and pausing a while
over my standish, I resolved in verse to paint forth my
passion.[2] Which best agreeing with the vein of my unrest, I
began to complain in this sort:

> Why is't damnation to despair and die,
> When life is my true happiness' disease?
> My soul, my soul, thy safety makes me fly
> The faulty means, that might my pain appease.
>   Divines and dying men may talk of hell,
>   But in my heart her several torments dwell.

> Ah, worthless wit, to train me to this woe,
> Deceitful arts, that nourish discontent:
> Ill thrive the folly that bewitched me so;
> Vain thoughts, adieu, for now I will repent.
>   And yet my wants persuade me to proceed,
>   Since none takes pity of a scholar's need.

> Forgive me, God, although I curse my birth,
> And ban the air, wherein I breathe a wretch;
> Since misery hath daunted all my mirth,
> And I am quite undone through promise-breach.
>   Oh friends, no friends, that then ungently frown,
>   When changing Fortune casts us headlong down.[3]

---

[1] Discite qui sapitis, non haec quae scimus inertes; Sed trepidas acies, et fera
bella sequi.
[2] Est aliquid fatale malum per verba levare,
[3] Pol me occidistis amici,

Without redress complains my careless verse,
And Midas-ears relent not at my moan;
In some far land will I my griefs rehearse,
'Mongst them that will be mov'd when I shall groan.
   England, adieu, the soil that brought me forth,
   Adieu, unkind, where skill is nothing worth.

These rhymes thus abruptly set down, I tossed my imaginations a thousand ways, to see if I could find any means to
relieve my estate; but all my thoughts consorted to this conclusion, that the world was uncharitable, and I ordained to be
miserable. Thereby I grew to consider how many base men,
that wanted those parts which I had, enjoyed content at will
and had wealth at command. I called to mind a cobbler, that
was worth five hundred pound; an hostler, that had built a
goodly inn, and might dispend forty pound yearly by his
land; a car-man in a leather pilch, that had whipped out a
thousand pound out of his horse tail: and have I more wit
than all these? thought I to myself, am I better born? am I
better brought up? yea, and better favoured? and yet am I a
beggar? What is the cause? how am I crossed? or whence is
this curse?

Even from hence, that men that should employ such as I
am, are enamoured of their own wits, and think whatever they
do is excellent, though it be never so scurvy; that learning
(of the ignorant) is rated after the value of the ink and paper,
and a scrivener better paid for an obligation, than a scholar for
the best poem he can make; and that every gross-brained idiot
is suffered to come into print, who if he set forth a pamphlet
of the praise of pudding-pricks, or write a treatise of Tom
Thumb or the exploits of Untruss, it is bought up thick and
threefold when better things lie dead.[1] How then can we
choose but be needy when there are so many drones amongst
us? or ever prove rich, that toil a whole year for fair looks?

[1] Scribimus indocti doctique poemata passim.

Gentle Sir Philip Sidney, thou knewest what belonged to a scholar, thou knewest what pains, what toil, what travail, conduct to perfection; well couldst thou give every virtue his encouragement, every art his due, every writer his desert; cause none more virtuous, witty, or learned than myself.

But thou art dead in thy grave and hast left too few successors of thy glory, too few to cherish the sons of the Muses or water those budding hopes with their plenty, which thy bounty erst planted.[1]

Believe me, gentlemen—for some cross mishaps have taught me experience—there is not that strict observation of honour, which hath been heretofore. Men of great calling take it of merit to have their names eternized by poets; and whatsoever pamphlet or dedication encounters them they put it up in their sleeves and scarce give him thanks that presents it. Much better is it for those golden pens to raise such ungrateful peasants from the dung-hill of obscurity and make them equal in fame to the worthies of old, when their doting self-love shall challenge it of duty and not only give them nothing themselves but impoverish liberality in others.

This is the lamentable condition of our times, that men of art must seek alms of cormorants, and those that deserve best be kept under by dunces, who count it a policy to keep them bare, because they should follow their books the better; thinking belike, that, as preferment hath made themselves idle, that were erst painful in meaner places, so it would likewise slacken the endeavours of those students, that as yet strive to excel in hope of advancement. A good policy to suppress superfluous liberality! But had it been practised when they were promoted the yeomanry of the realm had been better to pass than it is, and one drone should not have driven so many bees from their honeycombs.

"Ay, ay, we'll give losers leave to talk. It is no matter what *Sic probo* and his penniless companions prate, whilst we have

[1] Heu rapiunt mala fata bonos.

the gold in our coffers. This is it that will make a knave an honest man, and my neighbour Crampton's stripling a better gentleman than his grandsire." Oh, it is a trim thing when Pride, the son, goes before, and Shame, the father, follows after. Such precedents there are in our commonwealth a great many. Not so much of them whom learning and industry hath exalted (whom I prefer before *genus et proavos*) as of carterly upstarts, that out-face town and country in their velvets, when Sir Rowland Russet-coat, their dad, goes sagging every day in his round gaskins of white cotton, and hath much ado, poor penny-father, to keep his unthrift elbows in reparations.

Marry, happy are they (say I) that have such fathers to work for them whilst they play; for where other men turn over many leaves to get bread and cheese in their old age and study twenty years to distill gold out of ink, our young masters do nothing but devise how to spend, and ask counsel of the wine and capons how they may quickliest consume their patrimonies. As for me, I live secure from all such perturbations; for, thanks be to God, I am *vacuus viator*, and care not, though I meet the Commissioners of Newmarket Heath at high midnight, for any crosses, images, or pictures that I carry about me, more than needs.

Than needs, quoth I, nay I would be ashamed of it if *Opus* and *Usus* were not knocking at my door twenty times a week when I am not within; the more is the pity that such a frank gentleman as I should want; but, since the dice do run so untowardly on my side, I am partly provided of a remedy. For whereas those that stand most on their honour have shut up their purses and shift us off with court holy bread; and on the other side a number of hypocritical hotspurs, that have God always in their mouths, will give nothing for God's sake; I have clapped up a handsome supplication to the devil and sent it by a good fellow, that I know will deliver it.

And because you may believe me the better, I care not if I acquaint you with the circumstances.

I was informed of late days, that a certain blind retailer, called the devil, used to lend money upon pawns or anything and would let one for a need have a thousand pounds upon a statute merchant of his soul; or, if a man plied him thoroughly, would trust him upon a bill of his hand, without any more circumstance. Besides he was noted for a privy benefactor to traitors and parasites, and to advance fools and asses far sooner than any, to be a greedy pursuer of news, and so famous a politician in purchasing, that hell, which at the beginning was but an obscure village, is now become a huge city, whereunto all countries are tributary.

These manifest conjectures of plenty, assembled in one common-place of ability, I determined to claw Avarice by the elbow, till his full belly gave me a full hand, and let him blood with my pen (if it might be) in the vein of liberality; and so, in short time, was this paper-monster, *Pierce Penilesse*, begotten.

But, written and all, here lies the question; where shall I find this old ass, that I may deliver it? Mass, that's true; they say the lawyers have the devil and all; and it is like enough he is playing Ambodexter amongst them. Fie, fie, the devil a driver in Westminster Hall? It can never be.

Now, I pray, what do you imagine him to be? Perhaps you think it is not possible he should be so grave. Oh, then you are in an error, for he is as formal as the best scrivener of them all. Marry, he doth not use to wear a night-cap, for his horns will not let him; and yet I know a hundred as well-headed as he that will make a jolly shift with a court-cup on their crowns if the weather be cold.

To proceed with my tale. To Westminster Hall I went, and made a search of enquiry, from the black gown to the buckram bag, if there were any such sergeant, bencher, counsellor, attorney, or pettifogger, as *Signior Cornuto Diabolo* with the good face. But they all, *una voce*, affirmed that he was not there; marry, whether he were at the Exchange or no, amongst the rich merchants, that they could not tell; but it was likelier of the two that I should meet with him, or hear of him at the least, in those quarters. "I'faith, and say you so?" quoth I, "and I'll bestow a little labour more, but I'll hunt him out."

Without more circumstance, thither came I; and, thrusting myself, as the manner is, amongst the confusion of languages, I asked as before whether he were there extant or no? But from one to another, "*Non novi dæmonem,*" was all the answer I could get. At length, as fortune served, I lighted upon an old, straddling usurer, clad in a damask cassock, edged with fox fur, a pair of trunk slops, sagging down like a shoemaker's wallet, and a short threadbare gown on his back, faced with moth-eaten budge; upon his head he wore a filthy, coarse biggin, and next it a garnish of night-caps, which a sage button-cap, of the form of a cowshard, overspread very orderly. A fat chuff it was, I remember, with a gray beard cut short to the stumps, as though it were grimed, and a huge worm-eaten nose, like a cluster of grapes hanging downwards. Of him I demanded if he could tell me any tidings of the party I sought for.

"By my troth," quoth he, "stripling," and then he coughed, "I saw him not lately, nor know I certainly where he keeps: but thus much I heard by a broker, a friend of mine, that hath had some dealings with him in his time, that he is at home sick of the gout and will not be spoken withal under more than thou art able to give, some two or three hundred angels, at least, if thou hast any suit to him: and then, perhaps, he'll strain courtesy with his legs in child-bed, and come forth and talk with thee: but, otherwise, *non est domi*, he is busy with Mammon, and the prince of the North, how to build up his kingdom, or sending his spirits abroad to undermine the maligners of his government."

I, hearing of this cold comfort, took my leave of him very faintly, and, like a careless malcontent that knew not which way to turn, retired me to Paul's to seek my dinner with Duke

Humfrey; but when I came there the old soldier was not up. He is long a rising, thought I, but that's all one, for he that hath no money in his purse must go dine with Sir John Best-betrust at the sign of the Chalk and the Post.

Two hungry turns had I scarce fetched in this waste gallery, when I was encountered by a neat, pedantical fellow, in form of a citizen, who, thrusting himself abruptly into my company, like an intelligencer, began very earnestly to question with me about the cause of my discontent, or what made me so sad, that seemed too young to be acquainted with sorrow. I, nothing nice to unfold my estate to any whatsoever, discoursed to him the whole circumstance of my care, and what toil and pains I had took in searching for him that would not be heard of.

"Why, sir," quoth he, "had I been privy to your purpose before I could have eased you of this travail; for if it be the devil you seek for, know I am his man." "I pray, sir, how might I call you?" "A knight of the post," quoth he, "for so I am termed; a fellow that will swear you anything for twelve pence.[1] But, indeed, I am a spirit in nature and essence, that take upon me this human shape only to set men together by the ears and send souls by millions to hell."

"Now, trust me, a substantial trade; but when do you think you could send next to your master?" "Why, every day; for there is not a cormorant that dies or cut-purse that is hanged, but I despatch letters by his soul to him and to all my friends in the Low Countries; wherefore, if you have anything that you would have transported, give it me, and I will see it delivered."

"Yes, marry have I," quoth I, "a certain supplication here unto your master, which you may peruse if it please you." With that he opened it, and read as followeth.

---

[1] Non bene conducti vendunt periuria testes.

To the high and mighty Prince of Darkness, Donsell dell Lucifer, King of Acheron, Styx, and Phlegethon, Duke of Tartary, Marquis of Cocytus, and Lord High Regent of Limbo; his distressed orator, Pierce Penilesse, wisheth increase of damnation and malediction eternal, Per Iesum Christum Dominum nostrum.

Most humbly sueth unto your sinfulness, your single-soled orator, Pierce Penilesse; that whereas your impious excellence hath had the poor tenement of his purse any time this half year for your dancing school, and he, notwithstanding, hath received no penny nor cross for farm, according to the usual manner,[1] it may please your graceless majesty to consider of him, and give order to your servant Avarice he may be despatched; in so much as no man here in London can have a dancing school without rent, and his wit and knavery cannot be maintained with nothing. Or, if this be not so plausible to your honourable infernalship, it might seem good to your hellhood to make extent upon the souls of a number of uncharitable cormorants, who, having incurred the danger of a *præmunire* with meddling with matters that properly concern your own person, deserve no longer to live as men amongst men but to be incorporated in the society of devils. By which means the mighty controller of fortune and imperious subverter of destiny, delicious gold, the poor man's god, and idol of princes, that looks pale and wan through long imprisonment, might at length be restored to his powerful monarchy, and eftsoon be set at liberty, to help his friends that have need of him.

I know a great sort of good fellows that would venture far for his freedom,[2] and a number of needy lawyers, who now

[1] No; I'll be sworn upon a book have I not.
[2] *Id est*, for the freedom of gold.

F

mourn in threadbare gowns for his thraldom, that would go near to poison his keepers with false Latin, if that might procure his enlargement; but inexorable iron detains him in the dungeon of the night, so that now, poor creature, he can neither traffic with the mercers and tailors, as he was wont, nor domineer in taverns as he ought.

THE DESCRIPTION OF GREEDINESS

Famine, Lent, and Desolation sit in onion-skinned jackets before the door of his indurance, as a chorus in *The Tragedy of Hospitality*, to tell Hunger and Poverty there's no relief for them there. And in the inner part of this ugly habitation stands Greediness, prepared to devour all that enter, attired in a capouch of written parchment, buttoned down before with labels of wax, and lined with sheep's fells for warmness; his cap furred with cats' skins, after the Muscovy fashion, and all to-be-tasselled with angle-hooks, instead of aglets, ready to catch hold of all those to whom he shews any humbleness. For his breeches, they were made of the lists of broadcloths, which he had by letters patent assured him and his heirs, to the utter overthrow of bowcases and cushion makers; and bombasted they were, like beer barrels, with statute merchants and forfeitures. But of all, his shoes were the strangest, which, being nothing else but a couple of crab shells, were toothed at the toes with two sharp sixpenny nails that digged up every dunghill they came by for gold and snarled at the stones as he went in the street, because they were so common for men, women, and children to tread upon and he could not devise how to wrest an odd fine out of any of them.

Thus walks he up and down all his lifetime, with an iron crow in his hand instead of a staff, and a sergeant's mace in his mouth, which night and day he still gnaws upon, and either busies himself in setting silver lime twigs to entangle young gentlemen, and casting forth silken shraps to catch wood-cocks, or in sieving of muckhills and shop dust, whereof he will bolt a whole cartload to gain a bowed pin.

THE DESCRIPTION OF DAME NIGGARDIZE

On the other side, Dame Niggardize, his wife, in a sedge rug kirtle, that had been a mat time out of mind, a coarse hempen rail about her shoulders, borrowed of the one end of a hop bag, an apron made of almanacs out of date, such as stand upon screens, or on the backside of a door in a chandler's shop, and an old wife's pudding pan on her head, thrummed with the parings of her nails, sat barrelling up the droppings of her nose, instead of oil, to saim wool withal, and would not adventure to spit without half a dozen porringers at her elbow.

The house, or rather the hell, where these two earthworms encaptived this beautiful substance, was vast, large, strong built, and well furnished, all save the kitchen; for that was no bigger than the cook's room in a ship, with a little court chimney, about the compass of a parenthesis in proclamation print: then judge you what diminutive dishes came out of this dove's-nest. So likewise of the buttery; for whereas in houses of such stately foundation, that are built to outward shew so magnificent, every office is answerable to the hall, which is principal, there the buttery was no more but a blind coalhouse under a pair of stairs, wherein, uprising and downlying, was but one single, single kilderkin of small beer, that would make a man with a carouse of a spoonful run through an alphabet of faces. Nor used they any glasses or cups, as other men, but only little farthing ounce boxes, whereof one of them filled up with froth, in manner and form of an ale-house, was a meal's allowance for the whole household.

It were lamentable to tell what misery the rats and mice endured in this hard world; how, when all supply of victuals failed them, they went a boot-haling one night to Signior Greediness' bedchamber, where, finding nothing but emptiness and vastity, they encountered (after long inquisition) with a cod-piece, well dunged and manured with grease, which my pinch-fart penny-father had retained from his bachelorship, until the eating of these presents. Upon that they set, and with a courageous assault, rent it clean away from the breeches, and then carried it in triumph, like a coffin, on their shoulders betwixt them. The very spiders and dust-weavers, that wont to set up their looms in every window, decayed and undone through the extreme dearth of the place, that afforded them no matter to work on, were constrained to break, against their wills, and go dwell in the country, out of the reach of the broom and the wing; and generally, not a flea nor a cricket that carried any brave mind, that would stay there after he had once tasted the order of their fare. Only unfortunate gold, a predestinate slave to drudges and fools, lives in endless bondage there amongst them, and may no way be released, except you send the rot half a year amongst his keepers, and so make them away with a murrion, one after another.

The Complaint of Pride

Oh, but a far greater enormity reigneth in the heart of the Court. Pride, the perverter of all virtue, sitteth apparelled in the merchant's spoils, and ruin of young citizens; and scorneth learning, that gave their upstart fathers titles of gentry.

THE NATURE OF AN UPSTART

All malcontent sits the greasy son of a clothier, and complains, like a decayed earl, of the ruin of ancient houses; whereas the weaver's loom first framed the web of his honour, and the locks of wool, that bushes and brambles have took for toll of insolent sheep, that would needs strive for the wall of

a fir bush, have made him of the tenths of their tar, a squire
of low degree; and of the collections of their scatterings, a
Justice, *Tam Marti quam Mercurio*, of Peace and Quorum.
He will be humorous, forsooth, and have a brood of fashions
by himself. Sometimes, because Love commonly wears the
livery of Wit, he will be an *Inamorato Poeta*, and sonnet a
whole quire of paper in praise of Lady Swine-snout, his yellow-
faced mistress, and wear a feather of her rainbeaten fan for a
favour, like a fore-horse. All *Italio; ato* is his talk, and his
spade peak is as sharp as if he had been a pioneer before the
walls of Rouen. He will despise the barbarism of his own
country and tell a whole *Legend of Lies* of his travels unto
Constantinople. If he be challenged to fight, for his dilatory
excuse he objects that it is not the custom of the Spaniard or
the German to look back to every dog that barks. You shall
see a dapper jack, that hath been but over at Dieppe, wring
his face round about, as a man would stir up a mustard pot,
and talk English through the teeth, like Jaques Scabbed-hams
or Monsieur Mingo de Mousetrap; when, poor slave, he hath
but dipped his bread in wild boar's grease, and come home
again; or been bitten by the shins by a wolf; and saith, he hath
adventured upon the barricades of Gourney or Guingamp
and fought with the young Guise hand to hand.

THE COUNTERFEIT POLITICIAN

Some think to be counted rare politicians and statesmen, by
being solitary; as who should say, "I am a wise man, a brave
man, *Secreta mea mihi; Frustra sapit, qui sibi non sapit*, and
there is no man worthy of my company or friendship"; when,
although he goes ungartered like a malcontent cut-purse, and
wears his hat over his eyes like one of the cursed crew, yet
cannot his stabbing dagger, or his nitty love-lock, keep him
out of *The Legend of Fantastical Coxcombs*.

I pray ye, good Monsieur Devil, take some order, that the streets be not pestered with them so as they are. Is it not a pitiful thing that a fellow that eats not a good meal's meat in a week, but beggareth his belly quite and clean to make his back a certain kind of brokerly gentleman, and now and then, once or twice in a term, comes to the eighteen pence ordinary, because he would be seen amongst cavaliers and brave countiers, living otherwise all the year long with salt butter and Holland cheese in his chamber, should take up a scornful melancholy in his gait and countenance, and talk as though our commonwealth were but a mockery of government and our magistrates fools, who wronged him in not looking into his deserts, not employing him in state matters, and that, if more regard were not had of him very shortly, the whole realm should have a miss of him, and he would go (ay, marry, would he) where he should be more accounted of?

Is it not wonderful ill provided, I say, that this disdainful companion is not made one of the fraternity of fools, to talk before great states, with some old moth-eaten politician, of mending highways and leading armies into France?

THE PRODIGAL YOUNG MASTER

A young heir or cockney, that is his mother's darling, if he have played the waste-good at the Inns of the Court or about London, and that neither his student's pension nor his unthrift's credit will serve to maintain his college of whores any longer, falls in a quarrelling humour with his fortune, because she made him not King of the Indies, and swears and stares, after ten in the hundred, that ne'er a such peasant as his father or brother shall keep him under: he will to the sea, and tear the gold out of the Spaniards' throats, but he will have it, byrlady. And when he comes there, poor soul, he lies in brine, in ballast, and is lamentable sick of the scurvies;

his dainty fare is turned to a hungry feast of dogs and cats, or
haberdine and poor John at the most, and, which is lament-
blest of all, that without mustard.

As a mad ruffian, on a time, being in danger of shipwreck
by a tempest, and seeing all other at their vows and prayers,
that if it would please God, of his infinite goodness, to deliver
them out of that imminent danger, one would abjure this sin
whereunto he was addicted, another, make satisfaction for that
violence he had committed; he, in a desperate jest, began thus
to reconcile his soul to heaven.

"O Lord, if it may seem good to thee to deliver me from
this fear of untimely death, I vow before thy throne, and all
thy starry host, never to eat haberdine more whilst I live."

Well, so it fell out, that the sky cleared and the tempest
ceased, and this careless wretch, that made such a mockery of
prayer, ready to set foot a land, cried out; "Not without mustard, good Lord, not without mustard"; as though it had
been the greatest torment in the world to have eaten haberdine
without mustard.

But this by the way, what penance can be greater for Pride
than to let it swing in his own halter? *Dulce bellum inexpertis:*
there's no man loves the smoke of his own country, that hath
not been singed in the flame of another soil. It is a pleasant
thing, over a full pot, to read the fable of thirsty Tantalus;
but a harder matter to digest salt meats at sea, with stinking
water.

THE PRIDE OF THE LEARNED

Another misery of pride it is, when men that have good
parts and bear the name of deep scholars cannot be content to
participate one faith with all Christendom, but, because they
will get a name to their vainglory, they will set their self-love
to study to invent new sects of singularity, thinking to live
when they are dead, by having sects called after their names,

as Donatists of Donatus, Arians of Arius, and a number more new faith founders, that have made England the exchange of innovations, and almost as much confusion of religion in every quarter, as there was of tongues at the building of the Tower of Babel. Whence, a number that fetch the articles of their belief out of Aristotle, and think of heaven and hell as the heathen philosophers, take occasion to deride our ecclesiastical state and all ceremonies of divine worship as bugbears and scarecrows, because, like Herod's soldiers, we divide Christ's garment amongst us in so many pieces, and of the vesture of salvation make some of us babies' and apes' coats, others straight trusses and devil's breeches; some galligaskins or a shipman's hose, like the Anabaptists and adulterous Familists; others, with the Martinists, a hood with two faces, to hide their hypocrisy; and, to conclude, some, like the Barrowists and Greenwoodians, a garment full of the plague, which is not to be worn before it be new washed.

Hence atheists triumph and rejoice, and talk as profanely of the Bible, as of *Bevis of Hampton*. I hear say there be mathematicians abroad that will prove men before Adam; and they are harboured in high places, who will maintain it to the death that there are no devils.

It is a shame, Signior Beelzebub, that you should suffer yourself thus to be termed a bastard, or not approve to your predestinate children, not only that they have a father, but that you are he that must own them.[1] These are but the suburbs of the sin we have in hand: I must describe to you a large city, wholly inhabited with this damnable enormity.

THE PRIDE OF THE ARTIFICERS

In one place let me shew you a base artificer, that hath no revenues to boast on but a needle in his bosom, as brave as any pensioner or nobleman.

[1] The devil hath children, as other men, but few of them know their own father.

THE PRIDE OF MERCHANTS' WIVES

In another corner, Mistress Minx, a merchant's wife, that will eat no cherries, forsooth, but when they are at twenty shillings a pound, that looks as simperingly as if she were besmeared, and jets it as gingerly as if she were dancing the Canaries. She is so finical in her speech, as though she spoke nothing but what she had first sewed over before in her samplers, and the puling accent of her voice is like a feigned treble, or one's voice that interprets to the puppets. What should I tell how squeamish she is in her diet, what toil she puts her poor servants unto, to make her looking glasses in the pavement? How she will not go into the fields, to cower on the green grass, but she must have a coach for her convoy; and spends half a day in pranking herself if she be invited to any strange place? Is not this the excess of pride, Signior Satan? Go to, you are unwise, if you make her not a chief saint in your calendar.

THE PRIDE OF PEASANTS SPRUNG UP OF NOTHING

The next object that encounters my eyes is some such obscure upstart gallants as without desert or service are raised from the plough to be checkmates with princes. And these I can no better compare than to creatures that are bred *sine coitu*, as crickets in chimneys; to which I resemble poor scullions, that, from turning spit in the chimney corner, are on the sudden hoised up from the kitchen into the waiting chamber, or made barons of the beeves, and marquesses of the mary-bones; some by corrupt water, as gnats, to which we may liken brewers, that, by retailing filthy Thames water, come in a few years to be worth forty or fifty thousand pound; others by dead wine, as little flying worms, and so the vintners in like case; others by slime, as frogs, which may be alluded to

Mother Bunch's slimy ale, that hath made her and some other of her fill-pot faculty so wealthy; others by dirt, as worms, and so I know many gold-finders and hostlers come up: some by herbs, as cankers, and after the same sort our apothecaries; others by ashes, as scarabs, and how else get our colliers the pence? Others from the putrified flesh of dead beasts, as bees of bulls, and butchers by fly-blown beef; wasps of horses, and hackney-men by selling their lame jades to huntsmen for carrion.

Yet am I not against it, that these men by their mechanical trades should come to be sparage[1] gentlemen and chuff-headed burgomasters; but that better places should be possessed by coistrels, and the cobbler's crow, for crying but *Ave Cæsar*, be more esteemed than rarer birds, that have warbled sweeter notes unrewarded. But it is no marvel, for as hemlock fatteth quails and henbane swine, which to all other is poison, so some men's vices have power to advance them, which would subvert any else that should seek to climb by them; and it is enough in them, that they can pare their nails well to get them a living, whenas the seven liberal sciences and a good leg will scarce get a scholar a pair of shoes and a canvas doublet.

These whelps of the first litter of gentility, these exhalations, drawn up to the heaven of honour from the dunghill of abject fortune, have long been on horseback to come riding to your Devilship; but, I know not how, like Saint George, they are always mounted but never move. Here they outface town and country, and do nothing but bandy factions with their betters. Their big limbs yield the commonwealth no other service but idle sweat, and their heads, like rough-hewn globes, are fit for nothing but to be the blockhouses of sleep. Raynold, the fox, may well bear up his tail in the lion's den, but when he comes abroad he is afraid of every dog that barks. What cur will not bawl and be ready to fly in a man's face when he is

[1] Sparagus: a flower that never groweth but through a man's dung.

set on by his master, who, if he be not by to encourage him, he casts his tail betwixt his legs and steals away like a sheep-biter? Ulysses was a tall man under Ajax' shield; but by himself he would never adventure but in the night. Pride is never built but upon some pillars; and let his supporters fail him never so little, you shall find him very humble in the dust. Wit oftentimes stands instead of a chief arch to underprop it; in soldiers, strength; in women, beauty.

THE BASE INSINUATING OF DRUDGES AND THEIR PRACTICE TO ASPIRE

Drudges, that have no extraordinary gifts of body nor of mind, filch themselves into some nobleman's service, either by bribes or by flattery, and, when they are there, they so labour it with cap and knee, and ply it with privy whisperings, that they wring themselves into his good opinion ere he be aware. Then do they vaunt themselves over the common multitude, and are ready to outbrave any man that stands by himself. Their lord's authority is as a rebater to bear up the peacock's tail of their boasting, and anything that is said or done to the unhandsoming of their ambition is straight wrested to the name of treason. Thus do weeds grow up while no man regards them, and the Ship of Fools is arrived in the Haven of Felicity, whilst the scouts of Envy contemn the attempts of any such small barks.

But beware you that be great men's favourites; let not a servile insinuating slave creep betwixt your legs into credit with your lords; for peasants that come out of the cold of poverty, once cherished in the bosom of prosperity, will straight forget that ever there was a winter of want, or who gave them room to warm them. The son of a churl cannot choose but prove ingrateful, like his father. Trust not a villain that hath been miserable, and is suddenly grown happy. Virtue ascendeth by degrees of desert unto dignity: gold and lust may lead a man a nearer way to promotion: but he that hath neither comeliness nor coin to commend him undoubtedly strides over time by stratagems,[1] if of a molehill he grows to a mountain in a moment. This is that which I urge; there is no friendship to be had with him that is resolute to do or suffer anything rather than to endure the destiny whereto he was born; for he will not spare his own father or brother, to make himself a gentleman.

THE PRIDE OF THE SPANIARD

France, Italy and Spain, are all full of these false hearted Machiavellians; but, properly, pride is the disease of the Spaniard, who is born a braggart in his mother's womb. For, if he be but seventeen years old and hath come to the place where a field was fought—though half a year before—he then talks like one of the giants that made war against Heaven, and stands upon his honour, as much as if he were one of Augustus' soldiers, of whom he first instituted the order of heralds. And let a man soothe him in this vein of killcow vanity, you may command his heart out of his belly, to make you a rasher on the coals, if you will, next your heart.

THE PRIDE OF THE ITALIAN

The Italian is a more cunning proud fellow, that hides his humour far cleanlier, and indeed seems to take a pride in humility, and will proffer a stranger more courtesy than he means to perform. He hateth him deadly that takes him at his word; as, for example, if upon occasion of meeting, he request you to dinner or supper at his house, and that at the first or second entreaty you promise to be his guest, he will be the

[1] As by carrying tales, or playing the doughty pander.

mortalest enemy you have. But if you deny him, he will think
you have manners and good bringing up and will love you as
his brother. Marry, at the third or fourth time you must not
refuse him. Of all things he counteth it a mighty disgrace to
have a man pass jostling by him in haste on a narrow causey
and ask him no leave, which he never revengeth with less than
a stab.

THE PRIDE OF THE FRENCHMAN

The Frenchman (not altered from his own nature) is wholly
compact of deceivable courtship, and for the most part loves
none but himself and his pleasure; yet though he be the most
Grand Signeur of them all, he will say, *A vostre service et com-
mandemente Mounseur*, to the meanest vassal he meets. He
thinks he doth a great favour to that gentleman or follower
of his to whom he talks sitting on his close stool; and with
that favour, I have heard, the queen mother wonted to grace
the noblemen of France. And a great man of their nation
coming in time past over into England, and being here very
honourably received, he, in requital of his admirable entertainment, on an evening going to the privy, as it were to honour
extraordinarily our English lords appointed to attend him,
gave one the candle, another his girdle, and another the paper;
but they, not acquainted with this new kind of gracing,
accompanying him to the privy door, set down the trash and
so left him; which he, considering what kindness he extended
to them therein more than usual, took very heinously.

THE PRIDE OF THE DANE

The most gross and senseless proud dolts (in a different kind
from all these) are the Danes, who stand so much upon their
unwieldy burly-boned soldiery that they account of no man
that hath not a battle-axe at his girdle to hough dogs with,

or wears not a cock's feather in a red thrummed hat like a cavalier. Briefly, he is the best fool braggart under heaven. For besides nature hath lent him a flabberkin face, like one of the four winds, and cheeks that sag like a woman's dugs over his chin-bone, his apparel is so puffed up with bladders of taffaty, and his back like beef stuffed with parsley, so drawn out with ribbons and devices, and blistered with light sarsenet bastings, that you would think him nothing but a swarm of butterflies if you saw him afar off.[1] Thus walks he up and down in his majesty, taking a yard of ground at every step, and stamps on the earth so terrible, as if he meant to knock up a spirit, when, foul drunken bezzle, if an Englishman set his little finger to him, he falls like a hogs-trough that is set on one end. Therefore I am the more vehement against them, because they are an arrogant, ass-headed people, that naturally hate learning and all them that love it. Yea, and for they would utterly root it out from among them, they have withdrawn all rewards from the professors thereof. Not Barbary itself is half so barbarous as they are.

NO REWARDS AMONGST THEM FOR DESERT

First, whereas the hope of honour maketh a soldier in England; bishoprics, deaneries, prebendaries, and other private dignities animate our divines to such excellence; the civil lawyers have their degrees and consistories of honour by themselves, equal in place with knights and esquires; the common lawyers, suppose in the beginning they are but husbandmen's sons, come in time to be chief fathers of the land, and many of them not the meanest of the Privy Council: there, the soldier may fight himself out of his skin and do more exploits than he hath doits in his purse, before from a common mercenary he come to be corporal of the mould-

[1] If you know him not by any of these marks, look on his fingers and you shall be sure to find half a dozen silver rings, worth threepence apiece.

cheese, or the lieutenant get a captainship. None but the son of a corporal must be a corporal, nor any be captain but the lawful begotten of a captain's body. Bishoprics, deaneries, prebendaries, why, they know no such functions; a sort of ragged ministers they have, of whom they count as basely as water-bearers. If any of their noblemen refrain three hours in his life-time from drinking, to study the laws, he may perhaps have a little more government put into his hands than another; but otherwise, burgomasters and gentlemen bear all the sway of both swords, spiritual and temporal. It is death there for any but a husbandman to marry a husbandman's daughter, or a gentleman's child to join with any but the son of a gentleman. Marry, this; the King may well banish, but he cannot put a gentleman unto death in any cause whatsoever, which makes them stand upon it so proudly as they do. For fashion sake some will put their children to school, but they set them not to it till they are fourteen year old; so that you shall see a great boy with a beard learn his ABC and sit weeping under the rod when he is thirty years old.

WHAT IT IS TO MAKE MEN LABOUR WITHOUT HOPE

I will not stand to infer what a prejudice it is to the thrift of a flourishing state, to poison the growth of glory by giving it nought but the puddle water of penury to drink; to clip the wings of a high-towering falcon, who, whereas she wont in her feathered youthfulness, to look with an amiable eye upon her gray breast, and her speckled side sails, all sinewed with silver quills, and to drive whole armies of fearful fowl before her to her master's table; now she sits sadly on the ground, picking of worms, mourning the cruelty of those ungentle-manlike idle hands, that dismembered the beauty of her train.

You all know that man, insomuch as he is the image of God,

delighteth in honour and worship, and all Holy Writ warrants that delight, so it be not derogatory to any part of God's own worship: now, take away that delight, a discontented idleness overtakes him. For his hire, any handycraftman, be he carpenter, joiner, or painter, will ploddingly do his day labour. But to add credit and fame to his workmanship, or to win a mastery to himself above all other, he will make a further assay in his trade than ever hitherto he did. He will have a thousand flourishes, which before he never thought upon, and in one day rid more out of hand than erst he did in ten. So in arms, so in arts; if titles of fame and glory be proposed to forward minds, or that sovereignty, whose sweetness they have not yet felt, be set in likely view for them to soar to, they will make a ladder of cord of the links of their brains, but they will fasten their hands as well as their eyes on the imaginative bliss which they already enjoy by admiration. Experience reproves me for a fool for dilating on so manifest a case.

The Danes are bursten-bellied sots, that are to be confuted with nothing but tankards or quart pots, and Ovid might as well have read his verses to the Getes that understood him not, as a man talk reason to them that have no ears but their mouths, nor sense but of that which they swallow down their throats. God so love me as I love the quick-witted Italians and therefore love them the more because they mortally detest this surly, swinish generation.

I need not fetch colours from other countries to paint the ugly visage of Pride, since her picture is set forth in so many painted faces here at home. What drugs, what sorceries, what oils, what waters, what ointments, do our curious dames use to enlarge their withered beauties! Their lips are as lavishly red, as if they used to kiss an okerman every morning, and their cheeks sugar-candied and cherry-blushed so sweetly, after the colour of a new Lord Mayor's posts, as if the pageant of their wedlock holiday were hard at the door; so that if a painter were to draw any of their counterfeits on a table he needs no more but wet his pencil, and dab it on their cheeks, and he shall have vermilion and white enough to furnish out his work, though he leave his tar-box at home behind him. Wise was that sin-washing poet that made *The Ballad of Blue Starch and Poking Sticks*, for indeed the lawn of licentiousness hath consumed all the wheat of hospitality. It is said, Laurence Lucifer, that you went up and down London crying then like a lantern and candle man. I marvel no laundress would give you the washing and starching of your face for your labour, for God knows it is as black as the Black Prince.

It is suspected that you have been a great tobacco-taker in your youth, which causeth it to come so to pass; but Dame Nature, your nurse, was partly in fault, else she might have remedied it. She should have nointed your face overnight with *lac virginis*, which baking upon it in bed till the morning, she might have peeled off the scale like the skin of a custard, and making a posset of verjuice mixed with the oil of Tartary and camphor, bathed it in it a quarter of an hour, and you had been as fair as the flour of the frying pan. I warrant we have old hacksters in this great grandmother of corporations, Madame Troynovant, that have not backbited any of their neighbours with the tooth of envy this twenty year, in the wrinkles of whose face ye may hide false dice and play at cherry-pit in the dint of their cheeks: yet these aged mothers of iniquity will have their deformities new plastered over, and wear nosegays of yellow hair on their furies' foreheads, when age hath written, "Ho, God be here," on their bald, burnt-parchment pates. Pish, pish, what talk you of old age or bald pates? Men and women that have gone under the South Pole must lay off their furred night-caps in spite of their teeth, and become yeomen of the vinegar bottle. A close periwig hides all the sins of an old whore-master; but *Cucullus non facit monachum*, 'tis not their new bonnets will keep them from the old bone-ache. Ware when a man's sins are written on his eyebrows, and that there is not a hair-breadth betwixt them

G

and the falling sickness. The times are dangerous, and this is an iron age, or rather no iron age—for swords and bucklers go to pawn apace in Long Lane—but a tin age, for tin and pewter are more esteemed than Latin. You that be wise, despise it, abhor it, neglect it, for what should a man care for gold that cannot get it?

THE COMMENDATION OF ANTIQUARIES
LAUDAMUS VETERES, SED NOSTRIS UTIMUR ANNIS

An antiquary is an honest man, for he had rather scrape a piece of copper out of the dirt, than a crown out of Plowden's standish. I know many wise gentlemen of this musty vocation, who, out of love with the times wherein they live, fall a retailing of Alexander's stirrups, because, in verity, there is not such a strong piece of stretching leather made nowadays, nor iron so well tempered for any money. They will blow their nose in a box, and say it is the spittle that Diogenes spat in one's face; who, being invited to dinner to his house, that was neat and brave in all points as might be devised, and the grunting dog, somewhat troubled with the rheum, by means of his long fasting and staying for dinner more than wont, spat full in his host's face. And being asked the reason of it, said it was the foulest place he could spy out in all his house.

Let their mistress or some other woman give them a feather of her fan for her favour, and if one ask them what it is they make answer, "A plume of the Phœnix," whereof there is but one in all the world. A thousand gewgaws and toys have they in their chambers which they heap up together, with infinite expense, and are made believe of them that sell them that they are rare and precious things, when they have gathered them upon some dunghill, or raked them out of the kennel by chance. I know one sold an old rope with four knots on it

for four pouna, in that he gave it out it was the length and
breadth of Christ's tomb. Let a tinker take a piece of brass
worth a halfpenny, and set strange stamps on it, and I warrant
he may make it more worth to him of some fantastical fool,
than all the kettles that he ever mended in his life. This is the
disease of our newfangled humourists, that know not what to
do with their wealth. It argueth a very rusty wit, so to dote
on worm-eaten eld.

The Complaint of Envy

Out upon it, how long is Pride a dressing herself? Envy,
awake, for thou must appear before Nicolao Malevolo, great
muster-master of hell. Mark you this sly mate, how smoothly
he looks? The poets were ill advised, that feigned him to be
a lean, gag-toothed beldam, with hollow eyes, pale cheeks, and
snaky hair; for he is not only a man, but a jolly, lusty, old
gentleman, that will wink, and laugh, and jest drily, as if he
were the honestest of a thousand; and I warrant you shall not
hear a foul word come from him in a year. I will not contradict
it, but the dog may worry a sheep in the dark and thrust his
neck into the collar of clemency and pity when he hath done;
as who should say, "God forgive him, he was asleep in the
shambles, when the innocent was done to death." But openly,
Envy sets a civil, fatherly countenance upon it, and hath not
so much as a drop of blood in his face to attaint him of murder.

I thought it expedient in this my supplication, to place it
next to Pride; for it is his adopted son. And hence comes it,
that proud men repine at others' prosperity, and grieve that
any should be great but themselves. *Mens cuiusque, is est
quisque;* it is a proverb that is as hoary as Dutch butter, if a
man will go to the devil, he may go to the devil; there are a
thousand juggling tricks to be used at "Hey pass, come
aloft"; and the world hath cords enough to truss up a calf
that stands in one's way. Envy is a crocodile that weeps when

he kills, and fights with none but he feeds on. This is the nature of this quick-sighted monster, he will endure any pains to endamage another, waste his body with undertaking exploits that would require ten men's strengths, rather than any should get a penny but himself, blear his eyes to stand in his neighbour's light, and to conclude, like Atlas underprop heaven alone, rather than any should be in heaven that he liked not of, or come unto heaven by any other means but by him.

PHILIP OF SPAIN AS GREAT AN ENEMY TO MANKIND AS THE DEVIL

You, goodman wanderer about the world, how do ye spend your time, that you do not rid us of these pestilent members? You are unworthy to have an office if you can execute it no better. Behold another enemy of mankind, beside thyself, exalted in the South, Philip of Spain; who, not content to be the god of gold and chiefest commander of content that Europe affords, but now he doth nothing but thirst after human blood, when his foot is on the threshold of the grave. And as a wolf, being about to devour a horse, doth ballast his belly with earth that he may hang the heavier upon him, and then forcibly flies in his face, never leaving his hold till he hath eaten him up; so this wolvish, unnatural usurper, being about to devour all Christendom by invasion, doth cram his treasuries with Indian earth to make his malice more forcible, and then flies in the bosom of France and Belgia, never withdrawing his forces, as the wolf his fastening, till he hath devoured their welfare, and made the war-wasted carcases of both kingdoms a prey for his tyranny. Only poor England gives him bread for his cake, and holds him out at the arms' end. His Armadoes, that like a high wood over-shadowed the shrubs of our low ships, fled from the breath of our cannons, as vapours before the sun, or as the elephant

flies from the ram, or the sea-whale from the noise of parched
bones. The winds, envying that the air should be dimmed
with such a chaos of wooden clouds, raised up high bulwarks
of bellowing waves, whence death shot at their disordered
navy; and the rocks with their overhanging jaws eat up all the
fragments of oak that they left. So perished our foes; so the
heavens did fight for us. *Præterit Hippomenes, resonant spectacula
plausu.*

I do not doubt, Doctor Devil, but you were present in this
action, or passion rather, and helped to bore holes in ships
to make them sink faster, and rinse out galley-foists with salt
water, that stunk like fusty barrels with their masters' fear.
It will be a good while ere you do as much for the king, as
you did for his subjects. I would have ye persuade an army of
gouty usurers to go to sea upon a boon voyage. Try if you
can tempt Envy to embark himself in the maladventure and
leave troubling the stream, that poets and good fellows may
drink, and soldiers may sing *Placebo*, that have murmured so
long at the waters of strife.

But that will never be; for so long as Pride, Riot, and
Whoredom are the companions of young courtiers, they will
always be hungry and ready to bite at every dog that hath a
bone given him beside themselves. Jesu, what secret grudge
and rancour reigns amongst them, one being ready to despair
of himself if he see the Prince but give his fellow a fair look,
or to die for grief if he be put down in bravery never so little.
Yet this custom have our false hearts fetched from other
countries, that they will swear and protest love, where they
hate deadly, and smile on him most kindly, whose subversion
in soul they have vowed. *Fraus sublimi regnat in aula*; 'tis rare
to find a true friend in kings' palaces. Either thou must be so
miserable that thou fall into the hands of scornful pity, or
thou canst not escape the sting of envy. In one thought
assemble the famous men of all ages, and tell me which of
them all sat in the sunshine of his sovereign's grace, or waxed

great of low beginnings, but he was spite-blasted, heaved at, and ill spoken of; and that of those that bare them most countenance.

MURDER THE COMPANION OF ENVY

But were Envy nought but words, it might seem to be only women's sin; but it hath a lewd mate hanging on his sleeve, called Murder, a stern fellow, that, like a Spaniard in fight, aimeth all at the heart. He hath more shapes than Proteus, and will shift himself upon any occasion of revengement into a man's dish, his drink, his apparel, his rings, his stirrups, his nosegay.

O Italy,[1] the academy of manslaughter, the sporting place of murder, the apothecary-shop of poison for all nations; how many kind of weapons hast thou invented for malice? Suppose I love a man's wife, whose husband yet lives, and cannot enjoy her for his jealous overlooking; physic, or rather the art of murder, as it may be used, will lend one a medicine, which shall make him away, in the nature of that disease he is most subject to, whether in the space of a year, a month, half a year, or what tract of time you will, more or less.

THE PASQUIL THAT WAS MADE UPON THIS LAST POPE

In Rome the papal chair is washed, every five year at the furthest, with this oil of aconitum. I pray God, the king of Spain feasted not our holy father Sextus, that was last, with such a conserve of henbane; for it was credibly reported he loved him not, and this that is now, is a god made with his own hands; as it may appear by the pasquil that was set up of him, in manner of a note, presently after his election, *Sol, Re, Me, Fa,* that is to say, *Solus Rex me facit*; only the king of

---

[1] Italy the storehouse of all murderous inventions.

Spain made me Pope. I am no chronicler of our own country, but if probable suspicion might be heard upon his oath I think some men's souls would not be canonized for martyrs, that on the earth did sway it as monarchs.[1]

Is it your will and pleasure, noble Lantsgrave of Limbo, to let us have less carousing to your health in poison, fewer underhand conspirings, or open quarrels executed only in words, as they are in the world nowadays: and if men will needs carouse, conspire, and quarrel, that they may make Ruffians' Hall of hell, and there bandy balls of brimstone at one another's head, and not trouble our peaceable paradise with their private hurly-burlies about strumpets; where no weapon, as in Adam's Paradise, should be named, but only the angel of providence stand with a fiery sword at the gate, to keep out our enemies?

The Complaint of Wrath, a Branch of Envy

A perturbation of mind, like unto Envy, is Wrath, which looketh far lower than the former. For, whereas Envy cannot be said to be but in respect of our superiors, Wrath respecteth no degrees nor persons, but is equally armed against all that offend him. A hare-brained little dwarf[2] it is, with a swarth visage, that hath his heart at his tongue's end, if he be contraried, and will be sure to do no right nor take no wrong. If he be a judge or a justice (as sometimes the lion comes to give sentence against the lamb) then he swears by nothing but Saint Tyburn, and makes Newgate a noun substantive, whereto all his other words are but adjectives.[3] Lightly he is an old man, for those years are most wayward and teatish, yet be he never so old or so froward, since Avarice likewise is a fellow vice of those frail years, we must set one extreme to strive with

---

[1] As Cardinal Wolsey, for example.
[2] Little men for the most part are angry.
[3] Newgate, a common name for all prisons, as Homo is a common name for a man or a woman.

another and allay the anger of oppression by the sweet incense of a new purse of angels, or the doting planet may have such predominance in these wicked elders of Israel, that if you send your wife or some other female to plead for you she may get your pardon upon promise of better acquaintance. But whist, these are the works of darkness and may not be talked of in the day-time. Fury is a heat or fire, and must be quenched with maid's water.

A TALE OF A WISE JUSTICE

Amongst other choleric wise justices, he was one, that having a play presented before him and his township by Tarlton and the rest of his fellows, Her Majesty's Servants, and they were now entering into their first merriment, as they call it, the people began exceedingly to laugh when Tarlton first peeped out his head. Whereat the justice, not a little moved, and seeing with his becks and nods he could not make them cease, he went with his staff and beat them round about unmercifully on the bare pates, in that they, being but farmers and poor country hinds, would presume to laugh at the Queen's Men, and make no more account of her cloth in his presence.

THE NATURE OF THE IRISHMAN

The causes conducting unto wrath are as diverse as the actions of a man's life. Some will take on like a madman if they see a pig come to the table. Sotericus, the surgeon, was choleric at the sight of sturgeon. The Irishman will draw his dagger, and be ready to kill and slay, if one break wind in his company; and so some of our Englishmen that are soldiers, if one give them the lie. But these are light matters, whereof Pierce complaineth not.

Be advertised, Master *Os foetidum*, beadle of the blacksmiths, that lawyers cannot devise which way in the world to beg, they are so troubled with brabblements and suits every term of yeomen and gentlemen that fall out for nothing. If John a Nokes his hen do but leap into Elizabeth de Gappe's close, she will never leave to haunt her husband till he bring it to a *Nisi prius*. One while, the parson sueth the parishioner for bringing home his tithes; another while, the parishioner sueth the parson for not taking away his tithes in time.

A MERRY TALE OF A BUTCHER AND HIS CALVES

I heard a tale of a butcher, who driving two calves over a common, that were coupled together by the necks with an oaken withe, in the way where they should pass, there lay a poor, lean mare, with a galled back; to whom they coming, as chance fell out, one of one side, and the other of the other, smelling on her, as their manner is, the midst of the withe, that was betwixt their necks, rubbed her and grated her on the sore back, that she started and rose up, and hung them both on her back as a beam; which being but a rough plaster to her raw ulcer, she ran away with them, as she were frantic, into the fens, where the butcher could not follow them, and drowned both herself and them in a quagmire. Now the owner of the mare is in law with the butcher for the loss of his mare, and the butcher interchangeably indites him for his calves. I pray ye, Timothy Tempter, be an arbitrator betwixt them, and couple them both by the necks, as the calves were, and carry them to hell on your back, and then, I hope, they will be quiet.

The chief spur unto wrath is Drunkenness, which, as the touch of an ashen bough causeth a giddiness in the viper's head, and the bat, lightly struck with the leaf of a tree, loseth his remembrance, so they, being but lightly sprinkled with the juice of the hop, become senseless, and have their reason strucken blind, as soon as ever the cup scaleth the fortress of their nose. Then run their words at random, like a dog that hath lost his master, and are up with this man and that man, and generally inveigh against all men, but those that keep a wet corner for a friend, and will not think scorn to drink with a good fellow and a soldier. And so long do they practise this vein on their ale-bench, that when they are sober they cannot leave it. There be those that get their living all the year long by nothing but railing.

A TALE OF ONE FRIAR CHARLES, A FOUL-MOUTHED KNAVE

Not far from Chester, I knew an odd, foul-mouthed knave, called Charles the Friar, that had a face so parboiled with men's spitting on it, and a back so often knighted in Bridewell, that it was impossible for any shame or punishment to terrify him from ill-speaking. Noblemen he would liken to more ugly things than himself; some to "After my hearty commendations," with a dash over the head; others to gilded chines of beef, or a shoemaker sweating when he pulls on a shoe; another to an old verse in Cato, *Ad consilium ne accesseris, antequam voceris*; another to a Spanish codpiece; another, that his face was not yet finished, with suchlike innumerable absurd allusions. Yea, what was he in the court but he had a comparison instead of a capcase to put him in?

Upon a time, being challenged at his own weapon in a private chamber by a great personage (railing, I mean) he so far outstripped him in villainous words, and over-bandied him in bitter terms, that the name of sport could not persuade him patience, nor contain his fury in any degrees of jest, but needs he must wreak himself upon him. Neither would a common revenge suffice him, his displeasure was so infinite (and, it may be, common revenges he took before, as far as the whipcord would stretch, upon like provokements) wherefore he caused his men to take him, and bricked him up in a narrow chimney, that was *Neque maior neque minor corpore locato*; where he fed him for fifteen days with bread and water through a hole, letting him sleep standing if he would, for lie or sit he could not, and then he let him out to see if he could learn to rule his tongue any better.

It is a disparagement to those that have any true spark of gentility, to be noted of the whole world so to delight in detracting, that they should keep a venomous-toothed cur and feed him with the crumbs that fall from their table, to do nothing but bite everyone by the shins that pass by. If they will needs be merry, let them have a fool and not a knave to disport them, and seek some other to bestow their alms on than such an impudent beggar.

As there be those that rail at all men, so there be those that rail at all arts, as Cornelius Agrippa *De Vanitate Scientiarum*, and a treatise that I have seen in dispraise of learning, where he saith it is the corrupter of the simple, the schoolmaster of sin, the storehouse of treachery, the reviver of vices, and mother of cowardice; alleging many examples, how there was never man egregiously evil but he was a scholar; that when the use of letters was first invented the Golden World ceased, *Facinusque invasit mortales*; how study doth effeminate a man, dim his sight, weaken his brain, and engender a thousand diseases. Small learning would serve to confute so manifest a scandal, and I imagine all men, like myself, so unmovably resolved of the excellency thereof, that I will not, by the underpropping of confutation, seem to give the idle-witted adversary so much encouragement, as he should surmise his superficial arguments had shaken the foundation of it; against which he could never have lifted his pen if herself had not helped him to hurt herself.

AN INVECTIVE AGAINST ENEMIES OF POETRY

With the enemies of Poetry, I care not if I have a bout; and those are they that term our best writers but babbling ballad-makers, holding them fantastical fools that have wit, but cannot tell how to use it. I myself have been so censured among some dull-headed divines; who deem it no more cunning to write an exquisite poem, than to preach pure Calvin, or distill the juice of a commentary in a quarter sermon.[1] Prove it when you will, you slow-spirited saturnists, that have nothing but the pilferies of your pen to polish an exhortation withal; no eloquence but tautologies, to tie the ears of your auditory unto you; no invention but here is to be noted, "I stole this note out of Beza or Marlorat"; no wit to move, no passion to urge, but only an ordinary form of preaching, blown up by use of often hearing and speaking; and you shall find there goes more exquisite pains and purity of wit to the writing of one such rare poem as *Rosamond* than to a hundred of your dunstical sermons.[2]

Should we (as you) borrow all out of others, and gather nothing of ourselves, our names should be baffled on every bookseller's stall, and not a chandler's mustard-pot but would wipe his mouth with our waste paper. "New herrings, new," we must cry, every time we make ourselves public, or else we shall be christened with a hundred new titles of idiotism. Nor is Poetry an art whereof there is no use in a man's whole life, but to describe discontented thoughts and youthful desires; for there is no study, but it doth illustrate and beautify. How admirably shine those divines above the common mediocrity, that have tasted the sweet springs of Parnassus?

[1] Absit arrogantia, that this speech should concern all divines, but such dunces as abridge men of their lawful liberty, and care not how unprepared they speak to their auditory.

[2] Such sermons I mean as our sectaries preach in ditches, and other conventicles, when they leap from the cobbler's stall to their pulpits.

ENCOMIUM H. SMITHI

Silver-tongued Smith, whose well-tuned style hath made thy death the general tears of the Muses, quaintly couldst thou devise heavenly ditties to Apollo's lute, and teach stately verse to trip it as smoothly as if Ovid and thou had but one soul. Hence alone did it proceed, that thou wert such a plausible pulpit man, that before thou enteredst into the rough ways of theology, thou refinedst, preparedst, and purifidest thy mind with sweet poetry. If a simple man's censure may be admitted to speak in such an open theatre of opinions, I never saw abundant reading better mixed with delight, or sentences, which no man can challenge of profane affectation sounding more melodious to the ear or piercing more deep to the heart.

THE FRUITS OF POETRY

To them that demand what fruits the poets of our time bring forth or wherein they are able to prove themselves necessary to the state, thus I answer. First and foremost, they have cleansed our language from barbarism and made the vulgar sort here in London, which is the fountain whose rivers flow round about England, to aspire to a richer purity of speech than is communicated with the commonalty of any nation under heaven. The virtuous by their praises they encourage to be more virtuous, to vicious men they are as infernal hags, to haunt their ghosts with eternal infamy after death. The soldier, in hope to have his high deeds celebrated by their pens, despiseth a whole army of perils, and acteth wonders exceeding all human conjecture. Those that care neither for God nor the devil by their quills are kept in awe. *Multi famam*, saith one, *pauci conscientiam verentur*.[1] Let God see what he will, they would be loath to have the shame of

[1] Plin., lib. 3.

the world. What age will not praise immortal Sir Philip Sidney, whom noble Salustius, that thrice singular French poet, hath famoused, together with Sir Nicholas Bacon Lord Keeper, and merry Sir Thomas More, for the chief pillars of our English speech. Not so much but Chaucer's Host Bailey in Southwark, and his Wife of Bath he keeps such a stir with in his *Canterbury Tales*, shall be talked of whilst the bath is used or there be ever a bad house in Southwark.

THE DISPRAISE OF LAY CHRONIGRAPHERS

Gentles, it is not your lay chronigraphers, that write of nothing but mayors and sheriffs, and the dear year, and the great frost, that can endow your names with never dated glory. For they want the wings of choice words to fly to heaven, which we have. They cannot sweeten a discourse, or wrest admiration from men reading, as we can reporting the meanest accident. Poetry is the honey of all flowers, the quintessence of all sciences, the marrow of wit, and the very phrase of angels. How much better is it then to have an elegant lawyer to plead one's cause, than a stutting townsman, that loseth himself in his tale, and doth nothing but make legs; so much it is better for a nobleman, or gentleman, to have his honour's story related, and his deeds emblazoned, by a poet than a citizen.

Alas, poor Latinless authors, they are so simple they know not what they do. They no sooner spy a new ballad, and his name to it that compiled it, but they put him in for one of the learned men of our time. I marvel how the masterless men that set up their bills in Paul's for service, and such as paste up their papers on every post for arithmetic and writing schools, scape eternity amongst them. I believe both they and the Knight Marshal's men, that nail up mandates at the Court gate for annoying the palace with filth or making water, if they set their names to the writing, will shortly make up the

number of the learned men of our time, and be as famous as
the rest. For my part, I do challenge no praise of learning to
myself, yet have I worn a gown in the university, and so hath
caret tempus non habet moribus; but this I dare presume, that, if
any Maecenas bind me to him by his bounty, or extend some
round liberality to me worth the speaking of, I will do him
as much honour as any poet of my beardless years shall in
England. Not that I am so confident what I can do, but that
I attribute so much to my thankful mind above others, which,
I am persuaded, would enable me to work miracles.

On the contrary side, if I be evil entreated, or sent away
with a flea in mine ear, let him look that I will rail on him
soundly; not for an hour or a day, while the injury is fresh in
my memory, but in some elaborate polished poem, which I
will leave to the world when I am dead to be a living image
to all ages of his beggarly parsimony and ignoble liberality.
And let him not, whatsoever he be, measure the weight of
my words by this book, where I write *Quicquid in buccam
venerit* as fast as my hand can trot; but I have terms, if I be
vexed, laid in steep in *aquafortis* and gunpowder, that shall
rattle through the skies and make an earthquake in a peasant's
ears.

Put case, since I am not yet out of the theme of Wrath, that
some tired jade belonging to the press, whom I never wronged
in my life, hath named me expressly in print[1] (as I will not do
him) and accused me of want of learning, upbraiding me for
reviving, in an epistle of mine, the reverent memory of Sir
Thomas More, Sir John Cheeke, Doctor Watson, Doctor
Haddon, Doctor Carr, Master Ascham, as if they were no
meat but for his mastership's mouth, or none but some such
as the son of a ropemaker were worthy to mention them.
To shew how I can rail, thus would I begin to rail on him.

---

[1] I would tell you in what book it is, but I am afraid it would make his book
sell in his latter days, which hitherto hath lain dead, and been a great loss to
the printer.

Thou that hadst thy hood turned over thy ears, when thou wert a bachelor, for abusing of Aristotle, and setting him up on the school gates painted with asses' ears on his head; is it any discredit for me, thou great baboon, thou pigmy braggart, thou pamphleteer of nothing but pæans,[1] to be censured by thee, that hast scorned the Prince of Philosophers? Thou, that in thy dialogues soldst honey for a halfpenny, and the choicest writers extant for cues apiece, that camest to the Logic Schools when thou wert a freshman and writst phrases; off with thy gown and untruss, for I mean to lash thee mightily. Thou hast a brother, hast thou not, student in almanacs? Go to, I'll stand to it, he fathered one of thy bastards, a book I mean, which, being of thy begetting, was set forth under his name.

Gentlemen, I am sure you have heard of a ridiculous ass that many years since sold lies by the great, and wrote an absurd *Astrological Discourse* of the terrible conjunction of Saturn and Jupiter; wherein, as if he had lately cast the heavens' water or been at the anatomizing of the sky's entrails in Surgeon's Hall, he prophesieth of such strange wonders to ensue from stars' distemperature and the unusual adultery of planets, as none but he that is bawd to those celestial bodies could ever descry. What expectation there was of it both in town and country, the amazement of those times may testify; and the rather because he pawned his credit[2] upon it, in these express terms: "If these things fall not out in every point as I have wrote, let me for ever hereafter lose the credit of my astronomy."

Well, so it happened, that he happened not to be a man of his word. His astronomy broke his day with his creditors, and Saturn and Jupiter proved honester men than all the world took them for; whereupon the poor prognosticator was ready

---

[1] Look at the chandler's shop or at the flaxwife's stall, if you see no tow nor soap wrapped up in the title page of such a pamphlet as 'Incerti Authoris Io Paean.'

[2] Which at home iwis, was worth a dozen of halters at least, for if I be not deceived, his father was a ropemaker.

to run himself through with his Jacob's staff, and cast himself headlong from the top of a globe (as a mountain) and break his neck. The whole university hissed at him, Tarlton at the theatre made jests of him, and Elderton consumed his ale-crammed nose to nothing in bearbaiting him with whole bundles of ballads. Would you, in likely reason, guess it were possible for any shame-swollen toad to have the spit-proof face to live out this disgrace? It is, dear brethren, *Vivit, imo vivit*; and, which is more, he is a vicar.

Poor slave, I pity thee that thou hadst no more grace but to come in my way. Why could not you have sat quiet at home and writ catechisms, but you must be comparing me to *Martin*, and exclaim against me for reckoning up the high scholars of worthy memory? *Jupiter ingeniis præbet sua numina vatum*, saith Ovid, *seque celebrari quolibet ore sinit*. Which if it be so, I hope I am *Aliquis*, and those men, *quos honoris causa nominavi*, are not greater than gods. Methinks I see thee stand quivering and quaking, and even now lift up thy hands to heaven, as thanking God my choler is somewhat assuaged; but thou art deceived, for however I let fall my style a little, to talk in reason with thee that hast none, I do not mean to let thee scape so.

Thou hast wronged one for my sake, whom for the name I must love, T.N., the master-butler of Pembroke Hall, a far better scholar than thyself (in my judgment) and one that sheweth more discretion and government in setting up a size of bread, than thou in all thy whole book. Why man, think no scorn of him, for he hath held thee up a hundred times, while the Dean hath given thee correction, and thou hast capped and kneed him, when thou wert hungry, for a chipping. But that's nothing, for hadst thou never been beholding to him nor holden up by him, he hath a beard that is a better gentleman than all thy whole body, and a grave countenance, like Cato, able to make thee run out of thy wits for fear, if he look sternly upon thee.

H

I have read over thy sheepish discourse of the Lamb of God
and his enemies, and entreated my patience to be good to thee
while I read. But for all that I could do with myself (as I am
sure I may do as much as another man) I could not refrain,
but bequeath it to the privy, leaf by leaf as I read it, it was so
ugly, dorbellical, and lumpish. Monstrous, monstrous, and
palpable, not to be spoken of in a Christian congregation;
thou has scummed over the school-men, and of the froth of
their folly made a dish of divinity brewess, which the dogs will
not eat. If the printer have any great dealings with thee, he
were best to get a privilege betimes, *Ad imprimendum solum*,
forbidding all other to sell waste paper but himself, or else he
will be in a woeful taking. The Lamb of God[1] make thee a
wiser bell-weather than thou art, for else I doubt thou wilt
be driven to leave all, and fall to thy father's occupation,
which is, to go and make a rope to hang thyself. *Neque enim
lex æquior ulla est, quam necis artifices arte perire sua.* And so I
leave thee till a better opportunity, to be tormented world
without end of our poets and writers about London, whom
thou has called piperly make-plays and make-bates; not
doubting but he also, whom thou termest 'the vain Paphatchet,' will have a flurt at thee one day; all jointly driving thee
to this issue, that thou shalt be constrained to go to the chief
beam of thy benefice, and there beginning a lamentable speech
with *cur scripsi, cur perii*, end with *pravum prava decent, iuvat
inconcessa voluptas*, and so with a trice, truss up thy life in the
string of thy sancebell. "So be it," pray Pen, Ink, and Paper,
on their knees, that they may not be troubled with thee any
more.

Redeo ad vos, mei auditores, have I not an indifferent pretty
vein in spur-galling an ass? If you knew how extemporal it
were at this instant, and with what haste it is writ, you would
say so. But I would not have you think that all this that is set
down here is in good earnest, for then you go by St Giles,

[1] His own words.

the wrong way to Westminster: but only to shew how for a need I could rail, if I were thoroughly fired. So ho, Honiger Hammon, where are you all this while, I cannot be acquainted with you? Tell me, what do you think of the case? Am I subject to the sin of Wrath I write against, or no, in whetting my pen on this block? I know you would fain have it so, but it shall not choose but be otherwise for this once. Come on, let us turn over a new leaf, and hear what Gluttony can say for herself, for Wrath hath spit his poison, and full platters do well after extreme purging.

The Complaint of Gluttony

The Roman emperors that succeeded Augustus were exceedingly given to this horrible vice, whereof some of them would feed on nothing but the tongues of pheasants and nightingales; others would spend as much at one banquet as a king's revenues came to in a year; whose excess I would decipher at large, but that a new laureate hath saved me the labour, who, for a man that stands upon pains and not wit, hath performed as much as any story-dresser may do, that sets a new English nap on an old Latin apothegm. It is enough for me to lick dishes here at home, though I feed not mine eyes at any of the Roman feasts. Much good do it you, Master Dives, here in London; for you are he my pen means to dine withal. *Miserere mei*, what a fat churl it is! Why, he hath a belly as big as the round church in Cambridge, a face as huge as the whole body of a base viol, and legs that, if they were hollow, a man might keep a mill in either of them. *Experto crede, Roberto*, there is no mast like a merchant's table. *Bona fide*, it is a great misture, that we have not men swine as well as beasts, for then we should have pork that hath no more bones than a pudding and a side of bacon that you might lay under your head instead of a bolster.

NATURE IN ENGLAND IS BUT PLAIN DAME, BUT IN SPAIN AND ITALY, BECAUSE THEY HAVE MORE USE OF HER THAN WE, SHE IS DUBBED A LADY

It is not for nothing that other countries, whom we upbraid with drunkenness, call us bursten-bellied gluttons; for we make our greedy paunches powdering-tubs of beef, and eat more meat at one meal than the Spaniard or Italian in a month. Good thrifty men, they draw out a dinner with sallets, like a *Swart-rutters* suit, and make *Madona* Nature their best caterer. We must have our tables furnished like poulters' stalls, or as though we were to victual Noah's ark again wherein there was all sorts of living creatures that ever were, or else the good-wife will not open her mouth to bid one welcome. A stranger that should come to one of our *magnificoes'* houses, when dinner were set on the board, and he not yet set, would think the goodman of the house were a haberdasher of wild-fowl, or a Merchant Venturer of dainty meat, that sells commodity of good cheer by the great, and hath factors in Arabia, Turkey, Egypt, and Barbary, to provide him of strange birds, China mustard, and odd patterns to make custards by.

Lord, what a coil have we, with this course and that course, removing this dish higher, setting another lower, and taking away the third. A general might in less space remove his camp, than they stand disposing of their gluttony. And whereto tends all this gourmandise, but to give sleep gross humours to feed on, to corrupt the brain, and make it unapt and unwieldy for anything?

The Roman censors, if they lighted upon a fat corpulent man, they straight took away his horse, and constrained him to go afoot; positively concluding his carcase was so puffed up with gluttony or idleness. If we had such horse-takers amongst us, and that surfeit-swollen churls, who now ride on their foot-cloths, might be constrained to carry their flesh-budgets from place to place on foot, the price of velvet and cloth would fall with their bellies, and the gentle craft (*alias* the red herring's kinsmen) get more and drink less. *Plenus venter nil agit libenter, et plures gula occidit quam gladius.* It is as desperate a piece of service to sleep upon a full stomach as it is to serve in face of the bullet; a man is but his breath, and that may as well be stopped by putting too much in his mouth at once, as running on the mouth of the cannon. That is verified of us, which Horace writes of an outrageous eater in his time, *Quicquid quæsierat ventri donabat avaro*, whatsoever he could rap or rend, he confiscated to his covetous gut. Nay, we are such flesh-eating Saracens that chaste fish may not content us, but we delight in the murder of innocent mutton, in the unpluming of pullery, and quartering of calves and oxen. It is horrible and detestable, no godly fishmonger that can digest it.

A RARE WITTY JEST OF DOCTOR WATSON

Report, which our moderners cleppe flundering Fame, puts me in memory of a notable jest I heard long ago of Doctor Watson, very conducible to the reproof of these fleshly-minded Belials.[1] He being at supper on a fasting or fish night at least, with a great number of his friends and acquaintance, there chanced to be in the company an outlandish doctor, who, when all other fell to such victuals (agreeing to the time) as were before them, he overslipped them, and there being one joint of flesh on the table for such as had weak stomachs, fell freshly to it. After that hunger, half conquered, had restored him to the use of his speech, for his excuse he said to his friend that brought him thither, "*Profecto, Domine, ego sum malissimus piscator*," meaning by *piscator*, a fishman; (which is a

---

[1] Or rather Belly-alls, because all their mind is on their belly.

liberty, as also *malissimus*, that outlandish men in their familiar talk do challenge, at least above us). "*At tu es bonissimus carnifex*," quoth Doctor Watson, retorting very merrily his own licentious figures upon him. So of us may it be said, we are *malissimi piscatores*, but *bonissimi carnifices*. I would English the jest for the edification of the temporality, but that it is not so good in English as in Latin; and, though it were as good, it would not convert clubs and clouted shoon from the flesh pots of Egypt to the provant of the Low Countries; for they had rather (with the servingman) put up a supplication to the Parliament House that they might have a yard of pudding for a penny, than desire (with the baker) there might be three ounces of bread sold for a halfpenny.

THE MODERATION OF FRIAR ALPHONSO, KING PHILIP'S CONFESSOR

Alphonsus, King Philip's confessor, that came over with him to England, was such a moderate man in his diet, that he would feed but once a day, and at that time he would feed so slenderly and sparingly, as scarce served to keep life and soul together. One night, importunately invited to a solemn banquet, for fashion sake he sat down among the rest, but by no entreaty could be drawn to eat anything. At length, fruit being set on the board, he reached an apple out of the dish and put it in his pocket, which one marking, that sat right over against him, asked him, "*Domine, cur es solicitus in crastinum?*—Sir, why are you careful for the morrow?" Whereto he answered most soberly, "*Imo hoc facio, mi amice, ut ne sim solicitus in crastinum.* No, I do it, my friend, that I may not be careful for the morrow." As though his appetite were a whole day contented with so little as an apple, and that it were enough to pay the morrow's tribute to nature.

THE STRANGE ALTERATION OF THE COUNTY
MOLINES, THE PRINCE OF PARMA'S COMPANION

Rare, and worthy to be registered to all posterities, is the
County Moline's (sometime the Prince of Parma's companion)
altered course of life, who, being a man that lived in as great
pomp and delicacy as was possible for a man to do, and one
that wanted nothing but a kingdom that his heart could desire,
upon a day entering into a deep melancholy by himself, he fell
into a discursive consideration what this world was, how vain
and transitory the pleasures thereof, and how many times he
had offended God by surfeiting, gluttony, drunkenness, pride,
whoredom, and such like, and how hard it was for him, that
lived in that prosperity that he did, not to be entangled with
those pleasures. Whereupon he presently resolved, twixt
God and his own conscience, to forsake it and all his allure-
ments, and betake him to the severest form of life used in their
state. And with that called all his soldiers and acquaintance
together, and, making known his intent unto them, he distributed his living and possessions, which were infinite, amongst
the poorest of them; and having not left himself the worth of
one farthing under heaven, betook himself to the most
beggarly new erected Order of the Friar Capuchines. Their
institution is that they shall possess nothing whatsoever of
their own more than the clothes on their backs, continually to
go barefoot, wear hair shirts, and lie upon the hard boards,
winter and summer time. They must have no meat, nor ask
any but what is given them voluntarily, nor must they lay up
any from meal to meal, but give it to the poor, or else it is a
great penalty. In this severe humility lives this devout county,
and hath done this twelvemonth, submitting himself to all the
base drudgery of the house, as fetching water, making clean
the rest of their chambers, insomuch as he is the junior of the
order. Oh what a notable rebuke were his honourable lowliness

to succeeding pride, if this prostrate spirit of his were not the servant of superstition, or he mispent not his good works on a wrong faith.

Let but our English belly-gods punish their pursy bodies with this strict penance, and profess Capuchinism but one month, and I'll be their pledge they shall not grow so like dry-fats as they do. Oh, it will make them jolly long-winded, to trot up and down the dorter stairs, and the water-tankard will keep under the insurrection of their shoulders, the hair shirt will chase whoredom out of their bones, and the hard lodging on the boards take their flesh down a button-hole lower.

But if they might be induced to distribute all their goods amongst the poor, it were to be hoped Saint Peter would let them dwell in the suburbs of heaven, whereas otherwise they must keep aloof at Pancredge, and not come near the liberties by five leagues and above. It is your doing, Diotrephes Devil, that these stall-fed cormorants to damnation must bung up all the wealth of the land in their snap-hance bags, and poor scholars and soldiers wander in back lanes and the out-shifts of the city, with never a rag to their backs. But our trust is, that by some intemperance or other, you will turn up their heels one of these years together, and provide them of such unthrifts to their heirs, as shall spend in one week amongst good fellows what they got by extortion and oppression from gentlemen all their life-time.

The Complaint of Drunkenness

From gluttony in meats let me descend to superfluity in drink, a sin, that ever since we have mixed ourselves with the Low Countries is counted honourable, but before we knew their lingering wars, was held in that highest degree of hatred that might be. Then, if we had seen a man go wallowing in the streets, or lain sleeping under the board, we would have

spit at him as a toad, and called him foul, drunken swine, and
warned all our friends out of his company. Now, he is nobody
that cannot drink *super nagulum*,[1] carouse the hunter's hoop,
quaff *upsey freze cross*, with healths, gloves, mumps, frolics, and
a thousand such domineering inventions. He is reputed a
peasant and a boor that will not take his liquor profoundly.
And you shall hear a cavalier of the first feather, a princox
that was but a page the other day in the Court, and now is
all-to-be-frenchified in his soldier's suit, stand upon terms with
"God's wounds, you dishonour me, sir, you do me the disgrace if you do not pledge me as much as I drunk to you";
and, in the midst of his cups, stand vaunting his manhood,
beginning every sentence with, "When I first bore arms,"
when he never bare anything but his lord's rapier after him
in his life. If he have been over and visited a town of garrison,
as a traveller or passenger, he hath as great experience as the
greatest commander and chief leader in England. A mighty
deformer of men's manners and features is this unnecessary
vice of all other.

Let him be indued with never so many virtues, and have as
much goodly proportion and favour as nature can bestow
upon a man, yet if he be thirsty after his own destruction, and
hath no joy nor comfort but when he is drowning his soul in
a gallon pot, that one beastly imperfection will utterly obscure
all that is commendable in him, and all his good qualities sink
like lead down to the bottom of his carousing cups, where
they will lie, like lees and dregs, dead and unregarded of
any man.

Clim of the Clough, thou that usest to drink nothing but
scalding lead and sulphur in hell, thou art not so greedy of
thy night gear. Oh, but thou hast a foul swallow if it come
once to carousing of human blood; but that's but seldom,

[1] Drinking super nagulum, a device of drinking new come out of France;
which is, after a man hath turned up the bottom of the cup, to drop it on his
nail, and make a pearl with that is left; which, if it shed, and he cannot make
stand on by reason there's too much, he must drink again for his penance.

once in seven year, when there's a great execution, otherwise thou art tied at rack and manger, and drinkest nothing but the *aqua vitæ* of vengeance all thy life-time. The proverb gives it forth thou art a knave, and therefore I have more hope thou art some manner of good fellow. Let me entreat thee, since thou hast other iniquities enough to circumvent us withal, to wipe this sin out of the catalogue of thy subtleties; help to blast the vines, that they may bear no more grapes, and sour the wines in the cellars of merchants' store-houses, that our countrymen may not piss out all their wit and thrift against the walls.

KING EDGAR'S ORDINANCE AGAINST DRINKING

King Edgar, because his subjects should not offend in swilling and bibbing, as they did, caused certain iron cups to be chained to every fountain and well's side, and at every vintner's door, with iron pins in them, to stint every man how much he should drink; and he that went beyond one of those pins forfeited a penny for every draught. And, if stories were well searched, I believe hoops in quart pots were invented to that end, that every man should take his hoop, and no more.

THE WONDERFUL ABSTINENCE OF THE
MARQUIS OF PISANA, YET LIVING

I have heard it justified for a truth by great personages, that the old Marquis of Pisana, who yet lives, drinks not once in seven year; and I have read of one Andron of Argos, that was so seldom thirsty, that he travelled over the hot, burning sands of Lybia, and never drank. Then why should our cold clime bring forth such fiery throats? Are we more thirsty than Spain and Italy, where the sun's force is doubled? The Germans and Low Dutch, methinks, should be continually

kept moist with the foggy air and stinking mists that arise
out of their fenny soil; but as their country is over-flowen
with water, so are their heads always over-flowen with wine,
and in their bellies they have standing quagmires and bogs of
English beer.

THE PRIVATE LAWS AMONGST DRUNKARDS

One of their breed it was that writ the book *De Arte Bibendi*,
a worshipful treatise fit for none but Silenus and his ass to set
forth. Besides that volume, we have general rules and injunc-
tions, as good as printed precepts, or statutes set down by Act
of Parliament, that go from drunkard to drunkard; as still to
keep your first man, not to leave any flocks in the bottom of
the cup, to knock the glass on your thumb when you have
done, to have some shoeing horn to pull on your wine, as a
rasher off the coals or a red herring, to stir it about with a
candle's end to make it taste better, and not to hold your
peace while the pot is stirring.

THE EIGHT KINDS OF DRUNKENNESS

Nor have we one or two kinds of drunkards only, but
eight kinds. The first is ape drunk, and he leaps, and sings,
and holloes, and danceth for the heavens. The second is lion
drunk, and he flings the pots about the house, calls his hostess
whore, breaks the glass windows with his dagger, and is apt
to quarrel with any man that speaks to him. The third is swine
drunk, heavy, lumpish, and sleepy, and cries for a little more
drink and a few more clothes. The fourth is sheep drunk,
wise in his own conceit when he cannot bring forth a right
word. The fifth is maudlin drunk when a fellow will weep
for kindness in the midst of his ale, and kiss you, saying,
"By God, captain, I love thee; go thy ways, thou dost not

think so often of me as I do of thee; I would (if it pleased God) I could not love thee so well as I do." And then he puts his finger in his eye and cries. The sixth is martin drunk, when a man is drunk and drinks himself sober ere he stir. The seventh is goat drunk, when, in his drunkenness, he hath no mind but on lechery. The eighth is fox drunk, when he is crafty drunk, as many of the Dutchmen be, that will never bargain but when they are drunk. All these species, and more, I have seen practised in one company at one sitting, when I have been permitted to remain sober amongst them only to note their several humours. He that plies any one of them hard, it will make him to write admirable verses, and to have a deep casting head, though he were never so very a dunce before.

THE DISCOMMODITIES OF DRUNKENNESS

Gentlemen, all you that will not have your brains twice sodden, your flesh rotten with the dropsy, that love not to go in greasy doublets, stockings out at the heels, and wear ale-house daggers at your backs; forswear this slavering bravery, that will make you have stinking breaths, and your bodies smell like brewers' aprons; rather keep a snuff in the bottom of the glass to light you to bed withal, than leave never an eye in your head to lead you over the threshold. It will bring you in your old age to be companions with none but porters and car-men, to talk out of a cage, railing as drunken men are wont, a hundred boys wondering about them; and to die suddenly, as Fol Long the fencer did, drinking *aqua vitæ*. From which (as all the rest) good Lord deliver Pierce Penilesse.

The Complaint of Sloth

The nurse of this enormity (as of all evils) is Idleness, or Sloth, which, having no painful providence to set himself a-work, runs headlong, with the reins in his own hand, into all lasciviousness and sensuality that may be. Men, when they are idle, and know not what to do, saith one, "Let us go to the Steelyard, and drink Rhenish wine." "Nay, if a man knew where a good whorehouse were," saith another, "it were somewhat like." ''Nay,'' saith the third, "let us go to a dicing-house or a bowling-alley, and there we shall have some sport for our money." To one of these three ("at hand," quoth pick-purse) your evil angelship, master many-headed beast, conducts them; *ubi quid agitur*, betwixt you and their souls be it, for I am no drawer, box-keeper, or pander, to be privy to their sports.

If I were to paint Sloth (as I am not seen in the sweetening) by Saint John the Evangelist I swear I would draw it like a stationer that I know, with his thumb under his girdle, who, if a man come to his stall and ask him for a book, never stirs his head or looks upon him, but stands stone still and speaks not a word; only with his little finger points backwards to his boy, who must be his interpreter, and so all the day, gaping like a dumb image, he sits without motion, except at such times as he goes to dinner or supper; for then he is as quick as other three, eating six times every day.[1] If I would range abroad, and look in at sluggards' key-holes, I should find a number lying abed to save charges of ordinaries, and in winter, when they want firing, losing half a week's commons together, to keep them warm in the linen. And hold you content, this summer an under-meal of an afternoon long doth not amiss to exercise the eyes withal. Fat men and farmers' sons, that sweat much with eating hard cheese and drinking old wine, must have some more ease than young boys that take their pleasure all day running up and down.

[1] Videlicet, before he come out of his bed, then a set breakfast, then dinner, then afternoon's nunchings, a supper, and a rere-supper.

WHICH IS BETTER OF THE IDLE GLUTTON, OR VAGRANT UNTHRIFT

Setting jesting aside, I hold it a great, disputable question, which is a more evil man, of him that is an idle glutton at home, or a reckless unthrift abroad? The glutton at home doth nothing but engender diseases, pamper his flesh unto lust, and is good for none but his own gut. The unthrift abroad exerciseth his body at dancing school, fence school, tennis, and all such recreations; the vintners, the victuallers, the dicing-houses, and who not, get by him. Suppose he lose a little now and then at play, it teacheth him wit: and how should a man know to eschew vices, if his own experience did not acquaint him with their inconveniences? *Omne ignotum pro magnifico est:* that villainy we have made no assays in, we admire. Besides my vagrant reveller haunts plays and sharpens his wits with frequenting the company of poets; he emboldens his blushing face by courting fair women on the sudden, and looks into all estates by conversing with them in public places. Now tell me whether of these two, the heavy-headed, gluttonous house-dove, or this lively, wanton, young gallant, is like to prove the wiser man, and better member in the commonwealth? If my youth might not be thought partial, the fine qualified gentleman, although unstaid, should carry it clean away from the lazy clownish drone.

THE EFFECTS OF SLOTH

Sloth in nobility, courtiers, scholars, or any men, is the chiefest cause that brings them in contempt. For, as industry and unfatigable toil raiseth mean persons from obscure houses to high thrones of authority, so sloth and sluggish security causeth proud lords to tumble from the towers of their starry descents, and be trod underfoot of every inferior besonian.

Is it the lofty treading of a galliard, or fine grace in telling of a love tale amongst ladies, can make a man reverenced of the multitude? No, they care not for the false glistering of gay garments, or insinuating courtesy of a carpet peer; but they delight to see him shine in armour, and oppose himself to honourable danger, to participate a voluntary penury with his soldiers, and relieve part of their wants out of his own purse. That is the course he that will be popular must take, which, if he neglect, and sit dallying at home, nor will be awaked by any indignities out of his love-dream, but suffer every upstart groom to defy him, set him at nought, and shake him by the beard unrevenged, let him straight take orders and be a churchman, and then his patience may pass for a virtue; but otherwise, he shall be suspected of cowardice, and not cared for of any.

THE MEANS TO AVOID SLOTH

The only enemy to Sloth is contention and emulation; as to propose one man to myself, that is the only mirror of our age, and strive to out-go him in virtue. But this strife must be so tempered, that we fall not from the eagerness of praise, to the envying of their persons; for then we leave running to the goal of glory, to spurn at a stone that lies in our way; and so did Atalanta, in the midst of her course, stoop to take up the golden apple that her enemy scattered in her way, and was out-run by Hippomenes. The contrary to this contention and emulation is security, peace, quiet, tranquillity; when we have no adversary to pry into our actions, no malicious eye whose pursuing our private behaviour might make us more vigilant over our imperfections than otherwise we would be.

That state or kingdom that is in league with all the world and hath no foreign sword to vex it, is not half so strong or confirmed to endure, as that which lives every hour in fear of invasion. There is a certain waste of the people for whom there is no use, but war; and these men must have some employment still to cut them off. *Nam si foras hostem non habent, domi invenient:* if they have no service abroad, they will make mutinies at home. Or if the affairs of the state be such, as cannot exhale all these corrupt excrements, it is very expedient they have some light toys to busy their heads withal cast before them as bones to gnaw upon, which may keep them from having leisure to intermeddle with higher matters.

THE DEFENCE OF PLAYS

To this effect the policy of plays is very necessary, howsoever some shallow-brained censurers, not the deepest searchers into the secrets of government, mightily oppugn them. For whereas the afternoon being the idlest time of the day, wherein men that are their own masters (as gentlemen of the Court, the Inns of the Court, and the number of captains and soldiers about London) do wholly bestow themselves upon pleasure; and that pleasure they divide (how virtuously it skills not) either into gaming, following of harlots, drinking, or seeing a play: is it not then better, since of four extremes all the world cannot keep them but they will choose one, that they should betake them to the least, which is plays?

Nay, what if I prove plays to be no extreme; but a rare exercise of virtue? First, for the subject of them, for the most part it is borrowed out of our English Chronicles, wherein our forefathers' valiant acts, that have lain long buried in rusty brass and worm-eaten books, are revived, and they themselves raised from the grave of oblivion, and brought to plead their aged honours in open presence: than which, what can be a sharper reproof to these degenerate effeminate days of ours?

How would it have joyed brave Talbot, the terror of the French, to think that after he had lain two hundred years in his tomb, he should triumph again on the stage and have his

bones new embalmed with the tears of ten thousand spec-
tators at least (at several times), who, in the tragedian that
represents his person, imagine they behold him fresh bleeding!

I will defend it against any cullion, or club-fisted usurer of
them all, there is no immortality can be given a man on earth
like unto plays. What talk I to them of immortality, that are
the only underminers of honour, and do envy any man that is
not sprung up by base brokery like themselves? They care
not if all the ancient houses were rooted out, so that, like the
burgomasters of the Low Countries, they might share the
government amongst them as states, and be quarter-masters
of our monarchy. All arts to them are vanity; and if you tell
them what a glorious thing it is to have Henry the Fifth
represented on the stage, leading the French king prisoner,
and forcing both him and the Dauphin to swear fealty, "Aye,
but," will they say, "what do we get by it?", respecting
neither the right of fame that is due to true nobility deceased,
nor what hopes of eternity are to be proposed to adventurous
minds, to encourage them forward, but only their execrable
lucre, and filthy, unquenchable avarice.

They know when they are dead they shall not be brought
upon the stage for any goodness, but in a merriment of the
Usurer and the Devil, or buying arms of the herald, who
gives them the lion, without tongue, tail, or talons, because
his master, whom he must serve, is a townsman, and a man
of peace, and must not keep any quarrelling beasts to annoy
his honest neighbours.

THE USE OF PLAYS

In plays, all cozenages, all cunning drifts over-gilded with
outward holiness, all stratagems of war, all the cankerworms
that breed on the rust of peace, are most lively anatomized.
They shew the ill success of treason, the fall of hasty climbers,
the wretched end of usurpers, the misery of civil dissension,

I

and how just God is evermore in punishing of murder. And to prove every one of these allegations, could I propound the circumstances of this play and that play, if I meant to handle this theme otherwise than *obiter*. What should I say more? They are sour pills of reprehension, wrapped up in sweet words.

THE CONFUTATION OF CITIZENS' OBJECTIONS AGAINST PLAYERS

Whereas some petitioners of the Council against them object they corrupt the youth of the city, and withdraw prentices from their work, they [the players] heartily wish they might be troubled with none of their youth nor their prentices; for some of them (I mean the ruder handicrafts' servants) never come abroad, but they are in danger of undoing. And as for corrupting them when they come, that's false; for no play they have encourageth any man to tumults or rebellion, but lays before such the halter and the gallows; or praiseth or approveth pride, lust, whoredom, prodigality, or drunkenness, but beats them down utterly. As for the hindrance of trades and traders of the city by them, that is an article foisted in by the vintners, alewives, and victuallers, who surmise, if there were no plays, they should have all the company that resort to them lie boozing and beer-bathing in their houses every afternoon. Nor so, nor so, good Brother Bottle-ale, for there are other places besides, where money can bestow itself. The sign of the smock will wipe your mouth clean; and yet I have heard ye have made her a tenant to your tap-houses. But what shall he do that hath spent himself? Where shall he haunt? Faith, when dice, lust, and drunkenness and all have dealt upon him, if there be never a play for him to go to for his penny, he sits melancholy in his chamber, devising upon felony or treason, and how he may best exalt himself by mischief.

A PLAYER'S WITTY ANSWER TO AUGUSTUS

In Augustus' time, who was the patron of all witty sports, there happened a great fray in Rome about a player, insomuch as all the city was in an uproar. Whereupon, the emperor, after the broil was somewhat overblown, called the player before him, and asked what was the reason that a man of his quality durst presume to make such a brawl about nothing. He smilingly replied: "It is good for thee, O Caesar, that the people's heads are troubled with brawls and quarrels about us and our light matters; for otherwise they would look into thee and thy matters." Read Lipsius or any profane or Christian politician, and you shall find him of this opinion.

A COMPARISON TWIXT OUR PLAYERS AND THE PLAYERS BEYOND THE SEA

Our players are not as the players beyond sea, a sort of squirting bawdy comedians, that have whores and common courtezans to play women's parts, and forbear no immodest speech or unchaste action that may procure laughter; but our scene is more stately furnished than ever it was in the time of Roscius, our representations honourable, and full of gallant resolution, not consisting, like theirs, of a pantaloon, a whore, and a zany, but of emperors, kings and princes, whose true tragedies, *Sophocleo cothurno*, they do vaunt.

THE DUE COMMENDATION OF NED ALLEYN

Not Roscius nor Æsop, those admired tragedians that have lived ever since before Christ was born, could ever perform more in action than famous Ned Alleyn. I must accuse our poets of sloth and partiality, that they will not boast in large impressions what worthy men, above all nations, England affords. Other countries cannot have a fiddler break a string but they will put it in print, and the old Romans in the writings they published, thought scorn to use any but domestical examples of their own home-bred actors, scholars, and champions, and them they would extol to the third and fourth generation: cobblers, tinkers, fencers, none escaped them, but they mingled them all in one gallimaufry of glory.

Here I have used a like method, not of tying myself to mine own country, but by insisting in the experience of our time. And, if I ever write anything in Latin, as I hope one day I shall, not a man of any desert here amongst us, but I will have up. Tarlton, Ned Alleyn, Knell, Bently, shall be made known to France, Spain, and Italy; and not a part that they surmounted in, more than other, but I will there note and set down, with the manner of their habits and attire.

The Seventh and Last Complaint of Lechery

The child of Sloth is Lechery, which I have placed last in my order of handling; a sin that is able to make a man wicked that should describe it; for it hath more starting holes than a sieve hath holes, more clients than Westminster Hall, more diseases than Newgate. Call a leet at Bishopsgate, and examine how every second house in Shoreditch is maintained; make a privy search in Southwark and tell me how many she-inmates you find; nay, go where you will in the suburbs and bring me two virgins that have vowed chastity, and I'll build a nunnery.

Westminster, Westminster, much maidenhead hast thou to answer for at the day of judgment; thou hadst a sanctuary in thee once, but hast few saints left in thee now. Surgeons and apothecaries, you know what I speak is true, for you live, like summoners, upon the sins of the people; tell me, is there any place so lewd, as this Lady London? Not a wench sooner creeps out of the shell, but she is of the religion. Some wives will sow mandrake in their gardens, and cross-neighbourhood with them is counted good fellowship.

The Court I dare not touch, but surely there, as in the heavens, be many falling stars and but one true Diana. *Consuetudo peccandi tollit sensum peccati.* Custom is a law, and lust holds it for a law to live without law. Lais, that had so many poets to her lovers, could not always preserve her beauty with their praises. Marble will wear away with much rain; gold will rust with moist keeping; and the richest garments are subject to time's moth-frets. Clytemnestra, that slew her husband to enjoy the adulterer Ægisthus, and bathed herself in milk every day to make her young again, had a time when she was ashamed to view herself in a looking glass, and her body withered, her mind being green. The people pointed at her for a murderer, young children hooted at her as a strumpet: shame, misery, sickness, beggary, is the best end of uncleanness.

Lais, Cleopatra, Helen, if our clime hath any such, noble Lord Warden of the witches and jugglers, I commend them with the rest of our unclean sisters in Shoreditch, the Spital, Southwark, Westminster, and Turnbull Street, to the protection of your Portership: hoping you will speedily carry them to hell, there to keep open house for all young devils that come, and not let our air be contaminated with their sixpenny damnation any longer.

Yours Devilship's
bounden execrator
PIERCE PENILESSE

"A supplication callst thou this?" quoth the knight of the post, "It is the maddest supplication that ever I saw; methinks thou hast handled all the seven deadly sins in it, and spared none that exceeds his limits in any of them. It is well done to practise thy wit, but, I believe, our lord will con thee little thanks for it."

"The worse for me," quoth I, "if my destiny be such to lose my labour everywhere, but I mean to take my chance, be it good or bad." "Well, hast thou any more that thou wouldest have me to do?" quoth he. "Only one suit," quoth I, "which is this, that sith opportunity so conveniently serves you would acquaint me with the state of your infernal regiment: and what that hell is, where your lord holds his throne; whether a world like this, which spirits like outlaws do inhabit, who, being banished from heaven, as they are from their country, envy that any shall be more happy than they, and therefore seek all means possible, that wit or art may invent, to make other men as wretched as themselves; or whether it be a place of horror, stench, and darkness, where men see meat but can get none, or are ever thirsty and ready to swelt for drink yet have not the power to taste the cool streams that run hard at their feet: where, *permutata vicissitudine*, one ghost torments another by turns, and he that all his lifetime was a great fornicator, hath all the diseases of lust continually hanging upon him, and is constrained, the more to augment his misery, to have congress every hour with hags and old witches: and he that was a great drunkard here on earth, hath his penance assigned him, to carouse himself drunk with dish-wash and vinegar, and surfeit four times a day with sour ale and small beer: as so of the rest, as the usurer to swallow molten gold, the glutton to eat nothing but toads, and the murderer to be still stabbed with daggers, but never die: or whether, as some fantastical refiners of philosophy will needs persuade us, hell is nothing but error, and that none but fools and idiots and mechanical men, that have no learning, shall be damned. Of these doubts if you will resolve me, I shall think myself to have profited greatly by your company."

He, hearing me so inquisitive in matters above human

capacity, entertained my greedy humour with this answer.
"Poets and philosophers, that take a pride in inventing new
opinions, have sought to renown their wits by hunting after
strange conceits of heaven and hell; all generally agreeing that
such places there are, but how inhabited, by whom governed,
or what betides them that are transported to the one or other,
not two of them jump in one tale. We, that to our terror
and grief do know their dotage by our sufferings, rejoice to
think how these silly flies play with the fire that must burn
them.

But leaving them to the labyrinth of their fond curiosity,
shall I tell thee in a word what hell is? It is a place where the
souls of untemperate men and ill-livers of all sorts are detained
and imprisoned till the general resurrection, kept and possessed
chiefly by spirits, who lie like soldiers in garrison, ready to be
sent about any service into the world, whensoever Lucifer,
their Lieutenant General, pleaseth. For the situation of it in
respect of heaven, I can no better compare it than to Calais
and Dover. For, as a man standing upon Calais sands may
see men walking on Dover cliffs, so easily may you discern
heaven from the farthest part of hell, and behold the melody
and motions of the angels and spirits there resident, in such
perfect manner as if you were amongst them; which, how it
worketh in the minds and souls of them that have no power
to apprehend such felicity, it is not for me to intimate, because
it is prejudicial to our monarchy."

"I would be sorry," quoth I, "to importune you in any
matter of secrecy; yet this I desire, if it might be done without
offence, that you would satisfy me in full sort, and according
to truth, what the devil is whom you serve? As also how he
began, and how far his power and authority extends?"

"Percy, believe me, thou shrivest me very near in this
latter demand, which concerneth us more deeply than the
former and may work us more damage than thou art aware of;
yet in hope thou wilt conceal what I tell thee, I will lay open

our whole estate plainly and simply unto thee as it is. But first I will begin with the opinions of former times, and so hasten forward to that *manifeste verum* that thou seekest.

Some men there be that, building too much upon reason, persuade themselves that there are no devils at all, but that this word *dæmon* is such another moral of mischief, as the poets' Dame Fortune is of mishap. For as under the fiction of this blind goddess we aim at the folly of princes and great men in disposing of honours, that oftentimes prefer fools and disgrace wise men, and alter their favours in turning of an eye, as Fortune turns her wheel; so under the person of this old *gnathonical* companion, called the devil, we shroud all subtlety masking under the name of simplicity, all painted holiness devouring widows' houses, all gray-headed foxes clad in sheep's garments; so that the devil (as they make it) is only a pestilent humour in a man, of pleasure, profit, or policy, that violently carries him away to vanity, villainy, or monstrous hypocrisy. Under vanity I comprehend not only all vain arts and studies whatsoever, but also dishonourable prodigality, untemperate venery, and that hateful sin of self-love, which is so common amongst us. Under villainy I comprehend murder, treason, theft, cozenage, cut-throat covetise, and such like. Lastly, under hypocrisy, all machiavellism, puritanism, and outward glozing with a man's enemy, and protesting friendship to him that I hate and mean to harm, all underhand cloaking of bad actions with commonwealth pretences and, finally, all Italianate conveyances, as to kill a man and then mourn for him, *quasi vero* it was not by my consent; to be a slave to him that hath injured me, and kiss his feet for opportunity of revenge; to be severe in punishing offenders, that none might have the benefit of such means but myself; to use men for my purpose and then cast them off; to seek his destruction that knows my secrets; and such as I have employed in any murder or stratagem, to set them privily together by the ears, to stab each other mutually, for fear of bewraying me; or, if that fail, to hire them to humour one another in such courses as may bring them both to the gallows.

These, and a thousand more such sleights, hath hypocrisy learned by travelling strange countries. I will not say she puts them in practice here in England, although there be as many false brethren and crafty knaves here amongst us, as in any place. Witness the poor miller of Cambridge, that, having no room for his hen-loft but the tester of his bed (and it was not possible for any hungry poulterers to come there, but they must stand upon the one side of it and so not steal them but with great hazard) had in one night, notwithstanding, when he and his wife were a snorting, all the whole progeny of their pullery taken away, and neither of them heard any stirring. It is an odd trick, but what of that? We must not stand upon it, for we have graver matters in hand than the stealing of hens. Hypocrisy, I remember, was our text, which was one of the chief moral devils our late doctors affirm to be most busy in these days."

"And busy it is, in truth, more than any bee that I know."

"Now you talk of a bee, I'll tell you a tale of a battle-dore. The bear on a time, being chief burgomaster of all the beasts under the lion, gan think with himself how he might surfeit in pleasure, or best husband his authority to enlarge his delight and contentment. With that he began to pry and to smell through every corner of the forest for prey, to have a thousand imaginations with himself what dainty morsel he was master of, and yet had not tasted. Whole herds of sheep had he devoured, and was not satisfied; fat oxen, heifers, swine, calves, and young kids, were his ordinary viands. He longed for horse-flesh, and went presently to a meadow, where a fat cammell was grazing, whom, fearing to encounter with force, because he was a huge beast and well shod, he thought to betray under the colour of demanding homage, hoping that as he should stoop to do him trewage, he might seize upon his throat and stifle him before he should be able to recover himself from his false embrace. But therein he was deceived; for, coming unto this stately beast with this imperious message, instead of doing homage unto him, he lifted up one of his hind-most heels and struck him such a blow on the forehead that he overthrew him. Thereat not a little moved and enraged that he should be so dishonoured by his inferior, as he thought, he consulted with the ape how he might be revenged.

The ape abhorring him by nature, because he overlooked him so lordly and was by so many degrees greater than he was, advised him to dig a pit with his paws right in the way where this big-boned gentleman should pass, that so stumbling and falling in, he might lightly skip on his back, and bridle him, and then he [could] come and seize on him at his pleasure. No sooner was this persuaded than performed; for envy, that is never idle, could not sleep in his wrath or over-slip the least opportunity till he had seen the confusion of his enemy. Alas, goodly creature, that thou mightest no longer live! What availeth thy gentleness, thy prowess, or the plentiful pasture wherein thou wert fed; since malice triumphs over all thou commandest? Well may the mule rise up in arms, and the ass bray at the authors of thy death: yet shall their fury be fatal to themselves, before it take hold on these traitors. What needeth more words? The devourer feeds on his captive and is gorged with blood.

But as avarice and cruelty are evermore thirsty, so fared it with this hungry usurper; for having fleshed his ambition with this treacherous conquest, he passed along through a grove, where a herd of deer were a ranging; whom, when he had steadfastly surveyed from the fattest to the leanest, he singled out one of the fairest of the company, with whom he meant to close up his stomach instead of cheese. But because the woodmen were ever stirring thereabout, and it was not possible for one of his coat to commit such outrage undescried, and that if he were espied, his life were in peril (though not with the lion, whose eyes he could blind as he list, yet with the lesser sort of the brutish commonalty, whom no flattery might pacify) therefore he determined slily and privily to poison the stream where this jolly forester wonted to drink. And as he determined, so he did. Whereby it fell out that when the sun was ascended to his height and all the nimble citizens of the wood betook them to their lair, this youthful lord of the lawns, all faint and malcontent (as prophesying his near approaching mishap by his languishing) with a lazy wallowing pace, strayed aside from the rest of his fellowship and betook him all carelessly to the corrupted fountain that was prepared for his funeral.

Ah, woe is me, this poison is pitiless! What need I say more, since you know it is death with whom it encounters? And yet cannot all this expense of life set a period to insatiable murder; but still it hath some anvil to work upon, and overcasts all opposite prosperity, that may any way shadow his glory.

Too long it were to rehearse all the practices of this savage blood-hunter: how he assailed the unicorn as he slept in his den, and tore the heart out of his breast ere he could awake; how he made the lesser beasts lie in wait one for the other, and the crocodile to cope with the basilisk, that when they had interchangeably weakened each other he might come and insult over them both as he list. But these were lesser matters, which daily use had worn out of men's mouths, and he himself had so customably practised that often exercise had quite abrogated the opinion of sin, and impudency thoroughly confirmed an undaunted defiance of virtue in his face. Yet newfangled lust, that in time is weary of welfare and will be as soon cloyed with too much ease and delicacy, as poverty with labour and scarcity, at length brought him out of love with this greedy bestial humour; and now he affected a milder variety in his diet; he had bethought him what a pleasant thing it was to eat nothing but honey another while, and what great store of it there was in that country.

Now did he cast in his head, that if he might bring the husbandmen of the soil in opinion that they might buy honey cheaper than being at such charges in keeping of bees, or that those bees which they kept were most of them drones, and what should such idle drones do with such stately hives or lie sucking at such precious honeycombs; that if they were took away from them, and distributed equally abroad, they would relieve a great many of painful labourers that had need of them, and would continually live serviceable at their command, if they might enjoy such a benefit. Nay more, let them give wasps but only the wax and dispose of the honey as they think good, and they shall hum and buzz a thousand times louder than they, and have the hive fuller at the year's end (with young ones, I mean) than the bees are wont in ten year.

To broach this device the fox was addressed like a shepherd's dog, and promised to have his patent sealed to be the king's poulterer for ever, if he could bring it to pass. "Faith," quoth he, "and I'll put it in a venture, let it hap how it will." With that he grew in league with an old chameleon, that could put on all shapes, and imitate any colour as occasion served, and him he addressed, sometime like an ape to make sport, and then like a crocodile to weep, sometime like a serpent to sting, and by and by like a spaniel to fawn, that with these sundry forms, applied to men's variable humours, he might persuade the world he meant as he spake, and only intended their good, when he thought nothing less.

In this disguise, these two deceivers went up and down and did much harm under the habit of simplicity, making the poor silly swains believe they were cunning physicians and well seen in all cures, that they could heal any malady, though never so dangerous, and restore a man to life, that had been dead two days, only by breathing upon him. Above all things they persuaded them that the honey that their bees brought forth was poisonous and corrupt, by reason that those flowers

and herbs out of which it was gathered and exhaled were
subject to the infection of every spider and venomous canker,
and not a loathsome toad, how detestable soever, but reposed
himself under their shadow and lay sucking at their roots
continually; whereas in other countries, no noisome or
poisonous creature might live, by reason of the imputed
goodness of the soil, or careful diligence of the gardeners
above ours, as for example, Scotland, Denmark, and some more
pure parts of the seventeen provinces.

These persuasions made the good honest husbandmen to
pause, and mistrust their own wits very much, in nourishing
such dangerous animals. But yet, I know not how, antiquity
and custom so over-ruled their fear, that none would resolve
to abandon them on the sudden till they saw a further incon-
venience. Whereby my two cunning philosophers were driven
to study Galen anew, and seek out splenative simples, to purge
their popular patients of the opinion of their old traditions
and customs; which, how they wrought with the most part
that had least wit, it were a world to tell. For now nothing
was canonical but what they spake, no man would converse
with his wife but first asked their advice, nor pare his nails,
nor cut his beard, without their prescription. So senseless, so
wavering is the light unconstant multitude, that will dance
after every man's pipe; and sooner prefer a blind harper that
can squeak out a new hornpipe, than Alcinous' or Apollo's
variety, that imitates the right strains of the Dorian melody.
I speak this to amplify the novel folly of the headlong vulgar,
that making their eyes and ears vassals to the legerdemain of
these juggling mountebanks, are presently drawn to contemn
art and experience in comparison of the ignorance of a number
of audacious idiots.

The fox can tell a fair tale, and covers all his knavery under
conscience, and the chameleon can address himself like an
angel whensoever he is disposed to work mischief by miracles:
but yet in the end, their secret drifts are laid open, and Linceus'

eyes, that see through stone walls, have made a passage into the close coverture of their hypocrisy.

For one day, as these two devisers were plotting by themselves how to drive all the bees from their honeycombs by putting wormwood in all their hives, and strewing henbane and rue in every place where they resort, a fly that passed by and heard all their talk, stomaching the fox of old, for that he had murdered so many of his kindred with his flail-driving tail, went presently and buzzed in Linceus' ears the whole purport of their malice; who, awaking his hundred eyes at these unexpected tidings, gan pursue them wheresoever they went, and trace their intents as they proceeded into action; so that ere half their baits were cast forth, they were apprehended and imprisoned, and all their whole counsel detected. But long ere this, the bear, impatient of delays and consumed with an inward grief in himself that he might not have his will of a fat hind that outran him, he went into the woods all melancholy and there died for pure anger, leaving the fox and the chameleon to the destiny of their desert, and mercy of their judges. How they scaped I know not, but some say they were hanged, and so we'll leave them.

How likest thou of my tale, friend Percy? Have I not described a right earthly devil unto thee in the discourse of this bloody-minded bear? Or canst thou not attract the true image of hypocrisy under the description of the fox and the chameleon?"

"Yes, very well," quoth I, "but I would gladly have you return to your first subject, since you have moved doubts in my mind, which you have not yet discussed."

"Of the sundry opinions of the devil, thou meanest, and them that imagine him to have no existence, of which sort are they that first invented the proverb, *homo homini dæmon*: meaning thereby, that that power which we call the devil, and the ministering spirits belonging to him and to his kingdom, are tales and fables, and mere bugbears to scare boys; and that there is no such essence at all, but only it is a term of large content, describing the rancour, grudge, and bad dealing of one man toward another: as, namely, when one friend talks with another subtly, and seeks to dive into his commodity, that he may deprive him of it craftily; when the son seeks the death of the father, that he may be enfeoffed in his wealth; and the step-dame goes about to make away her son-in-law, that her children may inherit; when brothers fall at jars for portions, and shall, by open murder or privy conspiracy, attempt the confusion of each other, only to join house to house, and unite two livelihoods in one; when the servant shall rob his master, and men put in trust start away from their oaths and vows, they care not how.

In such cases and many more, may one man be said to be a devil to another, and this is the second opinion. The third is that of Plato, who not only affirmeth that there are devils, but divided them into three sorts, every one a degree of dignity above the other. The first are those whose bodies are compact of the purest airy element, combined with such transparent threads, that neither they do partake so much fire as should make them visible to sight, or have any such affinity with the earth, as they are able to be pressed or touched; and these he setteth in the highest incomprehensible degree of heaven. The second he maketh these whom Apuleius doth call reasonable creatures, passive in mind and eternal in time, being those *apostata* spirits that rebelled with Beelzebub; whose bodies, before their fall, were bright and pure all like to the former; but, after their transgression, they were obscured with a thick, airy matter, and ever after assigned to darkness. The third he attributes to those men that, by some divine knowledge or understanding, seeming to aspire above mortality, are called *dæmona*, (that is) gods: for this word *dæmon* containeth either, and Homer in every place doth use it both for that omnipotent power that was before all things, and the evil spirit that leadeth men to error: so doth Syrianus testify, that Plato was called *dæmon*, because he disputed of deep commonwealth matters, greatly available to the benefit of his country; and also Aristotle because he wrote at large of all things subject to moving and sense."

"Then belike," quoth I, "you make this word *dæmon* a capable name of gods, of men, and of devils, which is far distant from the scope of my demand; for I do only enquire of the devil, as this common appellation of the devil signifieth a malignant spirit, enemy to mankind, and a hater of God and all goodness."

"Those are the second kind," said he, "usually termed detractors or accusers, that are in knowledge infinite, insomuch as, by the quickness of their wits and agreeable mixtures of the elements, they so comprehend those seminary virtues to men unknown, that those things which, in course of time or by growing degrees, nature of itself can effect, they, by their art and skill in hastening the works of nature, can contrive and compass in a moment: as the magicians of Pharaoh, who, whereas nature, not without some interposition of time and ordinary causes of conception, brings forth frogs, serpents, or any living thing else, they, without all such distance of space, or circumscription of season, even in a thought, as soon as their king commanded, covered the land of Egypt with this monstrous increase.

Of the original of us spirits the scripture most amply maketh mention, namely, that Lucifer, before his fall an archangel, was a clear body, compact of the purest and brightest of the air, but after his fall he was veiled with a grosser substance, and took a new form of dark and thick air, which he still retaineth. Neither did he only fall, when he strove with Michael, but drew a number of angels to his faction; who, joint partakers of his proud revolt, were likewise partakers of his punishment, and all thrust out of heaven together by one judgment: who ever since do nothing but wander about the earth, and tempt and enforce frail men to enterprise all wickedness that may be, and commit most horrible and abominable things against God.

Marvel not that I discover so much of our estate unto thee; for the scripture hath more than I mention, as St Peter, where he saith that 'God spared not his angels that sinned'; and in another place, where he saith that 'they are bound with the chains of darkness, and thrown headlong into hell': which is not meant of any local place in the earth, or under the waters: for, as Austin affirmeth, we do inhabit the region under the moon, and have the thick air assigned us as a prison, from whence we may with small labour cast our nets where we list. Yet are we not so at our disposition, but that we are still commanded by Lucifer, although we are in number infinite, who, retaining that pride wherewith he arrogantly affected the majesty of God, hath still his ministering angels about him, whom he employs in several charges, to seduce and deceive as him seemeth best: as those spirits which the Latins call *Iovios* and *Antemeridianos*, to speak out of oracles, and make the people worship them as gods, when they are nothing but deluding devils that covet to have a false deity ascribed unto them, and draw men unto their love by wonders and prodigies, that else would hate them deadly, if they knew their malevolence and envy. Such a monarchizing spirit it was that said to Christ, 'If thou wilt fall down and worship me, I will give thee all the kingdoms of the earth.' And such a spirit it was that possessed the Lybian Psaphon, and the emperor Diocletian, who thought it the blessedest thing that might be, to be called god. For the one, being weary of human honour and inspired with a supernatural folly, taught little birds, that were capable of speech, to pronounce distinctly, *Magnus deus Psaphon*; that is to say, 'A great god is Psaphon'—which words, when they had learnt readily to carol and were perfect in their note, he let them fly at random, that so dispersing themselves everywhere, they might induce the people to count of him as a god. The other was so arrogant that he made his subjects fall

K

prostrate on their faces, and lifting up their hands to him, as to heaven, adore him as omnipotent.

The second kind of devils which he most employeth, are those northern *Marcii*, called the spirits of revenge, and the authors of massacres, and seedsmen of mischief; for they have commission to incense men to rapines, sacrilege, theft, murder, wrath, fury, and all manner of cruelties, and they command certain of the southern spirits, as slaves, to wait upon them, as also great Arioch, that is termed the spirit of revenge.

These know how to dissociate the love of brethren, and to break wedlock bands with such violence that they may not be united, and are predominant in many other domestical mutinies: of whom if thou list to hear more, read the thirty ninth chapter of *Ecclesiasticus*. The prophet Isaiah maketh mention of another spirit, sent by God to the Egyptians, to make them stray and wander out of the way, that is to say, the spirit of lying, which they call Bolychym. The spirits that entice men to gluttony and lust are certain watery spirits of the West, and certain southern spirits as Nefrach and Kelen, which for the most part prosecute unlawful loves and cherish all unnatural desires. They wander through lakes, fish-ponds, and fens, and overwhelm ships, cast boats upon anchors, and drown men that are swimming. Therefore are they counted the most pestilent, troublesome, and guileful spirits that are; for by the help of Alrynach, a spirit of the West, they will raise storms, cause earthquakes, whirlwinds, rain, hail, or snow in the clearest day that is: and if ever they appear to any man, they come in women's apparel. The spirits of the air will mix themselves with thunder and lightning, and so infect the clime where they raise any tempest, that suddenly great mortality shall ensue to the inhabitants from the infectious vapours which arise from their motions. Of such St John maketh mention in the ninth chapter of the *Apocalypse*. Their patron is Mereris, who beareth chief rule about the middle time of the day.

The spirits of the fire have their mansions under their regions of the moon, that whatsoever is committed to their charge they may there execute, as in their proper consistory, from whence they cannot start. The spirits of the earth keep, for the most part, in forests and woods, and do hunters much noyance, and sometime in the broad fields, where they lead travellers out of right way, or fright men with deformed apparitions, or make them run mad through excessive melancholy, like Ajax Telemonius, and so prove hurtful to themselves, and dangerous to others. Of this number the chief are Samaab and Achymael, spirits of the East, that have no power to do any great harm, by reason of the unconstancy of their affections. The under-earth spirits are such as lurk in dens and little caverns of the earth, and hollow crevices of mountains, that they may dive into the bowels of the earth at their pleasure. These dig metals and watch treasures, which they continually transport from place to place, that none should have use of them. They raise winds that vomit flames, and shake the foundation of buildings, they dance in rounds in pleasant lawns and green meadows, with noises of music and minstrelsy, and vanish away when any comes near them. They will take upon them any similitude but of a woman, and terrify men in the likeness of dead men's ghosts in the night-time: and of this quality and condition the necromancers hold Gaziel, Fegor, and Anarazel, southern spirits, to be.

Besides, there are yet remaining certain lying spirits, who, although all be given to lie by nature, yet are they more prone to that vice than the rest, being named Pythonists, of whom Apollo comes to be called Pytheus. They have a prince as well as other spirits, of whom mention is made in the *Third Book of Kings*, when he saith he will be a lying spirit in the mouth of all Ahab's prophets: from which those spirits of iniquity do little differ, which are called the vessels of wrath, that assist Belial (whom they interpret a spirit without yoke or controller) in all damnable devices and inventions. Plato reports them to be such as first devised cards and dice, and I am in the mind, that the monk was of the same order that found out the use of gunpowder and the engines of war thereto belonging. Those that write of these matters call this Belial Chodar of the East, that hath all witches' and conjurers' spirits under his jurisdiction, and gives them leave to help jugglers in their tricks, and Simon Magus to do miracles; always provided they bring a soul home to their master for his hire.

Yet are not these all, for there are spirits called spies and tale-carriers, obedient to Ascaroth, whom the Greeks call *daimona*, and St John, *the accuser of the brethren*: also tempters, who, for their interrupting us in all our good actions are called our evil angels. Above all things, they hate the light and rejoice in darkness, disquieting men maliciously in the night and sometimes hurt them by pinching them or blasting them as they sleep. But they are not so much to be dreaded as other spirits, because if a man speak to them they flee away and will not abide. Such a spirit Plinius Secundus telleth of, that used to haunt a goodly house in Athens that Athenodorus hired. And such another Suetonius describeth to have long hovered in Lamianus' garden, where Caligula lay buried, who, for because he was only covered with a few clods and unreverently thrown amongst the weeds, he marvellously disturbed the owners of the garden, and would not let them rest in their beds, till by his sisters, returned from banishment, he was taken up and entombed solemnly.

Pausanias avoucheth, amongst other experiments, that a certain spirit called Zazilus doth feed upon dead men's corses, that are not deeply interred in the earth as they ought. Which to confirm, there is a wonderful accident set down in the Danish history of Asuitus and Asmundus, who, being two famous friends well known in those parts, vowed one to another, that which of them two outlived the other should be buried alive with his friend that first died. In short space

Asuitus fell sick and yielded to nature; Asmundus, compelled by the oath of his friendship, took none but his horse and his dog with him, and transported the dead body into a vast cave under the earth, and there determined, having victualled himself for a long time, to finish his days in darkness and never depart from him that he loved so dearly.

Thus shut up and enclosed in the bowels of the earth, it happened Ericus, King of Sweveland, to pass that way with his army, not full two months after; who, coming to the tomb of Asuitus, and suspecting it a place where treasure was hidden, caused his pioneers with their spades and mattocks to dig it up. Whereupon was discovered the loathsome body of Asmundus, all to-besmeared with dead men's filth, and his visage most ugly and fearful; which, imbrued with congealed blood and eaten and torn like a raw ulcer, made him so ghastly to behold that all the beholders were affrighted. He, seeing himself restored to light, and so many amazed men stand about him, resolved their uncertain perplexity in these terms.

'Why stand you astonished at my unusual deformities, when no living man converseth with the dead but is thus disfigured? But other causes have effected this change in me; for I know not what audacious spirit, sent by Gorgon from the deep, hath not only most ravenously devoured my horse and my dog, but also hath laid his hungry paws upon me, and tearing down my cheeks, as you see, hath likewise rent away one of mine ears. Hence is it that my mangled shape seems so monstrous, and my human image obscured with gore in this wise. Yet scaped not this fell harpy from me unrevenged; for as he assailed me, I raught his head from his shoulders, and sheathed my sword in his body.'"

"Have spirits their visible bodies," said I, "that may be touched, wounded, or pierced? Believe me, I never heard that in my life before this."

"Why," quoth he, "although in their proper essence they are creatures incorporal, yet can they take on them the induments of any living body whatsoever, and transform themselves into all kind of shapes, whereby they may more easily deceive our shallow wits and senses. So testifies Basilius, that they can put on a material form when they list. Socrates affirmeth that his *dæmon* did oftentimes talk with him, and that he saw him and felt him many times. But Marcus Cherronesius, a wonderful discoverer of devils, writeth that those bodies which they assume are distinguished by no difference of sex, because they are simple, and the discernance of sex belongs to bodies compound. Yet are they flexible, motive and apt for any configuration; but not all of them alike; for the spirits of the fire and air have this power above the rest. The spirits of the water have slow bodies resembling birds and women, of which kind the Naids and Nereids are much celebrated amongst poets. Nevertheless, however they are restrained to their several similitudes it is certain that all of them desire no form or figure so much as the likeness of a man, and do think themselves in heaven when they are enfeoffed in that hue: wherefore I know no other reason but this, that man is the nearest representation to God, insomuch as the scripture saith, 'He made man after his own likeness and image'; and they, affecting by reason of their pride to be as like God as they may, contend most seriously to shroud themselves under that habit."

"But, I pray, tell me this, whether are there (as Porphyrius holdeth) good spirits as well as evil? "

"Nay, certainly," quoth he, "we are all evil, let Porphyrius, Proclus, Apuleius, or the Platonists dispute to the contrary as long as they will: which I will confirm to thy capacity by the names that are everywhere given us in the scripture. For the devil, which is the *summum genus* to us all, is called *diabolus*, *quasi deorsum ruens*, that is to say, falling downward, as he that aspiring too high, was thrown from the top of felicity to the lowest pit of despair; and Satan, that is to say, an adversary, who, for the corruption of his malice, opposeth himself ever against God, who is the chiefest good; in *Job*, Behemoth and Leviathan; and in the ninth chapter of the *Apocalypse*, Apolyon, that is to say, a subverter, because the foundation of those virtues, which our high maker hath planted in our souls, he undermineth and subverteth; a serpent for his poisoning, a lion for his devouring, a furnace, for that by his malice the elect are tried, who are vessels of wrath and salvation; in *Isaiah*, a siren, a lamia, a screech-owl, an ostrich; in the *Psalms*, an adder, a basilisk, a dragon; and lastly in the gospel, Mammon, prince of this world, and the governor of darkness. So that, by the whole course of condemning names that are given us, and no one instance of any favourable title bestowed upon us, I positively set down that all spirits are evil. Now, whereas the divines attribute unto us these good and evil spirits, the good to guide us from evil, and the evil to draw us from goodness, they are not called spirits, but angels; of which sort was Raphael, the good angel of Tobias, who exiled the evil spirit Asmodeus into the desert of Egypt, that he might be the more secure from his temptation."

"Since we have entered thus far into the devil's commonwealth, I beseech you certify me thus much, whether have they power to hurt granted them from God, or from themselves; can they hurt as much as they will?"

"Not so," quoth he, "for although that devils be most mighty spirits, yet can they not hurt but permissively, or by some special dispensation. As, when a man is fallen into the state of an outlaw, the law dispenseth with them that kill him, and the prince excludes him from the protection of a subject, so, when a man is a relapse from God and his laws, God withdraws his providence from watching over him, and authoriseth the devil, as his instrument, to assault him and torment him; so that whatsoever he doth is *limitata potestate*, as one saith; insomuch as a hair cannot fall from our heads, without the will of our heavenly father.

The devil could not deceive Ahab's prophets, till he was

licensed by God, nor exercise his tyranny over Job till he had given him commission, nor enter into the herd of swine till Christ bade them go. Therefore need you not fear the devil any whit, as long as you are in the favour of God, who reineth him so strait, that except he let him loose he can do nothing. This manlike proportion, which I now retain, is but a thing of sufferance, granted unto me to plague such men as hunt after strife, and are delighted with variance."

"It may be so very well, but whether have you that skill to foretell things to come, that is ascribed unto you?"

"We have," quoth he, "sometimes. Not that we are privy to the eternal counsels of God, but for that by the sense of our airy bodies, we have a more refined faculty of foreseeing than men possibly can have that are chained to such heavy earthly moulder; or else for that by the incomparable pernicity of those airy bodies, we not only outstrip the swiftness of men, beasts, and birds, whereby we may be able to attain to the knowledge of things sooner than those that by the dullness of their earthly sense come a great way behind us. Hereunto may we adjoin our long experience in the course of things from the beginning of the world, which men want, and therefore cannot have that deep conjecture that we have. Nor is our knowledge any more than conjecture; for prescience only belongeth to God, and that guess that we have, proceedeth from the compared disposition of heavenly and earthly bodies, by whose long observed temperature we do divine many times as it happens; and therefore do we take upon us to prophesy, that we may purchase estimation to our names, and bring men in admiration with that we do, and so be counted for gods. The miracles we work are partly contrived by illusion, and partly assisted by that supernatural skill we have in the experience of nature above all other creatures."

"But against these illusions of your subtlety, and vain terrors you inflict, what is our chief refuge?"

"I shall be accounted a foolish devil anon if I bewray the

secrets of our kingdom, as I have begun: yet I speak no more than learned clerks have written, and as much as they have set down will I shew thee.

Origen, in his treatise against Celsus, saith there is nothing better for him that is vexed with spirits, than the naming of Jesu, the true God, for he avoucheth he hath seen divers driven out of men's bodies by that means. Athanasius, in his book *De variis questionibus*, saith, 'The presentest remedy against the invasion of evil spirits, is the beginning of the sixty seventh Psalm, *Exsurgat Deus, et dissipentur inimici eius.*' Cyprian counsels men to adjure spirits only by the name of the true God. Some hold that fire is a preservative for this purpose, because when any spirit appeareth, the lights by little and little go out, as it were of their own accord, and the tapers are by degrees extinguished; others by invocating upon God by the name of *Vehiculum ignis superioris*, and often rehearsing the articles of our faith. A third sort are persuaded that the brandishing of swords is good for this purpose, because Homer feigneth that Ulysses, sacrificing to his mother, wafted his sword in the air to chase the spirits from the blood of the sacrifice; and Sibylla, conducting Æneas to hell, begins her charm in this sort:

Procul, o procul, este, prophani:
Tuque invade viam, vaginaque erripe ferrum.

Philostratus reporteth, that he and his companions meeting that devil which artists entitle Apollonius, as they came one night from banqueting, with such terms as he is cursed in holy writ, they made him run away howling. Many in this case extol perfume of *calamentum, pæonia, menta, palma Christi* and *appius*. A number prefer the carrying of red coral about them, or of *artemisia, hypericon, ruta, verbena*: and to this effect many do use the jingling of keys, the sound of the harp, and the clashing of armour. Some of old time put great superstition in characters, curiously engraved in their *pentagonon*, but they are all vain, and will do no good, if they be otherwise used than as signs of covenant between the devil and them. Nor do I affirm all the rest to be infallible prescriptions, though sometime they have their use: but that the only assured way to resist their attempts is prayer and faith, gainst which all the devils in hell cannot prevail."

"Enough, gentle spirit, I will importune thee no further, but commit this supplication to thy care; which, if thou deliver accordingly, thou shalt at thy return have more of my custom; for by that time I will have finished certain letters to divers orators and poets, dispersed in your dominions."

"That as occasion shall serve, but now I must take leave of you, for it is term time, and I have some business. A gentleman, a friend of mine that I never saw before, stays for me, and is like to be undone if I come not in to bear witness on his side: wherefore *Bazilez manus*, till our next meeting."

Gentle reader, *tandem aliquando* I am at leisure to talk to thee. I dare say thou hast called me a hundred times dolt for this senseless discourse: it is no matter, thou dost but as I have done by a number in my days. For who can abide a scurvy peddling poet to pluck a man by the sleeve at every third step in Paul's Churchyard, and when he comes in to survey his wares, there's nothing but purgations and vomits wrapped up in waste paper. It were very good the dog-whipper in Paul's would have a care of this in his unsavoury visitation every Saturday; for it is dangerous for such of the Queen's liege people, as shall take a view of them fasting.

Look to it, you booksellers and stationers, and let not your shops be infected with any such goose giblets or stinking garbage, as the jigs of newsmongers, and especially such of you as frequent Westminster Hall, let them be circumspect what dunghill papers they bring thither: for one bad pamphlet is enough to raise a damp that may poison a whole term, or at the least a number of poor clients, that have no money to

prevent ill air by breaking their fasts ere they come thither.
Not a base ink-dropper, or scurvy plodder at *Noverint*, but
nails his asses' ears on every post, and comes off with a long
circumquaque to the gentlemen readers; yea, the most excre-
mentory dish-lickers of learning are grown so valiant in
impudency, that now they set up their faces (like Turks) of
gray paper, to be spit at for silver games in Finsbury Fields.

Whilst I am talking, methinks I hear one say, "What a fop
is this, he entitles his book *A Supplication to the Devil*, and
doth nothing but rail on idiots, and tells a story of the nature
of spirits!" Have patience, good sir, and we'll come to you
by and by. Is it my title you find fault with? Why, have you
not seen a town surnamed by the principal house in the town,
or a nobleman derive his barony from a little village where he
hath least land? So fareth it by me in christening of my book.
But some will object, "Whereto tends this discourse of devils,
or how is it induced?" Forsooth, if thou wilt needs know my
reason, this it is. I bring Pierce Penilesse to question with the
devil, as a young novice would talk with a great traveller, who,
carrying an Englishman's appetite to enquire of news, will be
sure to make what use of him he may, and not leave anything
unasked, that he can resolve him of. If then the devil be
tedious in discoursing, impute it to Pierce Penilesse that was
importunate in demanding; or, if I have not made him so
secret and subtle in his art as devils are wont, let that of
Lactantius be mine excuse, *lib.* 2. *cap.* 16. *de Origenis errore*,
where he saith, the devils have no power to lie to a just man,
and if they adjure them by the majesty of the high God, they
will not only confess themselves to be devils, but also tell their
names as they are.

Deus bone, what a vein am I fallen into? "What an Epistle
to the Readers in the end of thy book? Out upon thee for an
arrant block, where learnedst thou that wit?" O sir, hold your
peace: a felon never comes to his answer before the offence be
committed. Wherefore, if I, in the beginning of my book,

should have come off with a long apology to excuse myself, it were all one as if a thief, going to steal a horse, should devise by the way as he went, what to speak when he came at the gallows. Here is a crossway, and I think it good here to part. Farewell, farewell, good Parenthesis, and commend me to Lady Vanity, thy mistress.

"Now, Pierce Penilesse, if for a parting blow thou hast ere a trick in thy budget more than ordinary, be not dainty of it for a good patron will pay for all." Ay, where is he? *Promissis quilibet dives esse potest.* But cap and thanks, is all our courtiers' payment; wherefore I would counsel my friends to be more considerate in their dedications, and not cast away so many months' labour on a clown that knows not how to use a scholar: for what reason have I to bestow any of my wit upon him, that will bestow none of his wealth upon me? Alas, it is easy for a goodly tall fellow that shineth in his silks, to come and outface a poor simple pedant in a threadbare cloak, and tell him his book is pretty, but at this time he is not provided for him: marry, about two or three days hence if he come that way, his page shall say he is not within, or else he is so busy with my Lord How-call-ye-him, and my Lord What-call-ye-him, that he may not be spoken withal. These are the common courses of the world, which every man privately murmurs at, but none dares openly upbraid, because all artists for the most part are base-minded and like the Indians that have store of gold and precious stones at command yet are ignorant of their value, and therefore let the Spaniards, the Englishmen and everyone load their ships with them without molestation; so they, enjoying and possessing the purity of knowledge, a treasure far richer than the Indian mines, let every proud Thraso be partaker of their perfections, repaying them no profit, and gild himself with the titles they give him, when he will scarce return them a good word for their labour. Give an ape but a nut, and he will look your head for it; or a dog a bone, and he'll wag his tail; but give me one of my young masters a book, and he will put off his hat and blush, and so go his way.

Yes, now I remember me, I lie; for I know him that had thanks for three years' work, and a gentleman that bestowed much cost in refining of music, and had scarce fiddler's wages for his labour. We want an Aretine here among us, that might strip these golden asses out of their gay trappings, and after he had ridden them to death with railing, leave them on the dunghill for carrion. But I will write to his ghost by my carrier, and I hope he'll repair his whip and use it against our English peacocks, that painting themselves with church spoils, like mighty men's sepulchres, have nothing but atheism, schism, hypocrisy, and vain-glory, like rotten bones lie lurking within them. Oh, how my soul abhors these buckram giants, that having an outward face of honour set upon them by flatterers and parasites, have their inward thoughts stuffed with straw and feathers, if they were narrowly sifted.

Far be it, bright stars of nobility and glistering attendants on the true Diana, that this my speech should be any way injurious to your glorious magnificence: for in you live those sparks of Augustus' liberality, that never sent any away empty; and science's seven-fold throne, well nigh ruined by riot and avarice, is mightily supported by your plentiful largess, which makes poets to sing such goodly hymns of your praise, as no envious posterity may forget.

But from general fame let me digress to my private experience, and, with a tongue unworthy to name a name of such worthiness, affectionately emblazon to the eyes that wonder, the matchless image of honour, and magnificent rewarder of virtue, Jove's eagle-borne Ganymede, thrice noble Amyntas. In whose high spirit, such a deity of wisdom appeareth, that if Homer were to write his Odyssey new (where, under the person of Ulysses, he describeth a singular man of perfection, in whom all ornaments both of peace and war are assembled in the height of their excellence) he need no other instance to

augment his conceit, than the rare carriage of his honourable
mind.   Many writers and good wits are given to commend their
patrons and benefactors, some for prowess, some for policy,
others for the glory of their ancestry and exceeding bounty
and liberality: but if my unable pen should ever enterprise
such a continuate task of praise, I would embowel a number
of those wind-puffed bladders and disfurnish their bald pates
of the periwigs poets have lent them, that so I might restore
glory to his right inheritance, and these stolen titles to their
true owners.   Which, if it would so fall out (as time may
work all things) the aspiring nettles, with their shady tops,
shall no longer overdrip the best herbs, or keep them from the
smiling aspect of the sun, that live and thrive by his comfortable beams; none but desert should sit in fame's grace, none but
Hector be remembered in the chronicles of prowess, none but
thou, most courteous Amyntas, be the second mystical argument of the knight of the Red Cross.

Oh decus atque ævi gloria summa tui.

And here, heavenly Spenser, I am most highly to accuse
thee of forgetfulness, that in that honourable catalogue of our
English heroes, which insueth the conclusion of thy famous
Faerie Queene, thou wouldst let so special a pillar of nobility
pass unsaluted.   The very thought of his far derived descent
and extraordinary parts, wherewith he astonisheth the world
and draws all hearts to his love, would have inspired thy for-
wearied Muse with new fury to proceed to the next triumphs
of thy stately goddess. But as I, in favour of so rare a scholar,
suppose, with this counsel he refrained his mention in this
first part, that he might with full sail proceed to his due commendation in the second.   Of this occasion long since I happened to frame a sonnet, which, being wholly intended to the
reverence of this renowned Lord, to whom I owe all the
utmost powers of my love and duty, I meant here for variety
of style to insert.

Perusing yesternight, with idle eyes,
 The fairy singer's stately tuned verse,
And viewing after chapmen's wonted guise,
 What strange contents the title did rehearse:
I straight leapt over to the latter end,
 Where like the quaint comedians of our time,
That when their play is done do fall to rhyme,
 I found short lines to sundry nobles penn'd;
Whom he as special mirrors singled forth,
 To be the patrons of his poetry:
I read them all, and reverenc'd their worth,
 Yet wonder'd he left out thy memory.
  But therefore guessed I he suppress'd thy name,
  Because few words might not comprise thy fame.

Bear with me, gentle poet, though I conceive not aright of thy purpose, or be too inquisitive into the intent of thy oblivion: for, however my conjecture may miss the cushion, yet shall my speech savour of friendship, though it be not allied to judgment.

Tantum hoc molior, in this short digression, to acquaint our countrymen that live out of the echo of the Court, with a common knowledge of his invaluable virtues, and show myself thankful (in some part) for benefits received: which since words may not countervail, that are the usual lip labour of every idle discourser, I conclude with that of Ovid.

 Accipe per longos tibi qui deserviat annos,
  Accipe, qui pura novit amare fide.

And if my zeal and duty, though all too mean to please, may by any industry be reformed to your gracious liking, I submit the simplicity of my endeavours to your service, which is all my performance may proffer, or my ability perform.

 Prœbeat Alcinoi poma benignus ager,
  Officium pauper numeret studiumque fidemque.

And so I break off this endless argument of speech abruptly.

FINIS

THE WONDERFUL YEAR

1603

*Wherein is shewed the picture of London lying
sick of the plague.*

*At the end of all, like a merry epilogue to a dull play,
certain tales are cut out in sundry fashions, of purpose
to shorten the lives of long winter's nights, that lie watching
in the dark for us.
Et me rigidi legant Catones.*

BY

THOMAS DEKKER

*To his well-respected, good friend, Mr Cuthbert
Thuresby, Water Bailiff of London*

BOOKS are but poor gifts, yet kings receive them: upon which
I presume you will not turn this out of doors. You cannot for
shame but bid it welcome, because it brings to you a great
quantity of my love; which, if it be worth little (and no marvel
if love be sold underfoot, when the god of love himself goes
naked) yet I hope you will not say you have a hard bargain,
sithence you may take as much of it as you please for nothing.
I have clapped the cognizance of your name on these scribbled
papers, it is their livery; so that now they are yours; being free
from any vile imputation, save only that they thrust themselves
into your acquaintance. But general errors have general
pardons; for the title of other men's names is the common

heraldry which all those lay claim to, whose crest is a pen and inkhorn. If you read, you may happily laugh; 'tis my desire you should, because mirth is both physical and wholesome against the plague; with which sickness, to tell truth, this book is, though not sorely, yet somewhat infected. I pray, drive it not out of your company for all that; for, assure your soul, I am so jealous of your health, that if you did but once imagine there were gall in mine ink I would cast away the standish and forswear meddling with any more Muses.

TO THE READER

And why to the reader? Oh good sir! There's as sound law to make you give good words to the reader, as to a constable when he carries his watch about him to tell how the night goes; though, perhaps, the one oftentimes may be served in for a goose, and the other very fitly furnish the same mess. Yet to maintain the scurvy fashion, and to keep custom in reparations, he must be honeyed and come-over with *Gentle Reader*, *Courteous Reader*, and *Learned Reader*, though he have no more gentility in him than Adam had, that was but a gardener; no more civility than a Tartar; and no more learning than the most arrant stinkard, that, except his own name, could never find anything in the hornbook.

How notoriously, therefore, do good wits dishonour not only their own calling, but even their creation, that worship glow-worms, instead of the sun, because of a little false glistering? In the name of Phœbus, what madness leads them unto it? For he that dares hazard a pressing to death (that's to say, to be a man in print) must make account that he shall stand, like the old weathercock over Paul's steeple, to be beaten with all storms. Neither the stinking tobacco-breath of a satin-gull, the aconited sting of a narrow-eyed critic, the faces of a fantastic stage-monkey, nor the "Indeed, la!" of a

L

puritanical citizen must once shake him. No, but desperately resolve, like a French post, to ride through thick and thin; endure to see his lines torn pitifully on the rack; suffer his Muse to take the bastoon, yea, the very stab, and himself, like a new stake, to be a mark for every haggler; and therefore, setting up all these rests, why should he regard what fool's bolt is shot at him? Besides, if that which he presents upon the stage of the world be good, why should he basely cry out with that old poetical madcap in his *Amphitruo*, "*Jovis summi causa clare plaudite?*—Beg a plaudit for God's sake!" If bad, who but an ass would entreat, as players do in a cogging epilogue at the end of a filthy comedy, that, be it never such wicked stuff, they would forbear to hiss, or to damn it perpetually to lie on a stationer's stall. For he that can so cozen himself, as to pocket up praise in that silly sort, makes his brains fat with his own folly.

But *hinc pudor!*, or rather *hinc dolor*, here's the devil! It is not the rattling of all this former hail-shot, that can terrify our band of Castalian penmen from entering into the field. No, no, the murdering artillery indeed lies in the roaring mouths of a company that look big, as if they were the sole and singular commanders over the main army of poesy, yet, if Hermes' muster-book were searched over, they'll be found to be most pitiful, pure, fresh-water soldiers. They give out, that they are heirs apparent to Helicon, but an easy herald may make them mere younger brothers; or, to say troth, not so much.

Bear witness all you whose wits make you able to be witnesses in this cause, that here I meddle not with your good poets, *Nam tales, nusquam sunt hic amplius;* if you should rake hell, or (as Aristophanes in his *Frog* says) in any cellar deeper than hell, it is hard to find spirits of that fashion. But those goblins whom I now am conjuring up, have bladder-cheeks puffed out like a Switzer's breeches, yet being pricked, there comes out nothing but wind, thin-headed fellows that live upon the scraps of invention, and travel with such vagrant souls, and so like ghosts in white sheets of paper, that the Statute of Rogues may worthily be sued upon them, because their wits have no abiding place, and yet wander without a passport.

Alas, poor wenches (the nine Muses!) how much are you wronged, to have such a number of bastards lying upon your hands? But turn them out a begging; or, if you cannot be rid of their rhyming company (as I think it will be very hard) then lay your heavy and immortal curse upon them, that whatsoever they weave in the motley loom of their rusty pates may, like a beggar's cloak, be full of stolen patches, and yet never a patch like one another; that it may be such true lamentable stuff, that any honest Christian may be sorry to see it. Banish these word-pirates, you sacred mistresses of learning, into the Gulf of Barbarism: doom them everlastingly to live among dunces: let them not once lick their lips at the Thespian bowl, but only be glad, and thank Apollo for it too, if hereafter (as hitherto they have always) they may quench their poetical thirst with small beer. Or, if they will needs be stealing your Heliconian nectar, let them, like the dogs of Nilus, only lap and away. For this goatish swarm are those that, where for these many thousand years you went for pure maids, have taken away your good names, these are they that deflower your beauties. These are those rank-riders of Art, that have so spur-galled your lusty winged Pegasus, that now he begins to be out of flesh, and, even only for provender-sake, is glad to shew tricks like Banks his curtal.

O you book-sellers, that are factors to the liberal sciences, over whose stalls these drones do daily fly humming, let Homer, Hesiod, Euripides, and some other mad Greeks with a band of the Latins, lie like musket-shot in their way, when these Goths and Getes set upon you in your paper fortifications. It is the only cannon, upon whose mouth they dare not venture; none but the English will take their parts, therefore fear them not, for such a strong breath have these cheese-eaters, that if they do but blow upon a book they imagine straight 'tis blasted: "*Quod supra nos; nihil ad nos,*" they say, "that which is above our capacity, shall not pass under our commendation."

Yet would I have these Zoilists, of all other, to read me, if ever I should write anything worthily; for the blame that known fools heap upon a deserving labour, does not discredit the same, but makes wise men more perfectly in love with it. Into such a one's hands therefore if I fortune to fall, I will not shrink an inch, but even when his teeth are sharpest and most ready to bite, I will stop his mouth only with this, *Haec mala sunt, sed tu, non meliora facis.*

READER

Whereas there stands in the rearward of this book a certain mingled troop of strange discourses, fashioned into tales, know that the intelligence which first brought them to light was only flying report; whose tongue, as it often does, if in spreading them it have tripped in any material point, and either slipped too far, or fallen too short, bear with the error; and the rather, because it is not wilfully committed.

Neither let anyone (whom those reports shall seem to touch) cavill, or complain of injury, sithence nothing is set down by a malicious hand. Farewell.

The Wonderful Year

Vertumnus,[1] being attired in his accustomed habit of change-able silk, had newly passed through the first and principal court gate of heaven; to whom for a farewell, and to shew how dutiful he was in his office, Janus, that bears two faces under one hood, made a very mannerly low leg; and, because he

[1] Vertumnus, god of the year.

was the only porter at that gate, presented unto this king of the months, all the New Year's gifts, which were more in number, and more worth, than those that are given to the Great Turk, or the Emperor of Persia.

DESCRIPTION OF THE SPRING

On went Vertumnus in his lusty progress, Priapus, Flora, the Dryads, and Hamadryads, with all the wooden rabble of those that dressed orchards and gardens, perfuming all the ways that he went with the sweet odours that breathed from flowers, herbs, and trees, which now began to peep out of prison. By virtue of which excellent airs, the sky got a most clear complexion, looked smug and smooth, and had not so much as a wart sticking on her face. The sun likewise was freshly and very richly apparelled in cloth of gold like a bridegroom; and instead of gilded rosemary, the horns of the Ram,[1] being the sign of that celestial bride-house where he lay to be married to the spring, were not like your common horns parcel-gilt, but double double-gilt with the liquid gold that melted from his beams. For joy whereof the lark sung at his window every morning, the nightingale every night; the cuckoo, like a single-sole fiddler, that reels from tavern to tavern, plied it all the day long; lambs frisked up and down in the valleys, kids and goats leapt to and fro on the mountains; shepherds sat piping, country wenches singing; lovers made sonnets for their lasses, whilst they made garlands for their lovers. And as the country was frolic, so was the city merry; olive trees, which grow nowhere but in the garden of peace, stood, as common as beech does at midsummer, at every man's door, branches of palm were in every man's hand. Streets were full of people, people full of joy; every house seemed to have a Lord of Misrule in it, in every house there was so much

[1] Upon the 23rd of March the spring begins by reason of the sun's entrance into Aries.

jollity. No screech-owl frighted the silly countryman at midnight, nor any drum the citizen at noon-day; but all was more calm than a still water, all hushed, as if the spheres had been playing in consort. In conclusion, heaven looked like a palace, and the great hall of the earth like a paradise.

THE QUEEN'S SICKNESS

But O the short lived felicity of man! O world, of what slight and thin stuff is thy happiness! Just in the midst of this jocund holiday, a storm rises in the west. Westward, from the top of a Richmount, descended a hideous tempest, that shook cedars, terrified the tallest pines, and cleft in sunder even the hardest hearts of oak. And if such great trees were shaken, what think you became of the tender eglantine, and humble hawthorn? They could not, doubtless, but droop, they could not choose but die with terror. The element, taking the Destinies' part, who indeed set abroach this mischief, scowled on the earth, and filling her high forehead full of black wrinkles, tumbling long up and down like a great-bellied wife, her sighs being whirlwinds, and her groans thunder, at length she fell in labour, and was delivered of a pale, meagre, weak child, named Sickness; whom Death (with a pestilence) would needs take upon him to nurse, and did so.

This starveling, being come to his full growth, had an office given him for nothing (and that's a wonder in this age) Death made him his herald, attired him like a courtier, and, in his name, charged him to go into the privy chamber of the English queen, to summon her to appear in the Star Chamber of heaven.

HER DEATH

The summons made her start, but, having an invincible spirit, did not amaze her; yet whom would not the certain news of parting from a kingdom amaze? But she knew where to find a richer, and therefore lightly regarded the loss of this, and thereupon made ready for that heavenly coronation, being (which was most strange) most dutiful to obey, that had so many years so powerfully commanded. She obeyed Death's messenger, and yielded her body to the hands of Death himself. She died, resigning her sceptre to posterity, and her soul to immortality.

THE GENERAL TERROR THAT HER DEATH BRED

The report of her death like a thunderclap was able to kill thousands, it took away hearts from millions. For having brought up, even under her wing, a nation that was almost begotten and born under her; that never shouted any other *Ave* than for her name, never saw the face of any prince but herself, never understood what that strange outlandish word *Change* signified; how was it possible, but that her sickness should throw abroad an universal fear, and her death an astonishment? She was the courtier's treasure, therefore he had cause to mourn; the lawyer's sword of justice, he might well faint; the merchant's patroness, he had reason to look pale; the citizen's mother, he might best lament; the shepherd's goddess, and should not he droop?

Only the soldier, who had walked a long time upon wooden legs, and was not able to give arms though he were a gentleman, had bristled up the quills of his stiff porcupine mustachio, and swore by no beggars that now was the hour come for him to bestir his stumps. Usurers and brokers, that are the devil's ingles and dwell in the Long Lane of Hell, quaked like aspen leaves at his oaths. Those that before were the only cutthroats in London, now stood in fear of no other death. But my *Signior Soldado* was deceived, the tragedy went not forward.

Never did the English nation behold so much black worn as there was at her funeral. It was then but put on to try if it were fit, for the great day of mourning was set down in the book of heaven to be held afterwards. That was but the dumb show, the tragical act hath been playing ever since. Her hearse as it was borne, seemed to be an island swimming in water, for round about it there rained showers of tears; about her death-bed none; for her departure was so sudden and so strange, that men knew not how to weep, because they had never been taught to shed tears of that making. They that durst not speak their sorrows, whispered them; they that durst not whisper sent them forth in sighs.

O what an earth-quake is the alteration of a state! Look from the Chamber of Presence to the farmer's cottage, and you shall find nothing but distraction. The whole kingdom seems a wilderness, and the people in it are transformed to wild men. The map of a country so pitifully distracted by the horror of a change, if you desire perfectly to behold, cast your eyes then on this that follows, which being heretofore in private presented to the King, I think may very worthily shew itself before you. And because you shall see them attired in the same fashion that they wore before his Majesty, let these few lines, which stood then as prologue to the rest, enter first into your ears.

> Not for applauses, shallow fools' adventure,
> I plunge my verse into a sea of censure;
> But with a liver drest in gall, to see
> So many rooks, catch-poles of poesy,
> That feed upon the fallings of high wit,
> And put on cast inventions, most unfit;
> For such am I pressed forth in shops and stalls,
> Pasted in Paul's, and, on the lawyers' walls,
> For every basilisk-eyed critic's bait,
> To kill my verse, or poison my conceit;

Or some smoked gallant, who at wit repines,
To dry tobacco with my wholesome lines,
And in one paper sacrifice more brain,
Than all his ignorant skull could ere contain:
But merit dreads no martyrdom, nor stroke,
My lines shall live, when he shall be all smoke.

Thus far the prologue, who leaving the stage clear, the fears that are bred in the womb of this altering kingdom do next step up, acting thus :

The great impostume of the realm was drawn
Even to a head: the multitudinous spawn
Was the corruption, which did make it swell
With hop'd sedition, the burnt seed of hell.
Who did expect but Ruin, Blood, and Death,
To share our kingdom, and divide our breath?
Religions without religion
To let each other blood, Confusion
To be next queen of England, and this year
The civil wars of France to be play'd here
By Englishmen, ruffians, and pandering slaves,
That fain would dig up gouty usurers' graves.
At such a time, villains their hopes do honey,
And rich men look as pale as their white money.
Now they remove, and make their silver sweat,
Casting themselves into a covetous heat;
And then, unseen, in the confederate dark,
Bury their gold, without or priest or clerk;
And say no prayers over that dead pelf,
True, Gold's no Christian, but an Indian elf.
Did not the very kingdom seem to shake
Her precious massy limbs? Did she not make
All English cities, like her pulses, beat
With people in their veins? The fear so great,

That had it not been physick'd with rare peace,
Our populous bower had lessen'd her increase.
The spring-time that was dry, had sprung in blood
A greater dearth of men, than e'er of food.
In such a panting time, and gasping year,
Victuals are cheapest, only men are dear.
Now each wise-acr'd landlord did despair,
Fearing some villain should become his heir;
Or that his son and heir before his time,
Should now turn villain, and with violence climb
Up to his life, saying, "Father you have seen
King Henry, Edward, Mary, and the Queen,
I wonder you'll live longer!" Then he tells him
He's loath to see him kill'd, therefore he kills him.
And each vast landlord dies like a poor slave,
Their thousand acres makes them but a grave.
At such a time great men convey their treasure
Into the trusty city; wait the leisure
Of blood and insurrection, which war clips,
When every gate shuts up her iron lips.
Imagine now a mighty man of dust
Stands in a doubt what servant he may trust
With plate worth thousands, jewels worth far more,
If he prove false, then his rich lord proves poor.
He calls forth one by one to note their graces,
Whilst they make legs, he copies out their faces,
Examines their eye-brow, construes their beard,
Singles their nose out, still he rests afear'd.
The first that comes by no means he'll allow,
'Has spied three hairs starting between his brow,
Quite turns the word, names it celerity,
For hares do run away and so may he.
A second shewn; him he will scarce behold,
His beard's too red, the colour of his gold.
A third may please him, but 'tis hard to say

A rich man's pleas'd when his goods part away.
And now do chirrup by fine golden nests
Of well hatch'd bowls, such as do breed in feasts,
For war and death cupboards of plate down pulls,
Then Bacchus drinks not in gilt bowls, but skulls.
Let me descend and stoop my verse a while,
To make the comic cheek of Poesy smile;
Rank penny-fathers scud, with their half hams
Shadowing their calves, to save their silver dams;
At every gun they start, tilt from the ground,
One drum can make a thousand usurers sound.
In unsought alleys and unwholesome places,
Back-ways and by-lanes, where appear few faces,
In shamble-smelling rooms, loathsome prospects,
And penny-lattice-windows, which rejects
All popularity, there the rich cubs lurk,
When in great houses ruffians are at work,
Not dreaming that such glorious booties lie
Under those nasty roofs; such they pass by
Without a search, crying, "There's nought for us,"
And wealthy men deceive poor villains thus.
Tongue-travelling lawyers faint at such a day,
Lie speechless, for they have no words to say.
Physicians turn to patients, their art's dry,
For then our fat men without physic die.
And to conclude, against all art and good,
War taints the doctor, lets the surgeon blood.

Such was the fashion of this land, when the great landlady
thereof left it. She came in with the fall of the leaf, and went
away in the spring; her life, which was dedicated to virginity,
both beginning and closing up a miraculous maiden circle;
for she was born upon a Lady Eve and died upon a Lady Eve,
her nativity and death being memorable by this wonder; the
first and last years of her reign by this, that a Lee was Lord

Mayor when she came to the crown, and a Lee Lord Mayor
when she departed from it. Three places are made famous by
her for three things, Greenwich for her birth, Richmond for
her death, and Whitehall for her funeral: upon her removing
from whence (to lend our tiring prose a breathing time) stay
and look upon these epigrams, being composed:

1. Upon the Queen's last Remove, being dead

> The Queen's remov'd in solemn sort,
> Yet this was strange and seldom seen,
> The queen us'd to remove the Court,
> But now the Court remov'd the Queen.

2. Upon her bringing by water to White Hall

> The Queen was brought by water to White Hall,
> At every stroke the oars tears let fall;
> More clung about the barge, fish under water
> Wept out their eyes of pearl, and swum blind after.
> I think the barge-men might with easier thighs
> Have row'd her thither in her people's eyes;
> For howsoe'er, thus much my thoughts have scann'd,
> S'had come by water, had she come by land.

3. Upon her lying dead at White Hall

> The Queen now lies at White Hall dead,
>   And now at White Hall living;
> To make this rough objection even,
>   Dead at White Hall at Westminster
> But living at White Hall in Heaven.

1603. *A MORE WONDERFUL YEAR THAN '88*

Thus you see that both in her life and her death, she was
appointed to be the mirror of her time. And surely, if, since

the first stone that was laid for the foundation of this great
house of the world, there was ever a year to be wondered at,
it is only this. The Sybil's *Octogesimus octavus annus*, that same
terrible '88, which came sailing hither in the Spanish Armada,
and made men's hearts colder than the frozen zone, when they
heard but an inkling of it; that '88 by whose horrible pre-
dictions almanack-makers stood in bodily fear their trade would
be utterly overthrown, and poor *Erra Pater* was threatened,
because he was a Jew, to be put to baser offices than the
stopping of mustard pots; that same '88 which had more
prophecies waiting at his heels than ever Merlin, the magician,
had in his head, was a year of jubilee to this. Plato's *mirabilis
annus* (whether it be passed already, or to come within these
four years) may throw Plato's cap at *mirabilis*, for that title of
wonderful is bestowed upon 1603. If that sacred aromatically-
perfumed fire of wit, out of whose flames Phœnix poesy doth
arise, were burning in any breast, I would feed it with no other
stuff for a twelve month and a day than with kindling papers
full of lines, that should tell only of the chances, changes, and
strange shapes that this Protean, climacterical year hath meta-
morphosed himself into. It is able to find ten chroniclers a
competent living, and to set twenty printers at work.

You shall perceive I lie not, if, with Peter Bales, you will
take the pains to draw the whole volume of it into the compass
of a penny. As first, to begin with the Queen's death, then the
kingdom's falling into an ague upon that. Next follows the
curing of that fever by the wholesome receipt of a proclaimed
king. That wonder begat more, for in an hour, two mighty
nations were made one; wild Ireland became tame on the
sudden; and some English great ones, that before seemed tame,
on the sudden turned wild, the same park which great Julius
Cæsar enclosed to hold in the deer, whom they before hunted,
being new circled by a second Cæsar with stronger pales to
keep them from leaping over. And last of all, if that wonder
be the last and shut up the year, a most dreadful plague. This

is the abstract, and yet, like Stowe's Chronicle of *decimo sexto* to huge Holinshed, these small pricks in this sea-card of ours represent mighty countries—whilst I have the quill in hand, let me blow them bigger.

The Queen being honoured with a diadem of stars, France, Spain, and Belgia lift up their heads, preparing to do as much for England by giving aim whilst she shot arrows at her own breast (as they imagined), as she had done many a year together for them. And her own nation betted on their sides, looking with distracted countenance for no better guests than civil sedition, uproars, rapes, murders, and massacres. But the wheel of Fate turned, a better lottery was drawn, *Pro Troia stabat Apollo*, God stuck valiantly to us. For behold, up rises a comfortable sun out of the North, whose glorious beams, like a fan, dispersed all thick and contagious clouds. The loss of a queen was paid with the double interest of a king and queen. The cedar of her government, which stood alone and bore no fruit, is changed now to an olive, upon whose spreading branches grow both kings and queens.

KING JAMES PROCLAIMED

Oh it were able to fill a hundred pair of writing tables with notes, but to see the parts played in the compass of one hour on the stage of this new-found world! Upon Thursday it was treason to cry "God save King James, King of England," and, upon Friday, high treason not to cry so. In the morning no voice heard but murmurs and lamentation, at noon nothing but shouts of gladness and triumph. St George and St Andrew, that many hundred years had defied one another, were now sworn brothers. England and Scotland (being parted only with a narrow river, and the people of both empires speaking a language less differing than English within itself, as though providence had enacted that one day those two nations should

marry one another) are now made sure together, and King
James his coronation is the solemn wedding day.

Happiest of all thy ancestors, thou mirror of all princes that
ever were or are, that at seven of the clock wert a king but
over a piece of a little island, and before eleven the greatest
monarch in Christendom. Now:

Silver crowds

Of blissful angels and tried martyrs tread
On the star-ceiling over England's head;
Now heaven broke into a wonder, and brought forth
Our *omne bonum* from the wholesome North,
Our fruitful sovereign, *James*, at whose dread name,
Rebellion swounded, and e'er since became
Grovelling and nerveless, wanting blood to nourish,
For Ruin gnaws herself when kingdoms flourish.
Now are our hopes planted in regal springs,
Never to wither, for our air breeds kings.
And in all ages from this sovereign time
England shall still be call'd the royal clime.
Most blissful monarch of all earthen powers,
Serv'd with a mess of kingdoms; four such bowers,
For prosperous hives and rare industrious swarms,
The world contains not in her solid arms.
O thou, that art the meter of our days,
Poets' Apollo! deal thy Daphnean bays
To those whose wits are bay-trees, ever green,
Upon whose high tops Poesy chirps unseen;
Such are most fit t'apparel kings in rhymes,
Whose silver numbers are the Muses' chimes,
Whose sprightly characters, being once wrought on,
Outlive the marble th'are insculpt upon.
Let such men chant thy virtue, then they fly
On Learning's wings up to eternity.
As for the rest that limp in cold desert,
Having small wit, less judgment, and least art,

Their verse 'tis almost heresy to hear,
Banish their lines some furlong from thine ear;
For 'tis held dangerous, by Apollo's sign,
To be infected with a leprous line.
O make some adamant act, ne'er to be worn,
That none may write but those that are true-born;
So when the world's old cheeks shall raze and peel,
Thy acts shall breathe in epitaphs of steel.

THE JOYS THAT FOLLOWED UPON HIS PROCLAIMING

By these comments it appears that by this time King James is proclaimed. Now does fresh blood leap into the cheeks of the courtier; the soldier now hangs up his armour, and is glad that he shall feed upon the blessed fruits of peace; the scholar sings hymns in honour of the Muses, assuring himself now that Helicon will be kept pure, because Apollo himself drinks of it. Now the thrifty citizen casts beyond the moon, and seeing the golden age returned into the world again, resolves to worship no saint but money. Trades that lay dead and rotten, and were in all men's opinion utterly damned, started out of their trance, as though they had drunk of *aqua cælestis*, or unicorn's horn, and swore to fall to their old occupation. Tailors meant no more to be called merchant-tailors, but merchants; for their shops were all led forth in leases to be turned into ships, and with their shears, instead of a rudder, would they have cut the seas, like Levant taffaty, and sailed to the West Indies for no worse stuff to make hose and doublets of than beaten gold. Or if the necessity of the time, which was likely to stand altogether upon bravery, should press them to serve with their iron and Spanish weapons upon their stalls, then was there a sharp law made amongst them, that no workman should handle any needle but that which had a pearl in his eye, nor any copper thimble, unless it were lined quite through, or bombasted with silver.

What mechanical hard-handed Vulcanist, seeing the dice of Fortune run so sweetly, and resolving to strike whilst the iron was hot, but persuaded himself to be a Master or Head Warden of his company ere half a year went about? The worst players' boy stood upon his good parts, swearing tragical and buskined oaths, that how villainously soever he ranted, or what bad and unlawful action soever he entered into, he would, in despite of his honest audience, be half a sharer at least at home; or else stroll, that's to say travel, with some notorious, wicked, floundering company abroad.

And good reason had these time-catchers to be led into this fools' paradise; for they saw mirth in every man's face, the streets were plumed with gallants, tobacconists filled up whole taverns, vintners hung out spick and span new ivy-bushes, because they wanted good wine, and their old rain-beaten lattices marched under other colours, having lost both company and colours before.

London was never in the high way to preferment till now. Now she resolved to stand upon her pantofles; now, and never till now, did she laugh to scorn that worm-eaten proverb of "Lincoln was, London is, and York shall be"; for she saw herself in better state than Jerusalem, she went more gallant than ever did Antwerp, was more courted by amorous and lusty suitors than Venice, the minion of Italy. More lofty towers stood, like a coronet or a spangled head-tire about her temples, than ever did about the beautiful forehead of Rome. Tyrus and Sidon to her were like two thatched houses to Theobalds: the grand Cayr was but a hogsty.

Hinc illæ lachrymæ, she wept her bellyful for all this. Whilst Troy was swilling sack and sugar, and mousing fat venison, the mad Greeks made bonfires of their houses. Old Priam was drinking a health to the wooden horse, and before it could be pledged had his throat cut. Corn is no sooner ripe, but for all

M

the pricking up of his ears he is pared off by the shins, and made to go upon stumps; flowers no sooner budded, but they are plucked up and die. Night walks at the heels of the day, and sorrow enters, like a tavern bill, at the tail of our pleasures. For in the Apennine height of this immoderate joy and security, that like Paul's steeple overlooked the whole city, behold, that miracle-worker, who in one minute turned our general mourning to a general mirth, does now again in a moment alter that gladness to shrieks and lamentation.

The Plague

Here would I fain make a full point, because posterity should not be frighted with those miserable tragedies, which now my Muse, as Chorus, stands read to present. Time, would thou hadst never been made wretched by bringing them forth! Oblivion, would in all the graves and sepulchres, whose rank jaws thou hast already closed up, or shalt yet hereafter burst open, thou couldst likewise bury them for ever.

A stiff and freezing horror sucks up the rivers of my blood; my hair stands on end with the panting of my brains; mine eye balls are ready to start out, being beaten with the billows of my tears. Out of my weeping pen does the ink mournfully, and more bitterly than gall, drop on the pale-faced paper, even when I do but think how the bowels of my sick country have been torn. Apollo, therefore, and you bewitching silver-tongued Muses, get you gone. I invocate none of your names. Sorrow and Truth, sit you on each side of me, whilst I am delivered of this deadly burden. Prompt me that I may utter ruthful and passionate condolement. Arm my trembling hand, that it may boldly rip up and anatomize the ulcerous body of this anthropophagized plague.[1] Lend me art, without any counterfeit shadowing, to paint and delineate to the life the whole story of this mortal and pestiferous battle. And you,

[1] Anthro-pophagi are Scythians, that feed on men's flesh.

the ghosts of those more (by many) than forty thousand, that with the virulent poison of infection have been driven out of your earthly dwellings; you desolate hand-wringing widows, that beat your bosoms over your departing husbands; you woefully distracted mothers, that with dishevelled hair are fallen into swounds, whilst you lie kissing the insensible cold lips of your breathless infants; you outcast and down-trodden orphans, that shall many a year hence remember more freshly to mourn, when your mourning garments shall look old and be forgotten; and you the genii of all those emptied families, whose habitations are now among the Antipodes; join all your hands together, and with your bodies cast a ring about me. Let me behold your ghastly visages, that my paper may receive their true pictures. Echo forth your groans through the hollow trunk of my pen, and rain down your gummy tears into mine ink, that even marble bosoms may be shaken with terror, and hearts of adamant melt into compassion.

What an unmatchable torment were it for a man to be barred up every night in a vast silent charnel-house; hung (to make it more hideous) with lamps dimly and slowly burning in hollow and glimmering corners? Where all the pavement should, instead of green rushes, be strewed with blasted rosemary, withered hyacinths, fatal cypress, and yew, thickly mingled with heaps of dead men's bones. The bare ribs of a father that begat him, lying there; here the chapless hollow skull of a mother that bore him. Round about him a thousand corses; some standing bolt upright in their knotted winding sheets; others half mouldered in rotten coffins, that should suddenly yawn wide open, filling his nostrils with noisome stench, and his eyes with the sight of nothing but crawling worms. And to keep such a poor wretch waking, he should hear no noise but of toads croaking, screech-owls howling, mandrakes shrieking. Were not this an infernal prison? Would not the strongest-hearted man beset with such a ghastly horror look wild? and run mad? and die?

And even such a formidable shape did the diseased city appear in. For he that durst, in the dead hour of gloomy midnight, have been so valiant as to have walked through the still and melancholy streets, what think you should have been his music? Surely the loud groans of raving sick men; the struggling pangs of souls departing; in every house grief striking up an alarum; servants crying out for masters, wives for husbands, parents for children, children for their mothers. Here he should have met some frantically running to knock up sextons; there, others fearfully sweating with coffins to steal forth dead bodies, lest the fatal handwriting of death should seal up their doors. And to make this dismal consort more full, round about him bells heavily tolling in one place, and ringing out in another. The dreadfulness of such an hour is unutterable: let us go further.

If some poor man suddenly starting out of a sweet and golden slumber should behold his house flaming about his ears, all his family destroyed in their sleeps by the merciless fire—himself in the very midst of it, woefully and like a madman calling for help—would not the misery of such a distressed soul appear the greater, if the rich usurer dwelling next door to him, should not stir, though he felt part of the danger, but suffer him to perish, when the thrusting out of an arm might have saved him? Oh, how many thousands of wretched people have acted this poor man's part! How often hath the amazed husband waking, found the comfort of his bed lying breathless by his side! his children at the same instant gasping for life! and his servants, mortally wounded at the heart by sickness! The distracted creature beats at death's doors, exclaims at windows, his cries are sharp enough to pierce heaven, but on earth no ear is opened to receive them.

And in this manner do the tedious minutes of the night stretch out the sorrows of ten thousand. It is now day, let us look forth and try what consolation rises with the sun. Not any, not any; for before the jewel of the morning be fully set

in silver, a hundred hungry graves stand gaping, and every
one of them, as at a breakfast, hath swallowed down ten or
eleven lifeless carcases. Before dinner, in the same gulf are
twice so many more devoured; and before the sun takes his
rest, those numbers are doubled. Threescore, that not many
hours before had every one several lodgings very delicately
furnished, are now thrust altogether into one close room; a
little noisome room, not fully ten foot square.

Doth not this strike coldly to the heart of a worldly miser?
To some the very sound of death's name is instead of a passing
bell. What shall become of such a coward, being told that the
self-same body of his, which now is so pampered with superfluous fare, so perfumed and bathed in odoriferous waters,
and so gaily apparelled in variety of fashions, must one day be
thrown, like stinking carrion, into a rank and rotten grave;
where his goodly eyes, that did once shoot forth such amorous
glances, must be beaten out of his head; his locks, that hang
wantonly dangling, trodden in dirt underfoot? This doubtless,
like thunder, must needs strike him into the earth. But,
wretched man, when thou shalt see, and be assured by tokens
sent thee from heaven, that tomorrow thou must be tumbled
into a muck-pit, and suffer thy body to be bruised and pressed
with threescore dead men lying slovenly upon thee, and thou
to be undermost of all! yea, and perhaps half of that number
were thine enemies! and see how they may be revenged, for
the worms that breed out of their putrefying carcases, shall
crawl in huge swarms from them, and quite devour thee; what
agonies will this strange news drive thee into? If thou art in
love with thyself, this cannot choose but possess thee with frenzy.

But thou art gotten safe out of the civil city Calamity to thy
parks and palaces in the country, lading thy asses and thy mules
with thy gold (thy god), thy plate, and thy jewels. And the
fruits of thy womb thriftily growing up but in one only son,
the young landlord of all thy careful labours, him also hast
thou rescued from the arrows of infection. Now is thy soul

jocund and thy senses merry. But open thine eyes, thou fool, and behold that darling of thine eye, thy son, turned suddenly into a lump of clay. The hand of pestilence hath smote him even under thy wing. Now dost thou rend thine hair, blaspheme thy creator, cursest thy creation and basely descendest into brutish and unmanly passions, threatening in despite of death and his plague, to maintain the memory of thy child in the everlasting breast of marble. A tomb must now defend him from tempests. And for that purpose, the sweaty hind, that digs the rent he pays thee out of the entrails of the earth, he is sent for, to convey forth that burden of thy sorrow. But note how thy pride is disdained. That weather-beaten, sun-burnt drudge, that not a month since fawned upon thy Worship like a spaniel, and, like a bond-slave, would have stooped lower than thy feet, does now stop his nose at thy presence, and is ready to set his mastiff as high as thy throat, to drive thee from his door. All thy gold and silver cannot hire one of those, whom before thou didst scorn, to carry the dead body to his last home. The country round about thee shun thee, as a basilisk, and therefore to London, from whose arms thou cowardly fledst away, post upon post must be galloping, to fetch from thence those that may perform that funeral office. But there are they so full of grave-matters of their own, that they have no leisure to attend thine. Doth not this cut thy very heart-strings in sunder? If that do not, the shutting up of the tragical act, I am sure, will. For thou must be enforced with thine own hands to wind up that blasted flower of youth in the last linen that ever he shall wear. Upon thine own shoulders must thou bear part of him, thy amazed servant the other. With thine own hands must thou dig his grave, not in the church or common place of burial, thou hast not favour, for all thy riches, to be so happy, but in thine orchard, or in the proud walks of thy garden, wringing thy palsy-shaking hands instead of bells, most miserable father, must thou search him out a sepulchre.

My spirit grows faint with rowing in this Stygian ferry, it can no longer endure the transportation of souls in this doleful manner; let us therefore shift a point of our compass, and, since there is no remedy, but that we must still be tossed up and down in this *mare mortuum*, hoist up all our sails, and on the merry wings of a lustier wind seek to arrive on some prosperous shore.

Imagine, then, that all this while, Death, like a Spanish leaguer, or rather like stalking Tamburlaine, hath pitched his tents (being nothing but a heap of winding-sheets tacked together) in the sinfully polluted suburbs. The Plague is muster-master and marshal of the field; burning fevers, boils, blains, and carbuncles, the leaders, lieutenants, sergeants, and corporals; the main army consisting, like Dunkirk, of a minglemangle, *viz*, dumpish mourners, merry sextons, hungry coffin-sellers, scrubbing bearers, and nasty grave-makers; but indeed they are the pioneers of the camp, that are employed only, like moles, in casting up of earth and digging of trenches. Fear and Trembling, the two catch-poles of Death, arrest everyone. No parley will be granted, no composition stood upon, but the alarum is struck up, the tocsin rings out for life, and no voice heard but "Tue, tue, kill, kill."

The little bells only, like small shot, do yet go off, and make no great work for worms, a hundred or two lost in every skirmish, or so. But, alas, that's nothing. Yet by those desperate sallies, what by open setting upon them by day, and secret ambuscadoes by night, the skirts of London were pitifully pared off, by little and little. Which they within the gates perceiving, it was no boot to bid them take their heels, for away they trudge, thick and threefold; some riding, some on foot; some without boots, some in their slippers; by water, by land; in shoals swum they westward. Marry, to Gravesend none went unless they be driven, for whosoever landed there never came back again. Hackneys, water-men, and wagons were not so terribly employed many a year; so that within a short time, there was not a good horse in Smithfield, nor a coach to be set eye on. For after the world had once run upon the wheels of the pest-cart, neither coach nor caroach durst appear in his likeness.

Let us pursue these runaways no longer, but leave them in the unmerciful hands of the country hard-hearted hobbinolls, who are ordained to be their tormentors, and return back to the siege of the city. For the enemy, taking advantage by their flight, planted his ordnance against the walls. Here the cannons, like their great bells, roared. The Plague took some pains for a breach; he laid about him cruelly, ere he could get it, but at length he and his tyrannous band entered. His purple colours were presently, with the sound of Bow-bell instead of a trumpet, advanced, and joined to the standard of the city. He marched even thorough Cheapside and the capital streets of Troynovant; the only blot of dishonour that stuck upon this invader being this, that he played the tyrant, not the conqueror, making havoc of all, when he had all lying at the foot of his mercy. Men, women, and children dropped down before him; houses were rifled, streets ransacked; beautiful maidens thrown on their beds and ravished by sickness; rich men's coffers broken open and shared amongst prodigal heirs and unthrifty servants; poor men used poorly but not pitifully; he did very much hurt, yet some say he did very much good.

Howsoever he behaved himself, this intelligence runs current, that every house looked like St Bartholomew's Hospital, and every street like Bucklersbury, for poor mithridatum and dragon-water (being both of them in all the world scarce worth threepence) were boxed in every corner, and yet were both drunk every hour at other men's cost. Lazarus lay groaning at every man's door; marry, no Dives was within to send him a crumb, for all your gold-finches were fled to the woods, nor a dog left to lick up his sores, for they, like curs, were knocked down like oxen, and fell thicker than acorns.

I am amazed to remember what dead marches were made of

three thousand trooping together; husbands, wives and children, being led as ordinarily to one grave, as if they had gone to one bed. And those that could shift for a time and shrink their heads out of the collar, as many did, yet went they most bitterly miching and muffled up and down with rue and wormwood stuffed in their ears and nostrils, looking like so many boars' heads stuck with branches of rosemary, to be served in for brawn at Christmas.

This was a rare world for the Church, who had wont to complain for want of living, and now had more living thrust upon her than she knew how to bestow. To have been clerk now to a parish clerk was better than to serve some foolish Justice of Peace, or than the year before to have had a benefice. Sextons gave out, if they might, as they hoped, continue these doings but a twelve-month longer, they and their posterity would all ride upon foot-clothes to the end of the world. Amongst which worm-eaten generation, the three bald sextons of limping Saint Giles', Saint Sepulchre's and Saint Olaf's, ruled the roast more hotly than ever did the *Triumviri* of Rome; Jehochanan, Simeon, and Eleazar never kept such a plaguy coil in Jerusalem among the hunger-starved Jews, as these three sharkers did in their parishes among naked Christians. Cursed they were, I am sure, by some, to the pit of hell, for tearing money out of their throats, that had not a cross in their purses. But alas! they must have it, it is their fee, and therefore give the devil his due. Only herb-wives and gardeners, that never prayed before unless it were for rain or fair weather, were now day and night upon their marybones, that God would bless the labours of those mole-catchers, because they suck sweetness by this; for the price of flowers, herbs, and garlands, rose wonderfully insomuch that rosemary, which had wont to be sold for twelve pence an armful, went now for six shillings a handful.

A fourth sharer likewise of these winding-sheet weavers, deserves to have my pen give his lips a Jew's letter; but because he worships the bakers' good lord and master, charitable St Clement, whereas none of the other three ever had to do with any saint, he shall scape the better. Only let him take heed that having all this year buried his prayers in the bellies of fat ones and plump capon-eaters (for no worse meat would down this sly fox's stomach) let him, I say, take heed, lest, his flesh now falling away, his carcase be not plagued with lean ones, of whom, whilst the bill of *Lord have mercy upon us* was to be denied in no place, it was death for him to hear.

In this pitiful, or rather pitiless, perplexity, stood London, forsaken like a lover, forlorn like a widow, and disarmed of all comfort. Disarmed I may well say, for five rapiers were not stirring all this time, and those that were worn had never been seen if any money could have been lent upon them, so hungry is the ostrich disease that it will devour even iron. Let us therefore with bag and baggage march away from this dangerous sore city, and visit those that are fled into the country. But alas! *Decidis in Scyllam*, you are peppered if you visit them, for they are visited already. The broad arrow of Death, flies there up and down, as swiftly as it doth here. They that rode on the lustiest geldings could not out-gallop the plague, it overtook them, and overturned them too, horse and foot.

You, whom the arrows of pestilence have reached at eighteen and twenty score, though you stood far enough as you thought from the mark, you, that sickening in the highway, would have been glad of a bed in an hospital, and dying in the open fields, have been buried like dogs, how much better had it been for you, to have lain fuller of boils and plague-sores than ever did Job, so you might in that extremity have received both bodily and spiritual comfort, which there was denied you? For those misbelieving pagans, the plough-drivers, those worse than infidels, that, like their swine, never look up so high as heaven, when citizens boarded them they wrung their hands, and wished rather they had fallen into the hands of the Spaniards. For the sight of a flat-cap was more dreadful to a lob, than the discharging of a caliver; a treble-ruff, being but once named the merchant's set, had power to cast a whole household in a cold sweat. If one new suit of sackcloth had been but known to have come out of Birchin Lane, being the common wardrobe for all their clownships, it had been enough to make a market town give up the ghost. A crow that had been seen in a sunshine day standing on the top of Paul's, would have been better than a beacon on fire, to have raised all the towns within ten mile of London, for the keeping her out.

Never let any man ask me what became of our physicians in this massacre; they hid their synodical heads as well as the proudest. And I cannot blame them, for their phlebotomies, lozenges, and electuaries, with their diacatholicons, diacodions, amulets, and antidotes, had not so much strength to hold life and soul together, as a pot of Pinder's ale and a nutmeg. Their drugs turned to dirt, their simples were simple things. Galen could do no more good than Sir Giles Goosecap. Hippocrates, Avicen, Paracelsus, Rasis, Fernelius, with all their succeeding rabble of doctors and water-casters, were at their wits' end, or, I think, rather at the world's end, for not one of them durst peep abroad; or, if anyone did take upon him to play the venturous knight, the plague put him to his *nonplus*. In such strange and such changeable shapes did this chameleon-like sickness appear that they could not, with all the cunning in their budgets, make purse-nets to take him napping.

Only a band of despervewes, some few empirical mad-caps, for they could never be worth velvet caps, turned themselves into bees, or more properly into drones, and went humming up and down, with honey-brags in their mouths, sucking the sweetness of silver, and now and then of *aurum potabile*, out of the poison of blains and carbuncles. And these jolly mounte-banks clapped up their bills upon every post, like a fencer's challenge, threatening to canvas the Plague, and to fight with him at all his own several weapons. I know not how they sped, but some they sped, I am sure, for I have heard them banned for the heavens because they sent those thither, that were wished to tarry longer upon earth.

I could in this place make your cheeks look pale and your hearts shake with telling how some have had eighteen sores at one time running upon them, others ten and twelve, many four and five; and how those that have been four times wounded by this year's infection, have died of the last wound, whilst others, that were hurt as often, go up and down now with sounder limbs than many that come out of France and the Netherlands. And, descending from these, I could draw forth a catalogue of many poor wretches, that in fields, in ditches, in common cages, and under stalls (being either thrust by cruel masters out of doors, or wanting all worldly succour but the common benefit of earth and air) have most miserably perished. But to chronicle these would weary a second Fabian.

We will therefore play the soldiers, who, at the end of any notable battle, with a kind of sad delight rehearse the memorable acts of their friends that lie mangled before them; some shewing how bravely they gave the onset; some, how politicly they retired; others, how manfully they gave and received wounds; a fourth steps forth, and glories how valiantly he lost an arm; all of them making by this means the remembrance even of tragical and mischievous events very delectable. Let us strive to do so, discoursing, as it were at the end of this mortal siege of the plague, of the several most worthy accidents and strange births which this pestiferous year hath brought forth; some of them yielding comical and ridiculous stuff, others lamentable, a third kind upholding rather admiration than laughter or pity.

As first, to relish the palate of lickerish expectation, and withal to give an item how sudden a stabber this ruffianly

swaggerer, Death, is, you must believe, that amongst all the
weary number of those, that, on their bare feet, have travelled
in this long and heavy vacation to the Holy Land, one (whose
name I could for need bestow upon you, but that I know
you have no need of it, though many want a good name) lying
in that common inn of sick men, his bed, and seeing the black
and blue stripes of the plague sticking on his flesh, which he
received as tokens from heaven that he was presently to go
dwell in the upper world, most earnestly requested, and in a
manner conjured his friend, who came to interchange a last
farewell, that he would see him go handsomely attired into the
wild Irish country of worms, and for that purpose to bestow
a coffin upon him. His friend loving him, not because he was
poor (yet he was poor) but because he was a scholar (alack
that the West Indies stand so far from universities! and that a
mind richly apparelled should have a threadbare body!) made
faithful promise to him, that he should be nailed up, he would
board him; and for that purpose went instantly to one of the
new-found trade of coffin-cutters, bespake one, and, like the
surveyor of death's buildings, gave direction how this little
tenement should be framed, paying all the rent for it before-
hand.

But note upon what slippery ground life goes! Little did he
think to dwell in that room himself which he had taken for
his friend. Yet it seemed the common law of mortality had
so decreed, for he was called into the cold company of his
grave neighbours an hour before his infected friend, and had
a long lease, even till doomsday, in the same lodging, which
in the strength of health he went to prepare for another.

What credit therefore is to be given to breath, which like a
harlot will run away with every minute? How nimble is sick-
ness, and what skill hath he in all the weapons he plays withal!
The greatest cutter that takes up the Mediterranean aisle in
Paul's for his gallery to walk in, cannot ward off his blows.
He's the best fencer in the world; Vincentio Saviolo is nobody

to him. He has his mandrittas, imbroccatas, stramazones, and stoccatas at his fingers' ends. He'll make you give him ground, though ye were never worth foot of land, and beat you out of breath, though Æolus himself played upon your wind-pipe.

To witness which, I will call forth a Dutchman (yet now he's past calling for, has lost his hearing, for his ears by this time are eaten off with worms) who, though he dwelt in Bedlam, was not mad; yet the very looks of the plague, which indeed are terrible, put him almost out of his wits. For when the snares of this cunning hunter, the Pestilence, were but newly laid, and yet laid, as my Dutchman smelt it out well enough, to entrap poor men's lives that meant him no hurt, away sneaks my clipper of the King's English; and, because musket-shot should not reach him, to the Low Countries, that are built upon butter-firkins and Holland cheese, sails this plaguy fugitive. But Death, who hath more authority there than all the seven electors, and to shew him that there were other Low Countries besides his own, takes a little frokin, one of my Dutch runaway's children, and sends her packing. Into those Netherlands she departed.

O how pitiful looked my burgomaster, when he understood that the sickness could swim! It was an easy matter to scape the Dunkirks, but Death's galleys made out after him swifter than the great Turk's. Which he perceiving, made no more ado, but drunk to the States five or six healths (because he would be sure to live well) and back again comes he, to try the strength of English beer. His old rendezvous of madmen was the place of meeting, where he was no sooner arrived, but the plague had him by the back, and arrested him upon an *Exeat Regnum*, for running to the enemy. So that for the mad tricks he played to cozen our English worms of his Dutch carcase, which had been fatted here, sickness and death clapped him up in Bedlam the second time, and there he lies. And there he shall lie till he rot before I'll meddle any more with him.

But being gotten out of Bedlam, let us make a journey to Bristol, taking an honest known citizen along with us, who with other company travelling thither, only for fear the air of London should conspire to poison him, and setting up his rest not to hear the sound of Bow-bell till next Christmas, was, notwithstanding, in the highway singled out from his company and set upon by the Plague, who bade him stand and deliver his life. The rest at that word shifted for themselves and went on. He, amazed to see his friends fly, and being not able to defend himself (for who can defend himself meeting such an enemy?) yielded; and, being but forty miles from London, used all the sleights he could to get loose out of the hands of Death, and so to hide himself in his own house. Whereupon, he called for help at the same inn, where not long before he and his fellow pilgrims obtained for their money (marry, yet with more prayers than a beggar makes in three terms) to stand and drink some thirty foot from the door. To this house of tippling iniquity he repairs again, conjuring the *Lares* or walking sprites in it, if they were Christians (that "if" was well put in) and in the name of God, to succour and rescue him to their power out of the hands of infection, which now assaulted his body. The devil would have been afraid of this conjuration, but they were not; yet afraid they were it seemed, for presently the doors had their wooden ribs crushed in pieces, by being beaten together; the casements were shut more close than an usurer's greasy velvet pouch; the drawing windows were hanged, drawn, and quartered; not a crevice but was stopped, not a mouse-hole left open, for all the holes in the house were most wickedly dammed up. Mine host and hostess ran over one another into the backside, the maids into the orchard, quivering and quaking, and ready to hang themselves on the innocent plum trees; for hanging to them would not be so sore a death as the plague. And to die maids too! Oh, horrible! As for the tapster, he fled into the cellar, rapping out five or six plain country oaths, that he would drown himself in a most villainous stand of ale if the sick Londoner stood at the door any longer.

But stand there he must, for to go away well he cannot, but continues knocking and calling in a faint voice, which in their ears sounded as if some staring ghost in a tragedy had exclaimed upon Rhadamanth. He might knock till his hands ached, and call till his heart ached, for they were in a worse pickle within than he was without; he being in a good way to go to heaven, they being so frighted, that they scarce knew whereabout heaven stood. Only they all cried out, "Lord, have mercy upon us," yet "Lord have mercy upon us" was the only thing they feared.

The doleful catastrophe of all is a bed could not be had for all Babylon; not a cup of drink, no, nor cold water be gotten, though it had been for Alexander the Great; if a draught of *aqua vitæ* might have saved his soul the town denied to do God that good service.

What misery continues ever? The poor man standing thus at death's door, and looking every minute when he should be let in, behold, another Londoner that had likewise been in the *frigida zona* of the country, and was returning, like Aeneas out of hell, to the heaven of his own home, makes a stand at this sight to play the physician. And seeing by the complexion of his patient that he was sick at heart, applies to his soul the best medicines that his comforting speech could make, for there dwelt no pothecary near enough to help his body. Being therefore driven out of all other shifts, he leads him into a field, a bundle of straw, which with much ado he bought for money, serving instead of a pillow.

But the Destinies, hearing the diseased party complain and take on because he lay upon a field-bed, when before he would have been glad of a mattress, for very spite cut the thread of his life; the cruelty of which deed made the other, that played Charity's part, at his wits' end, because he knew not where to purchase ten foot of ground for his grave. The church nor churchyard would let none of their lands. Master vicar was struck dumb, and could not give the dead a good word; neither clerk nor sexton could be hired to execute their office. No, they themselves would first be executed. So that he, that never handled shovel before, got his implements about him, ripped up the belly of the earth and made it like a grave, stripped the cold carcase, bound his shirt about his feet, pulled a linen night-cap over his eyes, and so laid him in the rotten bed of the earth, covering him with clothes cut out of the same piece. And learning by his last words his name and habitation, this sad traveller arrives at London, delivering to the amazed widow and children, instead of a father and a husband, only the outside of him, his apparel.

But, by the way, note one thing; the bringer of these heavy tidings, as if he had lived long enough when so excellent a work of piety and pity was by him finished, the very next day after his coming home, departed out of this world, to receive his reward in the spiritual court of heaven.

It is plain therefore by the evidence of these two witnesses, that Death, like a thief, sets upon men in the highway, dogs them into their own houses, breaks into their bedchambers by night, assaults them by day, and yet no law can take hold of him. He devours man and wife; offers violence to their fair daughters; kills their youthful sons, and deceives them of their servants. Yea, so full of treachery is he grown since this plague took his part, that no lovers dare trust him, nor by their good wills would come near him, for he works their downfall, even when their delights are at the highest.

Too ripe a proof have we of this, in a pair of lovers. The maid was in the pride of fresh blood and beauty; she was that (which to be now is a wonder) young and yet chaste. The gifts of her mind were great, yet those which fortune bestowed upon her, as being well descended, were not much inferior. On this lovely creature did a young man so steadfastly fix his eye, that her looks kindled in his bosom a desire whose flames

N

burnt the more brightly because they were fed with sweet and modest thoughts. Hymen was the god to whom he prayed day and night that he might marry her. His prayers were received and at length, after many tempests of her denial and frowns of kinsfolk, the element grew clear, and he saw the happy landing place where he had long sought to arrive. The prize of her youth was made his own, and the solemn day appointed when it should be delivered to him.

Glad of which blessedness (for to a lover it is a blessedness) he wrought by all the possible art he could use to shorten the expected hour and bring it nearer; for, whether he feared the interception of parents, or that his own soul with excess of joy was drowned in strange passions, he would often, with sighs mingled with kisses, and kisses half sinking in tears, prophetically tell her that sure he should never live to enjoy her.

To discredit which opinion of his, behold, the sun has now made haste and wakened the bridal morning. Now does he call his heart traitor, that did so falsely conspire against him; lively blood leaps into his cheeks. He's got up, and gaily attired to play the bridegroom. She likewise does as cunningly turn herself into a bride. Kindred and friends are met together; sops and muscadine run sweating up and down till they drop again, to comfort their hearts. And, because so many coffins pestered London churches that there was no room left for weddings, coaches are provided, and away rides all the train into the country.

On a Monday morning are these lusty lovers on their journey, and before noon are they alighted, entering, instead of an inn, for more state into a church, where they no sooner appeared but the priest fell to his business. The holy knot was a tieing, but he that should fasten it coming to this, "In sickness and in health," there he stopped, for suddenly the bride took hold of "in sickness," for "in health" all that stood by were in fear she should never be kept. The maiden blush, into which her cheeks were lately dyed, now began to lose colour; her voice, like a coward, would have shrunk away, but that her lover reaching her a hand, which he brought thither to give her (for he was not yet made a full husband) did with that touch somewhat revive her. On went they again so far, till they met with "For better, for worse," there was she worse than before, and had not the holy officer made haste the ground on which she stood to be married might easily have been broken up for her burial.

All ceremonies being finished, she was led between two, not like a bride, but rather like a corse, to her bed. That must now be the table, on which the wedding dinner is to be served up (being at this time, nothing but tears, and sighs, and lamentation) and Death is chief waiter. Yet, at length, her weak heart, wrestling with the pangs, gave them a fall, so that up she stood again and in the fatal funeral coach that carried her forth, was she brought back, as upon a bier, to the city.

But see the malice of her enemy that had her in chase! Upon the Wednesday following being overtaken, was her life overcome. Death rudely lay with her, and spoiled her of a maidenhead in spite of her husband. Oh, the sorrow that did round beset him! Now was his divination true; she was a wife yet continued a maid; he was a husband and a widower, yet never knew his wife; she was his own, yet he had her not; she had him, yet never enjoyed him. Here is a strange alteration, for the rosemary that was washed in sweet water to set out the bridal is now wet in tears to furnish her burial; the music that was heard to sound forth dances cannot now be heard for the ringing of bells; all the comfort that happened to either side being this, that he lost her before she had time to be an ill wife, and she left him ere he was able to be a bad husband.

Better fortune had this bride, to fall into the hands of the Plague, than one other of that frail female sex, whose picture is next to be drawn, had to scape out of them.

An honest cobbler (if at least cobblers can be honest, that live altogether amongst wicked soles) had a wife, who, in time of health treading her shoe often awry, determined in the agony of a sickness, which this year had a saying to her, to fall to mending as well as her husband did. The bed that she lay upon being (as she thought, or rather feared) the last bed that ever should bear her (for many other beds had borne her, you must remember) and the worm of sin tickling her conscience, up she calls her very innocent and simple husband out of his virtuous shop, where, like Justice, he sat distributing amongst the poor, to some halfpenny pieces, penny pieces to some, and twopenny pieces to others, so long as they would last; his provident care being always that every man and woman should go upright.

To the bed's side of his plaguy wife approaches Monsieur Cobbler, to understand what deadly news she had to tell him and the rest of his kind neighbours that there were assembled, such thick tears standing in both the gutters of his eyes, to see his beloved lie in such a pickle, that in their salt water all his utterance was drowned. Which she perceiving, wept as fast as he. But by the warm counsel that sat about the bed the shower ceased, she wiping her cheeks with the corner of one of the sheets, and he his sullied face with his leathern apron.

At last, two or three sighs, like a chorus to the tragedy ensuing, stepping out first, wringing her hands, which gave the better action, she told the pitiful *Actæon*, her husband, that she had often done him wrong. He only shook his head at this, and cried, "Humh!" Which "humh" she taking as the watchword of his true patience, unravelled the bottom of her frailty at length, and concluded, that with such a man (and named him, but I hope you would not have me follow her steps and name him too) she practised the universal and common art of grafting, and that upon her goodman's head, they two had planted a monstrous pair of invisible horns.

At the sound of the horns my cobbler started up like a March hare and began to look wild. His awl never ran through the sides of a boot, as that word did through his

heart. But being a politic cobbler, and remembering what
piece of work he was to under-lay, stroking his beard, like
some grave headborough of the parish, and giving a nod, as
who should say, "go on," bade her go on indeed, clapping to
her sore soul this general salve, that "All are sinners, and we
must forgive etc.," for he hoped by such wholesome physic,
as shoemaker's wax being laid to a boil, to draw out all the
corruption of her secret villainies.

She, good heart, being tickled under gills with the finger of
these kind speeches, turns up the white of her eye, and fetches
out another. "Another, O thou that art trained up in nothing
but to handle pieces! another hath discharged his artillery
against thy castle of fortification." Here was passion predominant. Vulcan struck the cobbler's ghost, for he was now
no cobbler, so hard upon his breast, that he cried, "Oh!"

His neighbours, taking pity to see what terrible stitches
pulled him, rubbed his swelling temples with the juice of
patience, which, by virtue of the blackish sweat that stood
reeking on his brows and had made them supple, entered very
easily into his now parlous-understanding skull: so that he left
winching, and sat quiet as a lamb, falling to his old vomit of
counsel, which he had cast up before, and swearing, because
he was in strong hope this shoe should wring him no more,
to seal her a general acquittance. Pricked forward with this
gentle spur, her tongue mends his pace, so that in her confession she overtook others, whose boots had been set all
night on the cobbler's last, bestowing upon him the posy of
their names, the time and place, to the intent it might be put
into his next wife's wedding ring. And although she had made
all these blots in his tables, yet the bearing of one man false,
whom she had not yet discovered, stuck more in her stomach
than all the rest.

"O valiant cobbler," cries out one of the auditors, "how
art thou set upon? how art thou tempted? Happy art thou,
that thou art not in thy shop, for instead of cutting out pieces

of leather thou wouldst doubtless now pare away thy heart; for I see, and so do all thy neighbours here, thy wife's ghostly fathers, see, that a small matter would now cause thee turn Turk, and to meddle with no more patches. But to live within the compass of thy wit, lift not up thy choler; be not horn mad; thank heaven that the murder is revealed; study thou Balthazar's part in *Jeronimo*, for thou hast more cause, though less reason, than he, to be glad and sad. Well, I see thou are worthy to have patient Griseld to thy wife, for thou bearest more than she. Thou shewst thyself to be a right cobbler, and no souter, that canst thus cleanly clout up the seam-rent sides of thy affection."

With this learned oration the cobbler was tutored, laid his finger on his mouth, and cried *paucos palabros*, he had sealed her pardon and therefore bid her not fear. Hereupon she named the malefactor (I could name him too but that he shall live to give more cobblers' heads the bastinado) and told that on such a night, when he supped there (for a lord may sup with a cobbler, that hath a pretty wench to his wife) when the cloth, O treacherous linen! was taken up, and Menelaus had for a parting blow, given the other his fist, down she lights, this half-sharer, opening the wicket, but not shutting him out of the wicket, but conveys him into a by-room, being the wardrobe of old shoes and leather; from whence—the unicorn cobbler, that dreamt of no such spirits, being over head and ears in sleep, his snorting giving the sign that he was cock-sure—softly out steals Sir Paris, and to Helena's teeth proved himself a true Trojan.

This was the cream of her confession, which being skimmed off from the stomach of her conscience, she looked every minute to go thither, where she should be far enough out of the cobbler's reach. But the Fates, laying their heads together, sent a reprieve; the plague, that before meant to pepper her, by little and little left her company. Which news being blown abroad—oh, lamentable!—never did the old buskined tragedy begin till now. For the wives of those husbands, with whom she had played at fast and loose, came with nails sharpened for the nonce like cats, and tongues forkedly cut like the stings of adders, first to scratch out false Cressida's eyes, and then, which was worse, to worry her to death with scolding.

But the matter was took up in a tavern. The case was altered, and brought to a new reckoning (marry, the blood of the Bordeaux grape was first shed about it) but in the end, all anger on every side was poured into a pottle pot and there burnt to death.

Now whether this recantation was true, or whether the steam of infection, fuming up like wine into her brains, made her talk thus idly, I leave it to the jury.

And whilst they are canvassing her case, let us see what doings the sexton of Stepney hath, whose warehouses being all full of dead commodities, saving one—that one he left open a whole night (yet it was half full too) knowing the thieves this year were too honest to break into such cellars; besides, those that were left there had such plaguy pates, that none durst meddle with them for their lives.

About twelve of the clock at midnight, when spirits walk, and not a mouse dare stir, because cats go a caterwauling, Sin, that all day durst not shew his head, came reeling out of an ale-house, in the shape of a drunkard, who no sooner smelt the wind, but he thought the ground under him danced the Canaries. Houses seemed to turn on the toe, and all things went round, insomuch that his legs drew a pair of indentures between his body and the earth, the principal covenant being that he for his part would stand to nothing whatever he saw. Every tree that came in his way did he jostle, and yet challenge it the next day to fight with him. If he had clipped but a quarter so much of the King's silver, as he did of the King's English, his carcase had long ere this been carrion for crows. But he lived by gaming, and had excellent casting, yet seldom won, for he drew reasonable good hands but had very bad feet, that were not able to carry it away. This setter-up of malt-men, being troubled with the staggers, fell into the self-same grave that stood gaping wide open for a breakfast next morning. And imagining, when he was in, that he had stumbled into his own house, and that all his bedfellows (as they were indeed) were in their dead sleep, he, never complaining of cold, nor calling for more sheet, soundly takes a nap till he snorts again.

In the morning the sexton comes plodding along and casting upon his fingers' ends what he hopes the dead pay of that day will come to by that which he received the day before, for sextons now had better doings than either taverns or bawdy-houses. In that silver contemplation, shrugging his shoulders together, he steps ere he be aware on the brims of that pit, into which this worshipper of Bacchus was fallen. Where finding some dead men's bones, and a skull or two, that lay scattered here and there, before he looked into this coffer of worms, those he takes up and flings them in. One of the skulls battered the sconce of the sleeper, whilst the bones played with his nose, whose blows waking his musty worship, the first word that he cast up was an oath, and thinking the cans had flyen about, cried, "Zounds, what do you mean to crack my mazer?"

The sexton, smelling a voice, fear being stronger than his heart, believed verily some of the corses spake to him, upon which, feeling himself in a cold sweat, took his heels, whilst the goblin scrambled up and ran after him. But it appears the sexton had the lighter foot, for he ran so fast, that he ran out of his wits which being left behind him, he died in a short time after, because he was not able to live without them.

A merrier bargain than the poor sexton's did a tinker meet withal in a country town; through which a citizen of London being driven to keep himself under the lee-shore in this tempestuous contagion, and casting up his eye for some harbour, spied a bush at the end of a pole, the ancient badge of a country ale-house. Into which, as good luck was, without any resistance of the barbarians, that all this year used to keep such landing places, vailing his bonnet he struck in.

The host had been a mad Greek (marry, he could now speak nothing but English) a goodly fat burgher he was, with a belly arching out like a beer-barrel, which made his legs, that were thick and short, like two piles driven under London Bridge, to straddle half as wide as the top of Paul's, which upon my knowledge hath been burnt twice or thrice. A leathern pouch hung at his side, that opened and shut with a snaphance, and was indeed a flask for gunpowder when King Henry went to Boulogne. An antiquary might have picked rare matter out of his nose but that it was worm-eaten (yet that proved it to be an ancient nose); in some corners of it there were bluish holes, that shone like shells of mother-of-pearl, and to do his nose right, pearls had been gathered out of them. Other were richly garnished with rubies, chrisolites, and carbuncles, which glistered so oriently, that the Hamburgers offered I know not how many dollars for his company in an East Indian voyage, to have stood a nights in the poop of their admiral, only to save the charge of candles. In conclusion, he was an host to be led before an emperor, and though he were one of the greatest men in all the shire, his bigness made him not proud, but he humbled himself to speak the base language of a tapster, and upon the Londoner's first arrival, cried, " Welcome; a cloth for this gentleman."

The linen was spread and furnished presently with a new cake and a can, the room voided, and the guest left, like a French lord, attended by nobody; who drinking half a can, in conceit, to the health of his best friend, the City, which lay extreme sick and had never more need of health, I know not what qualms came over his stomach, but immediately he fell down without uttering any more words, and never rose again.

Anon, as it was his fashion, enters my puffing host, to relieve with a fresh supply out of his cellar the shrinking can, if he perceived it stood in danger to be overthrown. But seeing

the chief leader dropped at his feet, and imagining at first he
was but wounded a little in the head, held up his gouty golls
and blessed himself, that a Londoner, who had wont to be the
most valiant rob-pots, should now be struck down only with
two hoops; and thereupon jogged him, fumbling out these
comfortable words of a soldier: "If thou art a man stand on
thy legs." He stirred not for all this. Whereupon the maids
being raised, as it had been with a hue and cry, came hobbling
into the room, like a flock of geese, and having upon search
of the body given up this verdict, that the man was dead, and
murdered by the Plague, Oh, daggers to all their hearts that
heard it!

Away trudge the wenches, and one of them, having had a
freckled face all her life-time, was persuaded presently that
now they were the tokens, and had liked to have turned up her
heels upon it. My gorbelly host, that in many a year could not
without grunting crawl over a threshold but two foot broad,
leapt half a yard from the corse (it was measured by a carpenter's rule) as nimbly as if his guts had been taken out by
the hangman. Out of the house he wallowed presently, being
followed with two or three dozen of napkins to dry up the
lard, that ran so fast down his heels, that all the way he went
was more greasy than a kitchen-stuff-wife's basket. You
would have sworn it had been a barrel of pitch on fire, if you
had looked upon him, for such a smoky cloud, by reason of his
own fatty, hot steam, compassed him round, that but for his
voice, he had quite been lost in that stinking mist. Hanged
himself he had without all question in this pitiful taking, but
that he feared the weight of his intolerable paunch would have
burst the rope, and so he should be put to a double death.

At length the town was raised, the country came down upon
him, and yet not upon him neither, for after they understood
the tragedy, every man gave ground, knowing my pursy ale-
conner could not follow them. What is to be done in this
strange alarum? The whole village is in danger to lie at the

mercy of God, and shall be bound to curse none but him for it. They should do well, therefore, to set fire on his house, before the Plague scape out of it, lest it forage higher into the country, and knock them down, man, woman, and child, like oxen, whose blood, they all swear, shall be required at his hands.

At these speeches, my tender-hearted host fell down on his marybones, meaning indeed to entreat his audience to be good to him. But they, fearing he had been peppered too, as well as the Londoner, tumbled one upon another, and were ready to break their necks for haste to be gone. Yet some of them, being more valiant than the rest, because they heard him roar out for some help very desperately stepped back, and with rakes and pitch-forks lifted the gulch from the ground; concluding after they had laid their hogsheads together to draw out some wholesome counsel, that whosoever would venture upon the dead man and bury him, should have forty shillings out of the common town purse, though it would be a great cut to it, with the love of the churchwardens and sidemen during the term of life.

This was proclaimed, but none durst appear to undertake the dreadful execution. They loved money well; marry, the plague hanging over any man's head that should meddle with it in that sort, they all vowed to die beggars, before it should be chronicled they killed themselves for forty shillings. And in that brave resolution, everyone with bag and baggage marched home, barricading their doors and windows with fir-bushes, fern, and bundles of straw, to keep out the pestilence at the stave's end.

At last a tinker came sounding through the town, mine host's house being the ancient watering-place where he did use to cast anchor. You must understand he was none of those base, rascally tinkers, that with a ban-dog and a drab at their tails, and a pike-staff on their necks, will take a purse sooner than stop a kettle. No, this was a devout tinker, he did honour god Pan; a musical tinker, that upon his kettle-drum could play any country dance you called for, and upon holidays had earned money by it, when no fiddler could be heard of. He was only feared when he stalked through some towns where bees were, for he struck so sweetly on the bottom of his copper instrument, that he would empty whole hives, and lead the swarms after him only by the sound.

This excellent, egregious tinker calls for his draught, being a double jug. It was filled for him, but before it came to his nose, the lamentable tale of the Londoner was told, the chamber door, where he lay, being thrust open with a long pole because none durst touch it with their hands, and the tinker bidden, if he had the heart, to go in and see if he knew him. The tinker, being not to learn what virtue the medicine had which he held at his lips, poured it down his throat merrily, and crying trillil he feared no plagues, in he stepped, tossing the dead body to and fro, and was sorry he knew him not. Mine host, that with grief began to fall away villainously, looking very ruefully on the tinker and thinking him a fit instrument to be played upon, offered a crown out of his own purse, if he would bury the party. A crown was a shrewd temptation to a tinker; many a hole might he stop, before he could pick a crown of it. Yet being a subtle tinker, and to make all sextons pray for him, because he would raise their fees, an angel he wanted to be his guide, and under ten shillings (by his ten bones) he would not put his finger into the fire.

The whole parish had warning of this presently. Thirty shillings was saved by the bargain, and the town like to be saved too, therefore ten shillings was levied out of hand, put into a rag, which was tied to the end of a long pole and delivered, in sight of all the parish, who stood aloof stopping their noses, by the headborough's own self in proper person to the tinker, who with one hand received the money, and with the other struck the board, crying, "Hey, a fresh double pot." Which armour of proof being fitted to his body, up he hoists the Londoner on his back like a schoolboy, a shovel and

pickaxe standing ready for him. And thus furnished, into a
field some good distance from the town he bears his deadly
load, and there throws it down, falling roundly to his tools,
upon which the strong beer having set an edge, they quickly
cut out a lodging in the earth for the citizen.

But the tinker, knowing that worms needed no apparel,
saving only sheets, stripped him stark naked, but first dived
nimbly into his pocket, to see what linings they had, assuring
himself that a Londoner would not wander so far without
silver. His hopes were of the right stamp, for from one of his
pockets he drew a leathern bag with seven pounds in it. This
music made the tinker's heart dance. He quickly tumbled his
man into the grave, hid him over head and ears in dust, bound
up his clothes in a bundle, and carrying that at the end of his
staff on his shoulder, with the purse of seven pounds in his
hand, back again comes he through the town, crying aloud,
"Have ye any more Londoners to bury, hey down a down
derry, have ye any more Londoners to bury?", the hobbinolls
running away from him, as if he had been the dead citizen's
ghost, and he marching away from them in all the haste he
could with that song still in his mouth.

You see, therefore, how dreadful a fellow Death is, making
fools even of wise men, and cowards of the most valiant. Yea,
in such a base slavery hath it bound men's senses that they
have no power to look higher than their own roofs, but seem
by their Turkish and barbarous actions to believe that there
is no felicity after this life, and that, like beasts, their souls
shall perish with their bodies. How many upon sight only of a
letter sent from London have started back, and durst have laid
their salvation upon it, that the plague might be folded in that
empty paper, believing verily that the arm of omnipotence
could never reach them unless it were with some weapon
drawn out of the infected city; insomuch that even the western
pugs receiving money there have tied it in a bag at the end of
their barge, and so trailed it through the Thames, lest plague-

sores sticking upon shillings, they should be nailed up for counterfeits when they were brought home?

More venturous than these blockheads was a certain Justice of Peace; to whose gate, being shut (for you must know that now there is no open house kept) a company of wild fellows being led for robbing an orchard, the stout-hearted constable rapped most courageously, and would have about with none but the Justice himself, who at last appeared in his likeness above at a window, inquiring why they summoned a parley. It was delivered why. The case was opened to his examining wisdom, and that the evil-doers were only Londoners. At the name of Londoners the Justice, clapping his hand on his breast, as who should say, "Lord have mercy upon us," started back, and, being wise enough to save one, held his nose hard between his forefinger and his thumb, and speaking in that wise (like the fellow that described the villainous motion of Julius Cæsar and the Duke of Guise, who—as he gave it out— fought a combat together) pulling the casement close to him, cried out in that quail-pipe voice, that if they were Londoners, away with them to Limbo. Take only their names, they were sore fellows, and he would deal with them when time should serve; meaning, when the plague and they should not be so great together. And so they departed, the very name of Londoners being worse than ten whetstones to sharpen the sword of Justice against them.

I could fill a large volume, and call it the second part of "The Hundred Merry Tales," only with such ridiculous stuff as this of the Justice, but *Dii meliora*, I have better matters to set my wits about. Neither shall you wring out of my pen, though you lay it on the rack, the villainies of that damned keeper who killed all she kept. It had been good to have made her keeper of the common jail, and the holes of both Counters, for a number lie there, that wish to be rid out of this motley world. She would have tickled them, and turned them over the thumbs.

I will likewise let the churchwarden in Thames Street sleep, for he's now past waking, who, being requested by one of his neighbours to suffer his wife or child, that was then dead, to lie in the churchyard, answered in a mocking sort he kept that lodging for himself and his household; and within three days after was driven to hide his head in a hole himself.

Neither will I speak a word of a poor boy, servant to a chandler, dwelling thereabouts, who being struck to the heart by sickness, was first carried away by water, to be left any where. But landing being denied by an army of brown-bill-men that kept the shore, back again was he brought, and left in an out-cellar; where lying grovelling and groaning on his face amongst faggots, but not one of them set on fire to comfort him, there continued all night and died miserably for want of succour.

Nor of another poor wretch in the parish of St Mary Overy's, who being in the morning thrown, as the fashion is, into a grave upon a heap of carcases, that stayed for their complement, was found in the afternoon, gasping and gaping for life.

But by these tricks imagining that many a thousand have been turned wrongfully off the ladder of life, and praying that Derrick or his executors may live to do those a good turn, that have done so to others; *Hic finis Priami*, here's an end of an old song.

Et iam tempus equum fumantia solvere colla.

FINIS

NOTES

The Third and Last Part of Cony Catching

Robert Greene (1558–92) was born in Norwich. In 1575 he matriculated at St John's College, Cambridge, and was admitted to the degree of B.A. in 1578. After leaving Cambridge Greene travelled on the Continent, where, according to his own account, he "practised such villainy as is abominable to declare."

Returning to England round about 1580, Greene began to write, and he also studied at Oxford, where he received the degree of M.A. in 1583. It was probably about this time that he married. Greene had a daughter by his wife, but then deserted her and went to London about the end of 1585. There he lived a Bohemian existence, associating with some of the most notorious rogues of the day. He supported himself by writing prose romances in the beautiful, ornate manner made fashionable by Lyly. The best-known of these romances are *Pandosto* (1588), the source of Shakespeare's *The Winter's Tale*, and *Menaphon* (1589).

About 1590 Greene turned away from the writing of romances to the production of the cony-catching pamphlets. How far this change was due to a desire for reformation on the part of Greene himself, and how far it was due to his realization that here was a new and profitable theme, it is hard to say. Greene certainly knew the underworld that he describes, but much of his material is drawn from earlier works, and especially from *A Manifest Detection of the most vyle and detestable use of Diceplay* (1552). The cony-catching pamphlets, together with his plays, which are difficult to date, occupied Greene till the end of his life. He died in poverty and misery on September 3, 1592.

The most interesting accounts of his life are to be found in his own works *Greene's Groatsworth of Witte* and *The Repentance of Robert Greene*, both published in 1592, though it has never been established precisely how much in them is fact and how much is fiction.

p. 34. *the two former published books.* I.e., *A Notable Discovery of Coosenage* and *The Second Part of Conny Catching*, both published in 1591.

p. 36. *Whittington College.* Founded by the executors of Sir Richard Whittington "with alms-houses for thirteen poor men, and divinity lectures to be read there for ever."—Stow's *Survey of London,* edited by Kingsford, vol. i, p. 109 and pp. 242–243.

p. 40. *Finsbury Fields.* At this time an open space outside the city, used for archery practice and as a place of recreation.

p. 40. *St Laurence Lane.* Led from West Cheap, where the citizen seems to have lived, to Catte Street. For the route followed see the map of London in Stow's *Survey,* edited by Kingsford.

p. 40. *the conduit in Aldermanbury.* "William Eastfield, mercer, 1438, appointed his executors of his goods to convey sweet water from Tyburn, and to build a fair conduit by Aldermanbury Church." —Stow's *Survey,* edited by Kingsford, vol. i, p. 109.

p. 45. *Tyburn.* The place of execution.

p. 45. *Paul's Church.* The chief meeting-place in the city, used for the transaction of business of all kinds, and a favourite haunt of those who had nothing else to do. Kingsford, in his edition of Stows' *Survey* (vol. ii, p. 316), quotes the following from the works of James Pilkington, Bishop of Durham, 1561: "The south alley for popery and usury, the north for simony, and the horse-fair in the midst for all kinds of bargains, meetings, brawlings, murders, conspiracies, and the font for ordinary payments of money, as well known to all men as the beggar knows his bush." *cf.* also note to *Pierce Penilesse* (p. 261).

p. 46. "*A game . . . mark the stand.*" Hunting terminology—"A fair game, a victim, keep an eye on him."

p. 46. *nipping the bung.* Thieves' cant for cutting a purse.

p. 49. For the collusion of cutpurse and ballad-singer see Ben Jonson's *Bartholomew Fair,* Act III, Scene v, where Nightingale sings a ballad warning his hearers to beware of the cutpurse, exactly as here.

p. 49. *Gracious Street.* I.e., Gracechurch Street.

p. 50. *I hear of their journey westward.* I.e., to Tyburn. *Cf.* p. 45.

p. 53. *term time.* I.e., during the law terms, when large numbers of clients came to London.

p. 54. *Ivy Bridge.* Bridge at Strand end of Ivy Lane, a passage which also served as a watercourse leading down to the Thames.

p. 56. *it was somewhat misreported before,* etc. I.e., in *The Second Part of Conny Catching,* where there is a different version of the story. See *The Works of Robert Greene,* edited by Grosart, vol. x, pp. 116–117.

p. 57. *the Bull within Bishopsgate.* One of the best known of the inns that became theatres early in the reign of Elizabeth. The earliest reference to it is in 1575. See Chambers' *Elizabethan Stage*, vol. ii, pp. 380–381.

p. 63. *Paul's Chain.* Short street or lane leading from the south side of St Paul's to Paul's Wharf Hill, and so down to the river.

p. 69. *into the tavern he went.* I.e., the tailor went.

p. 69. *the party offended with the broker.* I.e., the party offended by the broker.

Pierce Penilesse

Thomas Nashe (1567–1601?) was born at Lowestoft. His father was a parson, and Nashe always referred to himself as a "gentleman." In 1581 or 1582 Nashe went to St John's College, Cambridge, where he graduated B.A. in 1586. He seems to have left Cambridge about 1588, and probably went to London. His first published work, a preface to Greene's *Menaphon*, which shows that he was already acquainted with a number of literary men in London, appeared in 1589. About this time Nashe almost certainly took part in the campaign against Martin Marprelate.

Exactly how Nashe lived during these early years in London is not known. He seems to have depended much on the kindness of patrons, as most literary men did.

Pierce Penilesse, the most successful of his works in his own day, came out in 1592. This pamphlet largely initiated the literary quarrel between Nashe and Gabriel Harvey. Richard Harvey, Gabriel's brother, had said some harsh things about Nashe's preface to Greene's *Menaphon* in his work *The Lamb of God* (1590). In *Pierce Penilesse* Nashe retorted. The quarrel was then taken up by Gabriel Harvey in his *Foure Letters* (1592). Nash replied with *Strange Newes* (1593), and the verbal slanging match between the two culminated in Nashe's brilliant piece of vituperation *Have with You to Saffron-Walden* (1596). (For a full account of the quarrel see *The Works of Thomas Nashe*, edited by R. B. McKerrow, vol. v, pp. 65–110.)

In the meantime Nashe had written *The Unfortunate Traveller* (1594), which has some claims to being regarded as the first novel in English; a play, *Summer's Last Will and Testament*, published in 1600, but probably composed about 1592; and *Christ's Tears over Jerusalem* (1593), an attack on the vices of London.

In 1597 Nashe was engaged on a play, *The Isle of Dogs*. He did not finish it, and it was completed by Ben Jonson. As soon as it was put on the play was suppressed by the order of the Privy Council. Ben

Jonson was imprisoned for his share in it, and Nashe fled to Yarmouth. Out of this visit to Yarmouth came the most brilliant of all his works from a literary point of view, *Nashe's Lenten Stuffe* (1599). When and were Nashe died is not known, but he was dead in 1601.

p. 71. *Barbaria grandis habere nihil*, Ovid, *Amores* iii. 8. 4.

Ingenium quondam fuerat pretiosius auro
At nunc barbari est grandis, habere nihil.

"Culture was once more precious than gold, but now to be penniless is the worst form of barbarism."

p. 71. *A private Epistle, etc.* This is not in the first edition, which has a short preface, entitled, "The Printer to the Gentlemen Readers."

p. 71. *to the ghost of Robert Greene, etc.* Greene died at the beginning of September 1592, and according to Gabriel Harvey was buried on September 4; see Gabriel Harvey's *Foure Letters*, edited by G. B. Harrison, p. 22. After his death there appeared *Greene's Groatsworth of Witte*, *The Repentance of Robert Greene*, and Harvey's *Foure Letters*.

p. 72. *the fear of infection.* Plague broke out in London in August 1592.

p. 72. *that long-tailed title.* The title-page of the first edition has these words after the title: "Describing the over-spreading of Vice, and suppression of Virtue. Pleasantly interlaced with variable delights, and pathetically intermixed with conceited reproofs."

p. 72. *Paul's Churchyard.* Most of the booksellers' shops were in Paul's Churchyard.

p. 72. *the knight of the post.* A knight of the post was the name of a professional perjurer. *Cf.* p. 80.

p. 72. *Greene's Groatsworth of Witte.* Published after Greene's death, this pamphlet with its well-known attack on Shakespeare and others was almost certainly the work of Greene himself.

p. 72. *misinterpreting.* I.e., discovering allusions to individuals where none was intended. *Cf.* Ben Jonson's *Bartholomew Fair*, The Induction.

p. 72. *The antiquaries are offended.* Presumably by the passage at p. 98.

p. 73. "*The Black Book.*" Greene says in his *Disputation between a hee Conny Catcher and a shee Conny Catcher* that he had a *Black Book* in preparation, which would give the names of the chief thieves and scoundrels in London at the time.

p. 74. *Discite qui sapitis, etc.* Ovid, *Amores*, iii, 8, 25–26. "You, who are wise, should learn not the things that we poets have learnt in our lazy way, but to take part in the life of the army and the camp."

p. 74. *Est aliquid fatale malum per verba levare.* Ovid, *Tristia*, v, 1, 59. "There is some relief in finding expression for a deadly ill."

p. 74. *Pol me occidistis, amici.* Horace, *Epistles*, ii, 2, 138. "Indeed, my friends, you have killed me."

p. 75. *a pamphlet of the praise of pudding-pricks.* A treatise of *Tom Thumb—the exploits of Untruss.* None of these works is now extant. There was a ballad on the exploits of Untruss, probably the work of Anthony Munday.

p. 75. *Scribimus indocti doctique poemata passim.* Horace, *Epistles*, ii, 1, 117. "Unlearned and learned alike, we write poems everywhere."

p. 76. *Heu rapiunt mala fata bonos.* Ovid, *Amores* iii, 9, 35. "The malign Fates, alas, carry off the good."

p. 76. *Sic probo.* Nashe's name for a scholar.

p. 77. *genus et proavos.* Ovid, *Metamorphoses*, xiii, 140. "Family and ancestors."

p.77. *vacuus viator.* Juvenal, x, 22. *Cantabit vacuus coram latrone viator.* "The traveller whose pockets are empty can laugh at the highwayman."

p. 77. *the Commissioners of Newmarket Heath.* Highwaymen.

p. 77. *court holy bread.* Fair words. *Cf. King Lear*, Act III, Scene ii: "O nuncle, court holy-water in a dry house is better than this rain-water out o' door."

p. 78. *statute merchant.* "A bond of record, acknowledged before the chief magistrate of a trading town, giving to the obligee power of seizure of the land of the obligor if he failed to pay his debt at the appointed time."—(*Oxford English Dictionary*.)

p. 78. *Ambodexter.* An equivocator. Ambidexter is the name of the Vice in Thomas Preston's play *Cambises* (1569).

p. 78. *a driver.* McKerrow (vol. iv, p. 92) says that, while the exact sense is not clear, "there is evident allusion to the proverb *He must needs go when the devil drives.*" It seems likely, however, that this is the same word as that used by Massinger, *A New Way to Pay Old Debts*, Act II, Scene ii: "This term-driver, Marrall, This snip of an attorney"; where term-driver seems to mean a pettifogging lawyer, who drives hard bargains, a sense that fits 'driver' here.

p. 78. *a hundred as well-headed as he.* I.e., cuckolds, the usual Elizabethan joke.

p. 78. *from the black gown to the buckram bag.* From highest to lowest.

p. 79. *non novi dæmonem.* "I don't know the devil."

p. 79. *as though it were grimed.* 'It' would seem to refer to the merchant's face rather than his beard.

p. 79. *he'll strain courtesy with his legs in child-bed.* I take this to mean, "he'll treat his swollen legs unceremoniously."

p. 79. *non est domi.* "He is not at home."

p. 79. *the prince of the North.* Satan. The idea that Satan before his fall ruled the north part of heaven is based on Isaiah xiv, 13, 14.

pp. 79–80. *to seek my dinner with Duke Humfrey.* See Stow's *Survey*, edited by Kingsford, vol. i, p. 335. The tomb of Sir John Beauchamp in St Paul's was popularly supposed to be that of "good duke Humfrey."—.i.e, Humphrey, Duke of Gloucester (d. 1447). Those who remained in St Paul's during the dinner-hour, usually because they had no money to pay for a meal, were said to dine with Duke Humphrey.

p. 80. *at the sign of the Chalk and the Post.* I.e., on credit.

p. 80. *Non bene conducti vendunt perjuria testes.* Ovid, *Amores*, i, 10, 37. "It is not honourable for witnesses to swear false oaths for gain."

p. 80. *the Low Countries.* Hell. The same joke is used by Dekker, probably with this passage in mind. See p. 190.

p. 81. *your dancing school.* In *Strange Newes* Nashe writes, "*the devil's dancing school in the bottom of a man's purse that is empty*, hath been a gray-beard proverb two hundred years before Tarlton was born." In an empty purse there was no 'cross' (coin) to keep the devil out.

p. 81. *præmunire.* A writ, especially for the offence of acknowledging any foreign authority, such as the Pope.

p. 83. *a sedge rug kirtle.* 'Rug' is a coarse woollen stuff, or frieze. The *Oxford English Dictionary* suggests that 'sedge-rug' may be "a course material woven of sedge and resembling matting."

p. 83. *a parenthesis in proclamation print.* Round brackets ( ) in large type.

p. 83. *single, single.* Quibble on the two sense of the word: (i) single, as now; (ii) weak, thin, poor, especially referring to beer and ale.

p. 85. *Tam Marti quam Mercurio.* As much for the arts of wars as for those of peace.

p. 85. *Quorum.* "Certain justices of the peace, usually of eminent learning or ability, whose presence was necessary to constitute a bench."—*Oxford English Dictionary.*

p. 85. *Rouen.* Unsuccessfully besieged by Henry IV, from December 1591 to April 1592.

p. 85. *Gourney or Guingamp.* Scenes of battles during the French Civil Wars.

p. 85. *Secreta mea mihi, etc.* "My secrets are my own; he is wise to no purpose who does not keep his wisdom to himself."

p. 86. *the eighteen pence ordinary.* A very good-class eating-house.

p. 86. *swears and stares, after ten in the hundred.* Swears and swaggers for all he is worth.

p. 87. *Dulce bellum inexpertis.* "War is attractive to those who have not tried it."

p. 88. *Anabaptists . . . Familists . . . Barrowists and Greenwoodians.* Protestant sects.

p. 88. *mathematicians abroad that will prove men before Adam.* This looks like a reference to the mathematician Harriot, friend of Sir Walter Raleigh and Marlowe, who held advanced views. *Cf.* Richard Baines's accusations against Marlowe printed in C. F. Tucker-Brook's *Life of Marlowe and The Tragedy of Dido, Queen of Carthage* (Methuen's *Marlowe*, vol. 1, p. 98).

p. 88. *they are harboured in high places.* Probably Sir Walter Raleigh and his circle. See M. C. Bradbrooke's *The School of Night.*

p. 88. *pensioner.* One of the royal bodyguard of gentlemen instituted by Henry VIII.

p. 89. *one's voice that interprets to the puppets.* The voice of the man who does the talking in a puppet show.

p. 88. *sine coitu.* Without sexual intercourse.

p. 90. *Mother Bunch.* Allusions to her as the typical ale-wife are frequent. Whether she really existed or not is not known.

p. 90. *the cobbler's crow, for crying but Ave Cæsar.* McKerrow's note is as follows: "Alluding to a story told by Macrobius in *Saturnalia,* ii, 4, 29–30. On the return of Augustus from his victory over Antony some one brought to him a crow trained to cry, 'Ave, Cæsar, victor imperator.' This he purchased at a high price, as also a parrot and other birds similarly trained. A cobbler scenting in this an easily earned profit, purchased a crow and trained it to utter the same cry. It was, however, a troublesome task, and the cobbler frequently despairing of success exclaimed, 'Opera et impensa periit,' a phrase which the bird got by heart as well as the one intended. At last, however, the crow was perfect in its lesson, and the cobbler brought it to Augustus, only to be told that he had already enough talking birds and required no more. As he was about to retire in despair, the crow suddenly looked at him and said, 'Opera et impensa periit,' a remark which so pleased the emperor by its appositeness, that he purchased the bird at a higher rate than he had paid for any of the others."

p. 90. *the seven liberal sciences.* Grammar, rhetoric, and logic (the trivium); arithmetic, geometry, astronomy, and music (the quadrivium).

p. 90. *like Saint George.* Probably alluding to St George as pictured on inn-signs.

p. 91. *the Ship of Fools.* Alluding to Sebastian Brant's *Stultifera Navis* (1494), a long satirical poem translated into English by Alexander Barclay in 1509.

p. 92. *next your heart.* See Glossary.

p. 94. *like one of the four winds.* McKerrow explains "like one of the four winds as represented on maps," i.e., with the cheeks puffed out.

p. 96. *a new Lord Mayor's posts.* The door-posts of the Lord Mayor's house were painted red.

p. 97. *The Ballad of Blue Starch and Poking Sticks.* This ballad has not survived. A poking-stick was an instrument used in setting the pleats of a ruff.

p. 97. *the lawn of licentiousness hath consumed all the wheat of hospitality.* I.e., wheat is used for making starch instead of for making bread.

p. 97. *Madame Troynovant.* London, the new Troy.

p. 97. *Men and women that have gone under the South Pole, etc.* The exact meaning of all this is not very clear, but what Nashe is referring to is the loss of hair suffered by victims of venereal disease.

p. 97. *cucullus non facit monachum.* "The hood does not make the monk."

p. 98. *swords and bucklers go to pawn apace in Long Lane.* Swords and bucklers were being replaced by rapiers and daggers. Long Lane was the home of the second-hand dealers. *Cf.* p. 167 *and n.*

p. 98. *Latin.* Pun on 'latten,' a kind of brass.

p. 98. *Plowden's standish.* Edmund Plowden (1518–85) was an eminent jurist.

p. 98. *Laudamus veteres, sed nostris utimur annis.* Ovid, *Fasti*, i, 225. "We praise the past age, but we have to live in our own."

p. 99. *Mens cuiusque, is est quisque.* Cicero, *Respublica*, vi, 24. "The spirit of man is his true self."

p. 100. *gives him bread for his cake.* Answers him in kind, is a match for him.

p. 101. *Præterit Hippomenes, resonant spectacula plausu.* Ovid, *Metamorphoses*, x, 668. "Hippomenes gets ahead, and the amphitheatre resounds with applause."

p. 101. *Fraus sublimi regnat in aula.* Seneca, *Hippolytus*, 981. "Deceit is all-powerful in royal palaces."

p. 102. *our holy father Sextus.* Pope Sixtus V (1585–90).

p. 103. *As Cardinal Wolsey.* Nashe seems to be referring to the rumour that Wolsey committed suicide by poisoning himself.

p. 103. *Saint Tyburn.* See note to p. 45.

p. 104. *the doping planet.* Venus.

p. 104. *elders of Israel.* Exercised judicial powers. See *Deuteronomy*, xxii, 16.

p. 104. *Tarlton.* The most famous comic actor of the day, died in 1588.

p. 104. *Her Majesty's Servants . . . Queen's Men.* An acting company.

p. 105. *John a Nokes.* "A fictitious name for one of the parties in a legal action (usually coupled with John-a-Stiles.—*Oxford English Dictionary*. *Cf.* John Doe and Richard Doe.

p. 105. *Nisi prius.* First words of a writ impanelling a jury for the assizes. Hence they came to be used, as here, for a case at the assizes.

p. 106. *a back so often knighted in Bridewell.* Bridewell was a prison in Faringdon Ward Without. To be knighted in Bridewell was to be beaten there.

p. 106. *"After my hearty commendations."* Conventional phrase frequently used at the beginning of a letter. Presumably to liken one to "After my hearty commendations" means to liken one to a rather ridiculous commonplace.

p. 106. *Ad consilium ne accesseris, antequam voceris.* "Don't offer your advice till you are asked."

p. 107. *Neque maior meque corpore locato.* "Neither larger nor smaller than the body placed in it."

p. 107. *Facinusque invasit mortales.* "Crime laid hold upon men."

p. 108. *Os fœtidum.* "Stinking mouth," probably referring to the brimstone fumes the devil was supposed to breathe out.

p. 108. *Beza.* Theodore de Bèze (1519–1605), the successor of Calvin at Geneva.

p. 108. *Marlorat.* Augustin Marlorat (1506–63), another of the reformers at Geneva.

p. 108. *Rosamond.* Samuel Daniel's poem *The Complaint of Rosamond* (1592).

p. 108. *not a chandler's mustard-pot, etc.* References to the use of waste paper for covering mustard-pots are as frequent as those to its use for drying tobacco. *Cf.* p. 169 *and n.*

p. 109. *Smith.* Henry Smith, a popular preacher at St Clement Dane's, who died in 1591.

p. 109. *Multi famam, pauci conscientiam verentur.* "Many fear publicity, few their own conscience."

p. 110. *Noble Salustius.* Guillaume de Saluste du Bartas (1544–90), author of *Les Semaines*, an extremely popular poem in its day, translated into English by Joshua Sylvester. The passage referred to here runs as follows in Sylvester's translation:

> Our English Tongue three famous Knights sustain;
> Moore, Bacone, Sidney: of which former, twain
> (High Chancellors of England) weaned first
> Our infant phrase (till then but homely nurst);
> And childish toyes, and rudeness chasing thence,
> To civil knowledge, joyn'd sweet eloquence.
> And (world-mourn'd) Sidney, warbling to the Thames
> His swan-like tunes, so courts her coy proud streams,
> That (all with-child with Fame) his fame they bear
> To Thetis lap; and Thetis everywhere.
>
> *Du Bartas His Divine Weeks* (1633), p. 124

p. 111. *caret tempus non habet moribus.* McKerrow comments, "I have no idea what this means." Nor have I.

p. 111. *Quicquid in buccam venerit.* Martial, *Epigrams*, xii, 24, 4–5. "Whatever comes into my head."

p. 111. *some tired jade, etc.* Richard Harvey, who had attacked Nashe in his *Lamb of God* (1590). Both Greene, in *A Quip for an Upstart Courtier*, and Nashe make great play with the fact that the father of Gabriel, Richard, and John Harvey was a ropemaker at Saffron Walden.

p. 111. *an epistle of mine.* I.e., Nashe's *Preface* to Greene's *Menaphon* (1589).

p. 112. *Thou that hadst thy hood turned over thy ears, when thou wert a bachelor, for abusing of Aristotle.* McKerrow thinks that "to have thy hood turned over thy ears" means "to be deprived of your degree." It certainly implies some kind of public disgrace. The Harveys were supporters of Ramus, the French logician, who in 1536 began his attack on Aristotelian logic by defending the thesis that everything Aristotle had said was false.

p. 112. *a brother, student in almanacs.* John Harvey published an almanac for 1583 and another for 1589.

p. 112. *an absurd Astrological Discourse.* Richard Harvey's *Astrolo-*

gical Discourse upon the Conjunction of Saturn and Jupiter (1583). Harvey predicted a series of disasters which did not, in fact, occur.

p. 112. *Surgeon's Hall.* The company of Barber Surgeons were granted the bodies of four condemned criminals yearly for dissection.

p. 113. *Elderton.* A popular ballad-maker of the day. References to him are numerous, and usually stress his fondness for ale and the redness of his nose.

p. 113. *Vivit, imo vivit.* "He lives, aye, he lives."

p. 113. *Martin.* I.e., Martin Marprelate, the pseudonym of the author of a number of brilliant pamphlets directed against the bishops and the organization of the Church of England.

p. 113. *Jupiter ingeniis præbet, etc.* Ovid, *Tristia*, iv, 4, 17–18. "Jupiter gives his divine approval to the genius of poets, and allows any of them to sing his praises."

p. 113. *T.N., the master-butler of Pembroke Hall.* Richard Harvey in the *Epistle to the Reader*, prefixed to his *Lamb of God*, had written as follows: "Thomas Nash, one whom I never heard of before (for I cannot imagine him to be Thomas Nash our butler of Pembroke Hall, albeit peradventure not much better learned)."

p. 114. *ad imprimendum solum.* The formula *cum privilegio ad imprimendum solum* meant originally "with the royal privilege to print only," implying that no further privilege had been granted. By Nashe's time, however, it had come to mean "the sole right to print," implying copyright.

p. 114. *Neque enim lex, etc.* Ovid, *Ars Amatoria*, i, 655–656. "For there is no juster law than that the contrivers of murder should die by their own devices."

p. 114. '*the vain Paphatchet.*' I.e., the author of the anti-Martinist pamphlet *Pap with a Hatchet*, probably John Lyly.

p. 114. *cur scripsi, cur perii.* "Why did I have to write, why must I die?"

p. 114. *pravum prava decent, etc.* Ovid, *Amores*, iii, 4, 31. "Bad deeds fit a bad man; pleasures denied are welcome still."

p. 114. *Redeo ad vos, meo auditores.* "To come back to you, my readers."

p. 114. *you go by St Giles, the wrong way to Westminster.* The point of this lies in the fact that the Hospital of St Giles in the Field was on the way to Tyburn, not Westminster, and it was there that condemned criminals received their last refreshment in the form of a bowl of ale.

p. 116. *patterns to make custards by*. Designs for the pastry surrounding a custard.

p. 117. *the gentle craft*. Shoemakers.

p. 117. *Plenus venter, etc*. "A man with a full belly is not very active, and overeating is responsible for more deaths than the sword."

p. 117. "*Profecto, Domine*," etc. "To be sure, sir, I am a very poor eater of fish."

p. 118. "*At tu es bonissimus carnifex*." "But you are a very good executioner." (*Carnifex* is literally "one who makes meat," "a butcher.") The joke lies in the bad Latin.

p. 118. *clubs and clouted shoon*. Those who used clubs and wore patched shoes—i.e., the common people.

p. 120. *Pancredge*. St Pancras, at this time well outside the city.

p. 121. *been over*. I.e., over the Channel to France or the Low Countries.

p. 121. *Clim of the Clough*. The devil. Clim of the Clough was an archer well known in ballad literature, but there is nothing to connect him with the swallowing of hot lead. McKerrow concludes from references in Ben Jonson (*The Alchemist*, Act I, Scene ii) and elsewhere that it may also have been the name of a contemporary fire-swallower.

p. 123. *De Arte Bibendi*. A satirical poem 'on the art of drinking,' by Vincentius Obsopæus, published in 1536.

p. 125. *the Steelyard*. Originally the place granted to the merchants of the Hanse League for a trading settlement. It was on the north bank of the Thames a little above London Bridge. The settlement was suppressed in 1551, and in Nashe's day the Steelyard was celebrated for its winehouse.

p. 126. *Omne ignotum pro magnifico est*. Tacitus, *Agricola*, 30. "What is unknown is all the more attractive."

p. 128. *Nam si foras, etc*. Livy, xxx, 44, 9. "For if there is no enemy abroad they will find one at home."

p. 128. *The Defence of Plays*. For an account of the Puritan attack on the stage see E. K. Chambers, *The Elizabethan Stage*, vol. 1.

p. 128. *brave Talbot*. Almost certainly an allusion to *Henry VI*, Part I.

p. 129. *Henry the Fifth*. I.e., in the old play *The Famous Victories of Henry V*.

p. 130. *some of them . . . never come abroad, but they [the Players] are in danger of undoing*. A riot of apprentices in Southwark in June 1592 had led to the closing of the theatres.

p. 131. *Lipsius*. Justus Lipsius (1547–1606) was a famous Belgian scholar and historian.

p. 131. *the players beyond sea*. The Italian players of the Commedia dell Arte.

p. 131. *Sophocleo cothurno*. In the Sophoclean buskin—i.e., in a stately and dignified form of tragedy.

p. 131. *famous Ned Alleyn*. Edward Alleyn (1566–1626) was the greatest tragic actor of the age, until the appearance of Richard Burbage.

p. 132. *Knell, Bently*. Well-known actors of the day.

p. 133. *Diana*. The moon as a pattern of chastity, and, of course, Queen Elizabeth.

p. 133. *Consuetudo peccandi tollit sensum peccati*. "The habit of sinning takes away all sense of sin."

p. 134. *permutata vicissitudine*. "Change and change about."

p. 134. *some fantastical refiners of philosophy*. Probably the Walter Raleigh circle. See note to p. 88.

p. 136. *manifeste verum*. "Plain truth."

p. 136. *quasi vero*. "As if indeed."

p. 137. *"Now you talk of a bee, I'll tell you a tale of a battle-dore."* Alluding to the proverb "to tell a B. (or a bee) from a battle-dore." *Cf.* "to tell a B. from a bull's foot."

p. 137. *The bear, etc.* This story, as McKerrow points out, has much in common with Spenser's *Mother Hubbard's Tale*, and seems to be a political allegory, in which the bear is the Earl of Leicester, the fox is the Puritans, whom Leicester supported, and the bees are the ministers of the Church of England.

p. 137. *A fat cammell*. Some kind of horse.

p. 138. *The ape abhorring him by nature, etc.* The pronouns are confused here. The sense is as follows: The ape abhorring the horse, because the horse looked down on him and was bigger than he, advised the bear to dig a pit in the horse's path, so that when the horse fell into it the ape might skip on the horse's back and bridle him, and then the bear could come and seize the horse at his pleasure.

p. 139. *basilisk*. Mythical creature, also known as the cockatrice, that was believed to be able to petrify with fear anything that it looked at.

p. 142. *homo homini dæmon*. "Man a devil to man."

p. 150. *summum genus*. "The highest form."

p. 150. *diabolus, quasi deorsum ruens*. "Devil, from falling down from above." This etymology of the word is frequently alluded to by the Fathers.

p. 151. *limitata potestate*. "With limited power."

p. 153. *Exsurgat Deus, etc.* "Let God arise, and his enemies shall be scattered."

p. 153. *Vehiculum ignis superioris.* "The source of heavenly fire."

p. 153. *Procul, o procul, este prophani, etc.* Æned, vi, 258 and 260. "Away, away, all ye profane; and you [Æneas] take the path, and draw your sword from its sheath."

p. 154. *Bazilez manus.* Spanish *beso las manos,* "I kiss your hand." An affected form of salutation.

p. 154. *tandem aliquando.* "Now at last."

p. 154. *Paul's Churchyard.* Centre of the book-selling trade.

p. 154. *Westminster Hall.* The chief courts of the kingdom, including that of Chancery, the King's Bench, and the Star Chamber, all sat in Westminster Hall. See Stow's *Survey,* edited by Kingsford, vol. II, pp. 118–120.

p. 155. *Noverint.* The first words of a writ were *Noverint universi,* "Let all men know." Hence *plodders at Noverint* are petty lawyers.

p. 155. *Silver games in Finsbury Fields.* Would seem to be some kind of pitch and toss, in which a Turk's head cut out of grey paper was the mark. For Finsbury Fields see note to p. 40.

p. 156. *Promissis quilibet dives esse potest.* An adaptation of Ovid, *Ars Amatoria,* i, 444. "Anyone who wishes can be rich in promises."

p. 156. *Thraso.* A braggart, from Thraso, the braggart soldier in Terence's *Eunuchus.*

p. 156. *he will look your head.* I.e., examine your head for lice.

p. 157. *Aretine.* Pietro Aretino (1492–1554), the Italian satirist and erotic writer who enjoyed an enormous reputation in England at the end of the sixteenth century.

p. 157. *Amyntas.* Probably the Earl of Derby, who is addressed by this name in Spenser's *Colin Clout* (1595).

p. 158. *Knight of the Red Cross.* The hero of Book I of the *Faerie Queene.*

p. 158. *Oh decus atque ævi gloria summa tui.* Ovid, *Heroides,* xv, 94. "O ornament and greatest glory of your age."

p. 158. *that honourable catalogue.* The sonnets addressed to members of the English nobility published in the first edition of the *Faerie Queene.*

p. 159. *miss the cushion.* Go wrong, be mistaken. *Cf.* Greene's *Never Too Late* (1590), p. 54. "If thou thinkest, for that I am a woman, I am easy to be won with promises of love and protestations of loyalty, thou art, sweet servant, in a wrong box, and sittest far beside the cushion."

p. 159. *Tantum hoc molior.* "Thus much do I labour."

p. 159. *Accipe, per longos, etc.* Ovid, *Amores*, i, 3, 5–6. "Receive a man, to serve you for many long years; receive one, who knows how to love with a pure love."

p. 159. *Præbeat Alcinoï, etc.* Ovid, *Amores*, i, 10, 56–57. "Let the rich garden of Alcinous provide its fruits, the poor man can offer his duty, his zeal, and his loyalty."

The Wonderful Year

Thomas Dekker (1572?–1632) was born and bred in London. Little is known about his life, but it is improbable that he was ever at either of the universities. He is first heard of in 1597 as a playwright, and he continued to write plays during the rest of his life. His literary output was enormous. As well as having a share in a large number of plays Dekker wrote numerous pamphlets and pageants. Even so, he could not keep out of debt and was imprisoned on several occasions.

Dekker is essentially the poet of London. His best plays, such as *The Shoemakers' Holiday* (1600) and *The Honest Whore* (1604), are remarkable for their kindly humanity and for the minute and detailed observation of London life and manners which goes into them. This same knowledge of London appears again in Dekker's prose works, of which the best known are *The Wonderfull Yeare* (1603), *The Seven deadly Sinnes of London* (1606), and *The Guls Hornebooke* (1609). In the field of the pamphlet Dekker is, in fact, the natural successor of Greene and Nashe, uniting the sympathy and kindliness of the one with something of the inventiveness of the other.

p. 160. *Et me rigidi legant Catones.* "Even the most severe moralists may read me."

p. 161. *the old weathercock over Paul's steeple.* In 1603 there was no weathercock over St Paul's. Along with the steeple it had been burnt down by lightning in 1561 and never restored. See *Stow's Survey*, edited by Kingsford, vol. i, p. 331.

p. 162. *a new stake.* Used as a mark in archery practice.

p. 162. *setting up all these rests.* Risking everything. The phrase was derived from the card game of primero, the 'rest' being the final or reserved stakes.

p. 162. *that old poetical madcap.* Plautus.

p. 163. *the dogs of Nilus.* This anecdote, also referred to in Tourneur's *The Transformed Metamorphosis* (l. 551), goes back to Aelian, *Var. Hist.*, i, 4, where he says the dogs of Egypt, owing to their terror of the crocodiles, drink only by snatches and cannot quench their thirst.

p. 163. *Banks his curtal*. Thomas Banks's performing horse, Morocco, which could dance and count, had climbed to the top of St Paul's, and could, according to Nashe, distinguish between an Englishman and a Spaniard. See *Love's Labour's Lost*, Act I, Scene 2.

p. 164. *Haec mala sunt, etc*. "This is a poor piece of work, but you do no better."

p. 165. *a Lord of Misrule*. Special officer in the houses of the great, whose business it was to superintend the revels and pastimes of the Christmas season. See E. K. Chambers, *The Mediæval Stage*, vol. i, p. 403 *et seq*.

p. 166. *Westward, from the top of a Richmount, etc*. Queen Elizabeth died at Richmond on March 24, 1603.

p. 167. *to give arms*. To show armorial bearings. There is a quibble on 'to give alms.'

p. 167. *Long Lane*. A street stretching from Smithfield to Aldersgate, of which Stow says: "This lane is now lately builded on both the sides with tenements for brokers, tiplers, and such like." —Stow's *Survey*, edited by Kingsford, vol. ii, p. 28.

p. 169. *To dry tobacco*. Tobacco, when bought, was too moist for smoking and had to be dried. It was spread on a piece of paper and placed in an oven or held over a fire. There are many allusions to the use of waste paper for this purpose.

p. 171. *she was born upon a Lady eve, etc*. Elizabeth was born on September 7, 1533, the eve of the Nativity of the Virgin Mary, and died on March 24, 1603, the eve of the Annunciation.

p. 171. *a Lee was Lord Mayor, etc*. The Lord Mayor of London in 1558–59 was Sir Thomas Leigh, and in 1602–03 Robert Lee.

p. 173. *The Sybil's Octogesimus octavus annus. Cf*. Bacon's *Essays*, edited by Aldis Wright, p. 151 *and n*. The prophecy referred to is that of Regionmontanus, made in 1475, which went as follows:

> Post mille expletos a partu virginis annos,
> Et post quingentos rursus ab axe datos,
> Octovagesimus octavus mirabilis annus
> Ingruet, et secum tristia fata trahet.
> Si non hoc anno totus male concidet orbis,
> Si non in nihilum terra fretumque ruat,
> Cuncta tamen mundi sursum ibunt atque deorsum,
> Imperia, et luctus undique grandis erit.

"After the completion of a thousand years from the birth of

Christ, and of yet five hundred more, the wonderful year '88 will come rushing in, bringing fearful disasters with it. If the whole world does not come to a bad end in this year, and if land and sea are not confounded, yet all the kingdoms of the earth shall be turned upside down, and there shall be great lamentation everywhere."

p. 173. *Erra Pater.* The sixteenth- and seventeenth-century equivalent of "Old Moore." He was supposed to have been a Jew, but it is doubtful whether he ever really existed at all.

p. 173. *Plato's mirabilis annus, etc.* See *Timæus*, 39. Cornford, in *Plato's Cosmology*, explains the Great Year, or the Cyclic Year, as the period that must elapse from any given moment, before the sun, moon, and planets are once again in precisely the same relationship to one another.

p. 173. *throw Plato's cap at.* Fail to overtake; miss.

p. 173. *Peter Bales,* 1547?–1610. Calligraphist and shorthand writer, who in 1575 presented Queen Elizabeth with a penny on which he had engraved in Latin the Lord's Prayer, the Creed, and the Ten Commandments, together with "an excellent spectacle by him devised" to enable the Queen to read it.

p. 173. *wild Ireland became tame on the sudden.* The death of the Queen coincided with the submission of the Earl of Tyrone.

p. 173. *some English great ones.* Sir Walter Raleigh and Lord Cobham, who were suspected of conspiracy and sent to the Tower in July 1603. The Tower is "the same park which great Julius Cæsar enclosed."

p. 174. *huge Holinshed.* Holinshed's Chronicle is in folio.

p. 174. *Pro Troia stabat Apollo.* "Apollo was on the side of Troy."

p. 175. *Poets' Apollo.* James had written and published both in verse and prose.

p. 176. *aqua cælestis . . . unicorn's horn.* Two sovereign remedies at the time.

p. 176. *led forth in leases.* I.e., led forth on leashes, like dogs. 'Lease' is the normal sixteenth- and early seventeenth-century spelling of 'leash.' I have retained the original spelling, however, since it indicates a quibble on 'let forth on leases.'

p. 177. *Theobalds.* The great house of the Cecils at Cheshunt, in Hertfordshire.

p. 177. *the grand Cayr.* Cairo.

p. 179. *What an unmatchable torment, etc.* In this passage Dekker seems to be recalling *Romeo and Juliet*, Act IV, Scene 3.

P

p. 179. *mandrakes shrieking*. The forked root of the mandrake has a certain resemblance to the human form, and was popularly believed to utter a deadly shriek when plucked up from the ground. *Cf. Romeo and Juliet*, Act IV, Scene 3.

p. 180. *lest the fatal handwriting of death should seal up their doors*. A red cross was painted on the doors of an infected house and a paper, with the words "Lord have mercy upon us," fastened to the lintel. The house was shut up for twenty-eight days.

p. 181. *tokens sent thee from heaven*. The spots which appeared on the skins of victims of the plague were known as "God's tokens," and were regarded as a sure sign of death.

p. 182. *grave-matters*. Dekker is punning. *Cf. Gravesend* (p. 183).

p. 183. *like Dunkirk*. Dunkirk was a pirate stronghold. *Cf.* p. 190.

p. 184. *Bucklersbury*. Stow says, "This whole street called Buckles bury on both the sides throughout is possessed of grocers and apothecaries."—*Stow's Survey*, edited by Kingsford, vol. i, p. 260. *Cf. Merry Wives of Windsor*, Act III, Scene 4.

p. 184. *mithridatum and dragon-waker*. Popular remedies and antidotes.

p. 184. *gold-finches*. Rich men. *Cf.* Yellowhammer, the goldsmith in Middleton's play *A Chaste Maid in Cheapside*.

p. 184. *nor a dog left, etc.* Dogs were suspected of spreading the plague, and a dog-killer was appointed in each parish to kill all he could lay his hands on.

p. 185. *rue and wormwood*. Both regarded as prophylactics.

p. 185. *ride upon foot-clothes*. Foot-clothes were the trappings of the horses of the great, which reached down to the ground. To ride upon foot-clothes therefore means to be wealthy.

p. 185. *Jehochanan, Simeon, and Eleazar*. Leaders of Jewish factions inside Jerusalem during the siege of the city by Titus in A.D. 70. Dekker is probably remembering the description of their activities given by Nashe in *Christ's Tears over Jerusalem*. (*Works of Nashe*, edited by McKerrow, vol. ii, p. 63.)

p. 185. *rosemary*. Like rue and wormwood, used as a prophylactic.

p. 186. *St Clement*. The patron saint of the Bakers' Company in London. St Clement's was one of the parishes that suffered badly during the plague.

p. 186. *Decidis in Scyllam*. "You fall upon Scylla" in trying to avoid Charybdis.

p. 187. *a flat-cap*. The mark of a citizen.

p. 187. *Birchin Lane*. The home of drapers and hosiers. See Stow's *Survey*, edited by Kingsford, vol. i, p. 199.

p. 187. *Sir Giles Goosecap*. A foolish knight in the play *Sir Giles Goosecap*, which is probably by Chapman.

p. 187. *Hippocrates, Avicen, etc.* Hippocrates, Avicen, and Rasis are included in the list of great physicians given by Chaucer in the *Prologue*, ll. 430–434.

p. 187. *Fernelius.* Jean-François Fernel (1497–1558), a famous French physician.

p. 187. *aurum potabile.* "Drinkable gold," i.e., gold held in state of minute subdivision in some volatile oil. It was regarded as a sovereign remedy. *Cf.* Chaucer, *Prologue*, ll. 443–444:

> For gold in phisik is a cordial
> Therefore he loved gold in special.

p. 187. *clapped up their bills, etc.* Bills are public advertisements. See the commentators on *Much Ado about Nothing*, Act I, Scene 1.

p. 188. *a second Fabian.* Robert Fabyan, a draper and alderman of London, died in 1513. His work *The New Chronicles of England and France* appeared in 1516.

p. 189. *Vincentio Saviolo.* An Italian fencing master living in London at the time. His book *Vincentio Saviolo his Practise*, issued in 1595, was the first book in English to deal with the rapier.

p. 190. *Bedlam.* The hospital of St Mary of Bethlehem in Bishopsgate Ward, used as a lunatic asylum.

p. 190. *the Low Countries, that are built upon butter-firkins and Holland cheese.* The export of butter and cheese to England was one of the sources of Dutch wealth at this time.

p. 190. *the Dunkirks.* The Dunkirk pirates. *Cf.* p. 183 *and n.*

p. 192. *Rhadamanth.* Rhadamanthus, with Æcus and Minos, was the judge of the dead in the underworld. Dekker is probably thinking here of the *Induction to The Spanish Tragedy*, where the ghost of Andrea calls on Rhadamanth.—*Spanish Tragedy*, Act i, Scene 1.

p. 192. *"Lord have mercy upon us," was the only thing they feared. Cf.* note to p. 180.

p. 194. *sops and muscadine.* Muscadine wine with sops—i.e., cakes soaked in the wine—was drunk at weddings.

p. 196. *which this year had a saying to her.* Had something to say to her.

p. 196. *Actæon.* A cuckold. Actæon, who was turned into a stag because he saw Diana bathing, is always associated by the Elizabethans with the notion of horns and cuckoldry.

p. 198. *Balthazars' part in Jeronimo.* In Kyd's *Spanish Tragedy* Balthazar, who is in love with Lellimperia, discovers that she is in love with Horatio, whom he then murders.

p. 198. *paucos palabros.* Spanish *pocas palabras* ("few words").

p. 199. *the blood of the Bordeaux grape.* Claret; with a reference to the slang term 'claret'—'blood.'

p. 201. *the top of Paul's, which . . . hath been burnt, etc.* Stow says St Paul's was burnt in 1087, in 1444, and in 1561.

p. 201. *when King Henry went to Boulogne.* Henry VIII took Boulogne in 1544.

p. 202. *two or three dozen napkins to dry up the lard.* A reminiscence of Falstaff. *Cf. Henry IV*, Part I, Act II, Scene 2:

> Falstaff sweats to death,
> And lards the lean earth as he walks along.

p. 203. *God Pan.* A quibble is intended, of course.

p. 206. *nailed up for counterfeits.* It was customary for tradesmen to nail counterfeit money to the doors of their shops.

p. 206. *the villainous motion.* A motion is a puppet-show. For the conduct of a puppet-show see Ben Jonson's *Bartholomew Fair*, Act V, Scenes 4 and 5.

p. 206. *"The Hundred Merry Tales."* A popular jest-book. *Cf. Much Ado about Nothing.* Act II, Scene 1.

p. 206. *Dii meliora.* "God forbid."

p. 206. *the holes of both Counters.* The hole was the worst part of a prison. There were two prisons called the Counter, one in Wood Street and one in Southwark.

p. 206. *turned them over the thumb.* Gained complete control of them, done as she wished with them. *Cf.* 'to twist round one's finger.'

p. 207. *Derrick.* The name of the hangman at Tyburn.

p. 207. *Hic finis Priami.* Virgil, *Æneid*, II, 554. "This was the end of Priam."

p. 207. *Et iam tempus, etc.* Virgil, *Georgics II*, I, 542.

> Sed nos immensum spatiis confecimus æquor;
> Et iam tempus equum fumantia solvere colla.

"But we have covered an enormous distance, and it is now time to loose the smoking necks of the horses from the yoke."

BIBLIOGRAPHY

The following list of books is intended to help those who wish to know more about the work of Greene, Nashe, and Dekker, and about the world in which they lived:

Robert Greene

The only complete edition of Greene is *The Life and Complete Works*, edited by A. B. Grosart (London, 15 vols.; 1881–86).

The following pamphlets have been edited by G. B. Harrison for the "Bodley Head Quartos":

A Notable Discovery of Coosenage (1923).
The Second Part of Conny Catching (1923).
The Third and Last Part of Conny Catching (1923).
A Disputation between a hee Conny Catcher and a shee Conny Catcher (1923).
The Black Bookes Messenger (1924).
Greene's Groatsworth of Witte (1923).
The Repentance of Robert Greene (1923).

Thomas Nashe

The standard edition of Nashe is *The Works of Thomas Nashe*, edited by R. B. McKerrow (London, 5 vols.; 1904–10).

The following works have been published separately:

The Unfortunate Traveller, edited by H. F. B. Brett-Smith (1927).
Pierce Penilesse, edited by G. B. Harrison (1934).

Thomas Dekker

The Non-dramatic Works of Thomas Dekker, edited by A. B. Grosart (London, 5 vols.; 1884–86).

An edition by F. P. Wilson is being prepared.

The Plague Pamphlets of Thomas Dekker, edited by F. P. Wilson (Oxford, 1925).

The Wonderfull Yeare, edited by G. B. Harrison (1924).

The Seven Deadly Sinnes of London, edited by H. F. B. Brett-Smith (Oxford, 1922).

The Guls Horne-booke, edited by R. B. McKerrow (London, 1904).

Collections

The Elizabethan Underworld, edited by A. V. Judges (London, 1930), is an excellent collection of pamphlets, etc., from the sixteenth and early seventeenth centuries.

Life in Shakespeare's England, edited by J. Dover Wilson (Cambridge, 1911) gives a picture of the life of the times drawn from contemporary writings.

The Political Background

J. B. Black, *The Reign of Elizabeth* (Oxford, 1936).

The Social Background

G. M. Trevelyan, *English Social History* (1944).

R. H. Tawney, *Religion and the Rise of Capitalism* (London, 1926).

Sir Sidney Lee and C. T. Onions (editors), *Shakespeare's England* (Oxford, 1917).

The Intellectual Background

E. M. W. Tillyard, *The Elizabethan World Picture* (London, 1943).

The Classical Background

M. Cary and others (editors), *The Oxford Classical Dictionary* (1949).

GLOSSARY

aconitum, oil of, deadly poison, originally extracted from monk's-hood.

admiral (vb.), flagship.

address (vb.), dress, clothe.

admire, wonder at, marvel.

adventure (vb.), risk, venture.

aglet, metal tag at the end of a lace or ribbon to facilitate threading through eyelet-holes.

agood, thoroughly, heartily.

ale-conner, inspector or examiner of ale. Here equivalent to ale connoisseur.

alehouse dagger, dagger, or short sword, worn for use in alehouse brawls.

all to be, thoroughly, utterly, completely.

all amort, thoroughly dispirited, dejected.

ambuscado, ambush.

amort, see *all amort.*

angel, coin worth about ten shillings at this time. So called because it showed the archangel Michael standing upon the dragon.

angle-hook, fish-hook.

anthropophagized, man-eating, cannibal.

art, magic art.

artemisia, genus of plants, including wormwood and southern-wood, distinguished by a bitter taste.

artificial, skilful, artful, virtuoso.

artist, magician, astrologer.

attaint, convict, prove guilty.

attract, take in, realize.

aurum potabile, "drinkable gold," gold held in state of minute subdivision in some volatile oil, formerly in repute as a cordial. (See note at p. 226.)

Baby, doll.

backside, back premises of a building, out-buildings.

baffle, disgrace, treat with scorn.

ban, curse.

ban-dog, mastiff, bloodhound, any fierce dog.

bandora, musical instrument resembling guitar or lute. Modern banjo is a corruption of this word.

basilisk, fabulous reptile, also called a 'cockatrice.' Even its look was supposed to be mortal.

bastoon, bastinado, beating.

bazilez manus, I kiss your hand. (See note at p. 221.)

beldam, loathsome old woman, hag.

besmeared, befouled.

besonian, base fellow, rascal, knave.

better to pass, better off.

bezzle, hard drinker.

bibbing, tippling, hard drinking.

biggin, cap or hood for the head, nightcap.

blain, inflammatory swelling or sore.

blind, dark, obscure, hidden away.

bolt (vb.), to sift by passing through a sieve.

bombast (vb.), to stuff or pad out.

boon voyage, Fr., *bon voyage.* Used here in sense of a prosperous voyage.

boot-haling, to go a, to go looting, booty-seeking.

bottom, skein, or ball of thread.

bowed, bent, crooked.

box-keeper, keeper of dice and box at a gaming-house.

brabblement, noisy quarrelling or dispute.

break, to become bankrupt, or perhaps in this case to break away, to leave.

brewess, broth, liquor in which beef and vegetables have been boiled.

broker, middleman, agent, second-hand dealer, retailer.

brokerly, like a broker, huckstering.

brokery, business of a broker.

buckram, coarse linen or cloth stiffened with gum. A buckram giant is an effigy of the kind used in pageants.

budge (sb.), lambskin with the wool left on and worn on the outside.

budget, pouch, bag, wallet.

bung, thieves' cant for 'purse.'

bursten-bellied, broken-bellied, or with belly filled to bursting.

buskined, literally buskins were half-boots, then the word was used as the equivalent of *cothurnus,* the high boot worn by the actors

in Athenian tragedy. *Cf. Sophocleo cothurno* (p. 131). Here
equivalent to stately, dignified.

butter-firkin, butter-barrel.

button-cap, small flat cap.

byrlady, contraction of 'by our Lady,' used as an oath.

Cage, a local gaol, lock-up.

calamentum, calamint. A genus of aromatic herbs formerly in
repute as a medicine.

caliver, a light kind of musket.

cammell, some kind of horse.

Canaries, a lively Spanish dance.

cap (vb.), to take off the cap as a token of respect.

capable, comprehensive, all-inclusive.

cap-case, a travelling-case, bag, or wallet.

capouch, a hood or cowl, seems to be used here for the cloak to
which the hood was attached.

carder, a card-player.

car-man, carter, carrier.

caroach, coach of a stately kind.

carpet-peer, contemptuous term for a peer whose exploits were
confined to the carpeted chamber rather than the field.

carterly, ill-bred, of low birth.

Castalian, inspired. Castalia was the spring on Mount Parnassus,
the home of the Muses.

casting, calculating, scheming.

casting, *i.e.*, of the dice. Throwing.

cause (conj.), because.

catch-pole, sheriff's officer, bum-bailiff.

causey, causeway, paved part of a street.

Cayr (the grand), Cairo.

censure, judgment.

chapless, without the chap or lower jaw.

chapman, merchant, trader, dealer.

checkmate, equal, match, rival.

cherry-pit, a children's game in which cherry-stones were thrown
into a small pit or hole.

chipping, a paring of the crust of a loaf.

chronigrapher, chronicler.

chuff, a coarse, churlish fellow.

chuff-headed, swollen-headed. With big, fat heads.

circumquaque, circumlocution, tedious and prolix address.

civil, having proper public and social order.

Clim of the Clough, one of Nashe's jesting names for the devil. (See note at p. 219.)

cleppe, call, name.

clip (vb.), embrace.

clip (vb.), to clip a piece off a coin, a common offence before the use of milled-edges.

close, secret, covert.

close-stool, chamber-pot enclosed in a stool or box.

club-fisted, close-fisted.

cock and pie, form of oath. The precise meaning of this phrase is doubtful.

cockney, a milksop, mother's darling.

cod-piece, "a bagged appendage to the front of the close-fitting hose or breeches worn by men from the fifteenth to the seventeenth century."—*Oxford English Dictionary*.

cog (vb.), cheat, deceive.

coil, noisy disturbance, fuss.

coistrel, rascal, varlet.

commodity, profit, parcel of goods, anything that one trades in.

communicated with, imparted to, granted to.

compacter, confederate.

con. (con . . . thanks), to thank, to express thanks.

conceit, thought, idea, imagination.

complice, accomplice, associate in crime.

consistories, councils.

consort, concert, music produced by a combination of instruments.

conspiration, conspiracy, plot.

construe, scan, examine carefully.

content (of large content), comprehensive.

continuate, continuous, lasting.

convey, make away with.

cony, victim, dupe.

cony-catchers, the rogues and cheats of the London underworld who lived by their wits.

cony-catching, trickery, cheating.

copes-mate, confederate, accomplice.

corse, corpse.

cormorant, avaricious man, usurer.

countenance (p. 43), continuance; (p. 61), moral support, patronage, favour.

Counter, gaol in the City of London.

counterfeit, picture, portrait.

county, count.

court chimney, "small stove(?)"—*Oxford English Dictionary.*

court-cup, a dish made of ash-wood.

court holy bread, flattery, smooth words.

cowshard, cow-dung.

cozen, cheat, dupe.

cozenage, sleight, confidence trick.

crew (cursed), class of ruffians.

cross, coin, so called from the fact that coins had a cross stamped on one side.

cross-biter, swindler, blackmailer, one who 'double-crosses.'

crow, crow-bar.

cue, "the sum of half a farthing, formerly denoted in College accounts by the letter *q*, originally for quadrans."—*Oxford English Dictionary.*

cullion, rascal, base fellow.

cunning (sb.), skill, cleverness, ability.

cupboard, sideboard, piece of furniture for the display of plate.

cuttle, knife.

Dagger (alehouse), see *alehouse dagger.*

decipher, to make plain, reveal.

despervewe, "poor beggar."—*Oxford English Dictionary.* Here seems to have rather the sense of 'desperado.'

devil's breeches, a kind of close-fitting hose.

diacatholicon, a laxative, a general remedy.

diacodion, syrup prepared from poppy-heads, used as an opiate.

discover, reveal, uncover, disclose.

dispend, to receive, to have an income of.

doit, small Dutch coin worth half a farthing; hence any trifling coin or sum of money.

donsell, squire or page.

dorbellical, foolish, stupid, clumsy.

dorter, bed-chamber, dormitory.

dragon-water, a medicinal preparation popular in the seventeenth century.

draw (in phrase *to draw to one's purse*), to feel for.

drift (sb.), device, plot, stratagem.

driver, pettifogging lawyer. (See note at p. 212.)

dry-fat, a large cask or box used to hold dry things as opposed to liquids.

Eftsoon, soon afterwards, forthwith.

egregiously, remarkably, outstandingly, unusually.

eld, antiquity.

engine, instrument.

enterprise (vb.), undertake.

erst, formerly, once, first.

eternize, immortalize.

exeat regnum, permission to leave the country, passport.

extent, to make, seize upon, confiscate.

Fadge, prosper, succeed, come off.

fantastical, crotchety, with a bee in his bonnet.

farm (sb.), rent.

fetch (sb.), trick, stratagem, device.

figure, horoscope.

filch (filch themselves into), introduce themselves stealthily into, steal into.

flabberkin, puffed out, puffy.

flat-cap, round cap with low, flat crown, worn by citizens of London in sixteenth and seventeenth centuries.

fleece, share of the booty—obtained by 'fleecing' some one, swag.

flocks, dregs.

flurt, fillip, rap, gibe.

foot-cloth, richly ornamented cloth hanging from the back of a horse and reaching to the ground on either side. A mark of wealth and distinction.

frenchify (all to the frenchified), to make French, utterly French in manners and ways.

fresh-water, raw, unskilled, untrained.

frokin, a Dutch child.

frolic, "(?) Humorous verses circulated at a feast."— *Oxford English Dictionary.*

fronting, prefacing, introducing.

Gag-toothed, having a projecting or prominent tooth.

galley-foist, a State barge.

galliard, a quick and lively dance in triple time.

gallimaufray, medley, heterogeneous mixture.

galligaskins, a kind of wide hose or breeches.

gaskins, wide hose or breeches.

Getes, Getae, a Thracian tribe of the lower Danube, among whom Ovid lived when in exile.

glove, drinking term. Precise meaning not known.

glozing, dissimulation.

gnathonical, parasitical.

goblin, mischievous and ugly demon.

gold-finch, a rich man.

gold-finder, scavenger, one who emptied privies.

gold-finer, a refiner of gold.

goll, a hand.

gorbelly, fat-bellied.

grafting, cuckolding.

great sale; great, by the, wholesale.

greek, merry rogue, madcap, roysterer.

groat, coin worth fourpence.

gulch, glutton or drunkard.

Haberdine, salt or sun-dried cod.

hackster, prostitute.

haggler, clumsy, awkward archer.

hatched, inlaid with silver or gold.

headborough, parish officer equivalent to petty constable.

hey pass, come aloft, juggler's exclamation commanding an object to move. *Cf.* 'hey presto.'

his (passive), possessive of 'it.' Modern 'its,' as well as 'his.'

hobbinoll, countryman, rustic. Derived from character Hobbinoll in Spenser's *Shepherd's Calendar.*

holy bread, court, smooth words, flattery.

honey-brag, trap for honey.

hoop, the amount of liquor between two of the hoops on a quart pot.

hornbook, sheet of paper containing the alphabet and Lord's Prayer, protected by a plate of horn. A primer.

hotspur, zealot, fanatic. (Sense not noted by *Oxford English Dictionary*).

hough, to hamstring.

humourist, faddist, a whimsical or fantastical person.

hunter's hoop, drinking term.

hypericon, drug prepared from plants of the genus hypericum—i.e., St John's wort.

Imbroccata, pass or thrust in fencing.

inch, at an, close at hand, closely.

indifferent, impartial, fair.

indument, material body or form.

indurance, imprisonment.

ingle, familiar, intimate.

institution, rule, constitution.

intelligence, news.

intelligencer, informer, spy, secret agent.

Jack, fellow, knave.

Jacob's staff, instrument formerly used for taking the altitude of the sun.

jet, to walk ostentatiously, to trip.

Jew's letter, text inscribed in Hebrew on a phylactery, regarded as the outward symbol of a Jew.

jump, agree, coincide.

keeper, nurse.

kennel, gutter, surface drain of a street.

kilderkin, cask, containing sixteen to eighteen gallons.

killcow, bragging, boastful.

kitchen-stuff-wife, woman who collected kitchen refuse, dripping, etc.

knee (vb.), bow or kneel to some one in token of respect.

knight of the post, professional perjurer.

Lac virginis, some kind of cosmetic.

lamia, witch, she-demon, fabulous monster, supposed to have the body of a woman and to prey on human beings.

lantern and candle man, watchman, bellman.

Lantsgrave, Landgrave.

Latin, punning on 'latten,' a kind of brass.

leaguer, a military camp, a besieging force.

learn (being not to learn), needing no instruction.

leet, special kind of court held by the lords of certain manors.

liberty, district, extending beyond the bounds of a city, subject to the control of the municipal authority.

lickerish, greedy, longing.

lift, to steal something from a shop. *Cf.* modern 'shop-lifting.'

lightly, usually, as a general rule.

lob, country bumpkin, rustic.

Low Countries, Hell. (See note at p. 213.)

Make-bate, mischief maker, breeder of strife, libeller.

make extent, to seize upon, to confiscate.

malt-men, maltsters.

mandritta, a cut from right to left in fencing.

manifeste verum, plain truth.

martin, a kind of monkey.

marybone, literally 'marrowbone,' the knee.

mass, form of oath, literally 'by the mass.'

mast, literally acorns, beechnuts, etc., used in fattening pigs. Here equivalent to rich food.

masterless men, unemployed servants.

mazer, mazard, head.
mechanical men, labouring men, manual workers.
menta, generic name for plants of the mint family.
miche, to skulk, to lurk out of sight.
mingle-mangle, a confused medley.
misture, loss, privation.
mithridatum, a composition of many ingredients, regarded as an
  antidote to infectious diseases.
moral, allegory, symbol.
moth-fret, hole caused by moths.
motion, puppet show.
mouldcheese, mouldy cheese.
moulder, mould, clay, dust.
mouse (vb.), to tear, to bite.
mump, grimace.
muster-master, officer responsible for the muster roll of part of an
  army.
murrion, plague, pestilence.
Nest (of bowls), a set in graduated sizes so as to fit one inside
  another.
next your heart, on an empty stomach.
nice, pernickety, scrupulous, hesitant.
nip (sb.), cutpurse or pickpocket.
nip (vb.), to cut (a purse), to steal.
nipper, thief, or pickpocket.
nisi prius, lawsuit. (See note at p. 216.)
nitty, lousy, infested with nits.
noint, annoint.
noverint, a writ. (See note at p. 221.)
Obligation, legal document. Written contract or bond under seal.
occupier, trader, merchant, dealer.
okerman, one who deals in ochre.
onion-skinned, so thin as to be transparent.
ordinary, eating house.
oriently, brilliantly, lustrously.
other (prn.), form of plural as well as singular.
ought, owned.
outlandish, foreign.
outshifts, outskirts.
overdrip, to drip over, overshadow.
over-flowen, flooded, inundated.
overslip, slip past.

overtake, to overreach, take in.

owe, to own.

Paeonia, peony—formerly in regard as a medicine.

painful, painstaking, laborious.

pair (of stairs), flight.

palma Christi, castor-oil plant.

paltry (sb.), trivial, worthless thing.

pantofle, high heeled shoes. *To stand on one's pantofles* is to stand on one's dignity.

parcel-gilt, partly gilded.

participate, share.

pasquil, squib, satire, lampoon.

pass, better to, better off.

passion, act of suffering. *Cf.* Christ's Passion.

pavement, floor (of a house).

pawn (sb.), pledge. *Cf.* pawnbroker.

peak, beard. *Spade peak,* a beard shaped like a pointed spade.

pedantical, formal, precise.

pencil, paint-brush.

penny-father, an old miser, niggard, skinflint.

pensioner, one of royal bodyguard called Gentlemen Pensioners, gentleman-at-arms.

pentagonon, pentagram or pentangle, a five-pointed star used as a mystical symbol and credited with magical powers.

pernicity, swiftness, celerity.

pike staff, a staff with a metal point at the lower end.

pilch, rough outer garment of leather or wool.

pillow-bere, pillow-case.

pinch-fart, mean, avaricious.

placebo, to sing, to flatter, be sycophantic.

plaguy, plague-stricken.

plausible, deserving of applause, commendable.

policy, cunning, trickery.

politic, cunning.

politician, one who is cunning, who achieves his ends by doubtful and devious means.

politicly, craftily, shrewdly.

poor John, salt hake.

popularity, publicity.

post, knight of the, professional perjurer.

posy, short motto inscribed on a knife or within a ring. Here equivalent to list.

pothecary, apothecary.

pottle-pot, two-quart pot or tankard.

powdering-tub, tub in which meat was salted or pickled.

praemunire, writ or summons.

prefer, to advance.

presently, (passim), at once, immediately.

priding, showing pride, self opinionated.

prig (vb.), to steal.

princox, coxcomb, conceited, young man.

professor, practiser, expert, professional.

pudding, kind of sausage. *Cf.* black-pudding.

pudding-prick, wooden skewer for fastening the ends of the gut containing a pudding.

pug, bargeman. *Western pugs* were the men who navigated barges down the Thames to London.

pullery, poultry.

purchase, booty, loot, spoil.

purchasing, acquiring possessions by unfair or illegal means.

Quaintly, skilfully.

quarter sermon, quarterly sermon.

queen, wench.

Rail, a piece of cloth worn about the neck by women.

rank-rider, rapid, reckless rider.

rap, seize, snatch.

raught, (from *to reach*). Struck, cut off.

reach (sb.), stratagem, device, trick.

rebater, wire framework supporting a ruff. More usual form, rebato.

regiment, rule, government.

rest, to set up one's, to risk one's all. (See note at p. 222.)

roguing mate, companion in roguery.

rot (sb.), a wasting disease.

round (vb.), to whisper.

Ruffians Hall, Smithfield. *Oxford English Dictionary* quotes Blount (1674), "*Ruffians Hall,* so that part of Smithfield was anciently called, which is now the Horse market, where trials of skill were played by ordinary ruffianly people, with sword and buckler."

rug, coarse woollen stuff.

ruta, a bitter herb, rue. Formerly regarded as valuable medicinally.

Sack, white wine imported from Spain and the Canaries.

sage, sage-coloured.

saim, to grease.

sallet, (i) a headpiece, (ii) a salad.

salt, salt-cellar.

sance-bell, sanctus bell. Bell rung after pealing had ceased.

satin-gull, dandified fool.

saturnist, one born under the influence of Saturn, and therefore morose and saturnine.

saying, to have a saying to one, to have something to say to one.

scald (adj.), paltry, contemptible, 'scurvy.'

scrubbing (adj.), squalid, beggarly.

sea-card, chart of the sea, map.

seen, qualified, expert, skilled.

seminary, seminal.

sergeant's mace, sergeant's rod of office (with a pun on the other sense of mace—spice).

set, the arrangement of a ruff in pleats.

shadow (vb.), conceal.

sharer, a member of a company of players, who paid the expenses and received the profits.

sheepbiter, dog that worries sheep.

shift off, put off with an excuse, get rid of.

shrap, bait of chaff or seed laid for birds.

shrive, to question, to examine.

sign of the smock, brothel.

simple (sb.), herb.

sinewed, covered over with, ornamented.

single-sole(d), poverty stricken.

sithence, since.

size (of bread), allowance, ration.

skill (vb.), to matter, to be of importance.

smooth (vb.), to make plausible.

snaphance, spring catch, snap lock.

snuff (sb.), portion of drink left at the bottom of a cup; a heel-tap.

soothe, to declare or maintain a thing to be true.

souter, shoemaker.

sparage, asparagus.

speed (vb.) (i) to succeed in getting, to obtain; (ii) to send packing, to kill.

splenative, acting on the spleen.

spur-gall, to gall a horse with the spur.

squirting, mean, contemptible.

stall, bench in front of a shop on which wares were displayed.

stand (sb.), barrel set on end.

standish, a stand containing pen, ink, etc.

starting-hole, way of escape, loophole.

state, person of importance, noble, prince.

statute merchant, form of bond. (See note at p. 212.)

still (adv.), constantly, continually.

stinkard, one who stinks. Term of abuse.

stoccata, a thrust or stab in fencing.

stomach (vb.), to be offended at, to resent.

strain courtesy, used both in the sense of being excessively courteous (p. 42), and of not being courteous enough (p. 79).

stramazone, a slicing or cutting blow in fencing.

stutting, stuttering.

swartrutter, "One of a class of irregular troopers, with black dress
and armour and blackened faces, who infested the Netherlands in
the sixteenth and seventeenth centuries."—*Oxford English Dictionary.*

swelt, to die, to perish.

swound, fainting fit, swoon.

swound (vb.), to faint.

Table, writing-tablet, canvas.

tall, bold.

tar-box, literally box used by shepherds to hold tar. Here used
jocularly for a paint-box.

teatish, peevish, irritable, bad-tempered.

temperature, behaviour, disposition.

temporality, temporality, lay people.

term, lawyers and their clients who had come together for one of
the law terms.

thick and threefold, in large quantities.

thrummed, trimmed, ornamented.

time-catcher, opportunist.

tokens (see note at p. 181).

toy, trifle.

train, plot, plan, stratagem.

treacher, traitor, knave, rogue.

trewage, homage, fealty.

Troynovant, London (the new Troy).

trug, prostitute, trull.

trusses, close-fitting breeches.

turn up their heels, cause them to die. *Cf.* "to turn up one's
toes."

Underlay, to fit shoes with an additional sole. Here figurative.
undermeal, afternoon nap.
unfatigable, indefatigable.
unhandsoming, defacing, lessening.
unpluming, plucking.
unthrift, spendthrift, prodigal.
uprising and downlying, altogether, all in all.
upsey freze cross, drinking term, "after the Frisian fashion," i.e.,
    deeply, heavily.
Vail, to take off one's hat.
vastity, desolation, emptiness.
verjuice, the acid liquor obtained from crushed crab-apples.
virginals, a keyed musical instrument resembling a spinet, set in a
    box or case without legs.
void (vb.), to clear.
Vulcanist, blacksmith.
Wastegood, spendthrift.
white money, silver.
winching, wincing of a galled horse.
wing, the wing of a goose used as a brush.
withe, a band made of twisted osiers as in the handle of a basket.
woodcock, simpleton, gull, fool.
wooden, sylvan, of the woods.
Younker, young man.
Zoilist, a carping critic. So called from Zoilus, critic and gram-
    marian of fourth century B.C.